Invitation to
INDUSTRIAL
RELATIONS

WITHDRAWN

INVITATION SERIES

Invitation to Archaeology	Philip Rahtz
Invitation to Economics	David Whynes
Invitation to Engineering	Eric Laithwaite
Invitation to Linguistics	Richard Hudson
Invitation to Philosophy	Martin Hollis
Invitation to Politics	Michael Laver
Invitation to Social Work	Bill Jordan
Invitation to Statistics	Gavin Kennedy

Other titles in preparation

Invitation to Anthropology	Maurice Bloch
Invitation to Astronomy	Jacqueline and Simon Mitton
Invitation to Law	Brian Simpson
Invitation to Management	Peter Lawrence
Invitation to Mathematics	John Bowers
Invitation to Medicine	Douglas Black
Invitation to Nursing	June Clark
Invitation to Psychology	Philip Johnson-Laird
Invitation to Teaching	Trevor Kerry

Invitation to
INDUSTRIAL
RELATIONS

Tom Keenoy

BASIL BLACKWELL

First published 1985
Basil Blackwell Ltd
108 Cowley Road, Oxford OX4 1JF, UK

Basil Blackwell Inc.
432 Park Avenue South, Suite 1505,
New York, NY 10016, USA

British Library Cataloguing in Publication Data

Keenoy, Tom
    Invitation to industrial relations.
    1. Industrial relations
    I. Title
    331   HD6971

    ISBN 0–631–14104–9
    ISBN 0–631–14105–7 Pbk

Library of Congress Cataloging in Publication Data

Keenoy, Tom.
    Invitation to industrial relations.

    Bibliography: p.
    Includes index.
    1. Industrial relations.   I. Title.
HD6971.K392   1985   331   85–11100
ISBN 0–631–14104–9
ISBN 0–631–14105–7 (pbk.)

Typeset by Oxford Publishing Services, Oxford
Printed in Great Britain by
Whitstable Litho Ltd., Whitstable, Kent

For my parents

Contents

Preface

Given contemporary public opinion, an invitation to industrial relations may sound like a request to join me in national mourning, for the character of British industrial relations is thought by many to carry a heavy responsibility for the parlous state of our economy. Sadly, public images have a tendency to reflect little but the surface ripples of social life, and industrial relations is about far more than unruly pickets and seemingly irrational demarcation disputes. At the core of industrial relations is work and the employment relationship.

Work dominates our lives. We all spend – or, these days, hope to spend – roughly one-half of our waking hours in some form of gainful employment. Work not only pays the bills but gives us status, is a source of our ambitions and plays a critical role in providing us with a social identity. Knowing what someone 'does for a living' is like being in possession of their social fingerprints. Most work, these days, is performed within the context of an employment relationship. Doctors, plumbers, social workers, surveyors, models, vicars, insurance clerks and footballers are all employed by someone or some institution to perform work in return for some form of reward. In exchanging our labour for these rewards we invariably accept that part of the deal involves allowing the employer to control and direct what we do; and, while happy to accept the rewards, there are numerous instances when we resent being told what to do. This is a permanent underlying source of tension in all employment relationships and, on occasion, may result in open conflict. Work, in other words, is not always a happy and harmonious experience, no matter what the profit.

In seeking to lay the basis for understanding industrial relations, this book tries to sidestep all the ideological quicksands: there will be no gnashing of teeth over our economic decline, no bewailing the shortcomings of management or trade unions and no attempt to sell you any hopeful solutions to our problems, real or imagined. What is on offer is a *way of seeing*: a method through which we can cut through the candyfloss prescriptions of political expediency and examine the skeletal structure which lies below the surface of what passes for everyday knowledge about industrial relations.

The way in which we *see* the social world is a fundamental influence on how we come to understand and explain the social world. For example, consider the differences of opinion as to what has 'gone wrong' with industrial relations and what ought to be done to 'put them right'. These range from abolishing trade unions, legally restricting their activities, talking to them, allowing them a significant influence on political policy and, according to some newspapers, permitting them to run the country. If none of these is to your taste, there is another possibility: the revolutionary overthrow of the existing social order. All these different 'solutions' reflect differences in the way the protagonists 'see' the social world and what they think is necessary to improve it or, at the least, rid us of our industrial relations 'problems'. It is vitally important to recognise that, insofar as it is possible to come to any judgement, our agreement or disagreement with any of these proposals will be intimately related to how *we* see the social world.

So, no instant solutions, however well-meaning. The way of seeing developed in the pages which follow is designed to provide not only a disciplined framework for understanding industrial relations and how certain forms of behaviour, such as strikes, come to be defined as 'problems', but also attempts to create a more insightful method of assessing the 'solutions' on offer from politicians, employers, trade unions and other assorted soothsayers.

SOME DEBTS

Many people have contributed to the writing of this book. My teachers, students and colleagues have been a primary source of stimulation and encouragement. Geoff Mungham and Bob Price, the publisher's reader, read the whole manuscript; both provided highly constructive comment and did their best to curb stylistic excesses and the tendency to over-generalise. Barbara Clargo, Lindsey Nicholas and, in particular, Mair Price, were responsible for typing successive drafts and displaying remarkable patience. Special thanks are due to Celia Crowther, Marie Keenoy and Jenny Lewis who undertook to test-read the book and provided invaluable advice on where the text became turgid or incomprehensible. My children, Kevin and Maeve, interfered just enough to keep me sane; and my wife, Judy, contributed a constant and essential supply of 'mindful loving kindness'. To all these, and more, my sincere thanks.

List of Abbreviations

ACAS	Advisory, Conciliation and Arbitration Service
APT	Association of Professional Teachers
ASLEF	Associated Society of Locomotive Engineers and Firemen
ASTMS	Association of Scientific, Technical and Managerial Staffs
AUEW	Amalgamated Union of Engineering Workers
AUT	Association of University Teachers
BACM	British Association of Colliery Management
BIM	British Institute of Management
BMA	British Medical Association
CBI	Confederation of British Industry
CIR	Commission on Industrial Relations
CSEU	Confederation of Shipbuilding and Engineering Unions
EEF	Engineering Employers' Federation
EETPU	Electrical, Electronic, Telecommunication and Plumbing Union
GMBTU	General, Municipal, Boilermakers and Allied Trades Union
GMWU	General and Municipal Workers' Union

IPM	Institute of Personnel Management
MDW	Measured day work
MSC	Manpower Services Commission
NACODS	National Association of Colliery Overmen, Deputies and Shotfirers
NALGO	National and Local Government Officers' Association
NBPI	National Board for Prices and Incomes
NCB	National Coal Board
NEDC	National Economic Development Council
NGA	National Graphical Association
NIRC	National Industrial Relations Court
NUM	National Union of Mineworkers
NUPE	National Union of Public Employees
NUR	National Union of Railwaymen
NUT	National Union of Teachers
RCN	Royal College of Nursing
TGWU	Transport and General Workers' Union
TICA	Thermal Insulation Contractors' Association
TUC	Trades Union Congress
USDAW	Union of Shop, Distributive and Allied Workers

1

The Laggers' Tale

These days, industrial relations can boast few megastars. However, one among the many unsung heroes of contemporary industry is the great British Lagger. This is an occupation which can be traced back to the 19th century, when laggers were employed to insulate steam-boilers with a carefully prepared mixture of cow-dung and wood. In these days of advanced technology such crude materials have been replaced by felt, asbestos, various plastics and metal mouldings; and laggers are to be found wherever the manufacturing process requires thermal insulation. Oil refineries, chemical plants and power stations are among the workplaces which have laggers as a permanent part of the workforce.

Against all expectation, in an age when the vast majority of manual jobs and occupations are becoming progressively less demanding in terms of the required skills, the laggers have achieved the impossible: they have become skilled workers. By the early 1970s they had established a 4-year apprenticeship and thus managed to add lagging to the honourable list of manual occupations enjoying the status of a craft. Despite the historical audacity of this achievement, as a media event, it produced nothing but scorn and criticism for – in securing their historical new status – the laggers were involved in a bitter year-long dispute at the Isle of Grain where a new power station was being built.

This then is the laggers' tale. Not, however, an account of the latter strike, but a story of six laggers in an earlier almost unheard-of affair which illustrates the complexities, the uncertainty and the subtlety of the social experience called industrial relations. The events described are almost hypothetical and only the names have been changed to protect the guilty.

ChemTar International Inc. is a multinational chemical and petro-chemical company with a variety of plants and factories throughout the United Kingdom as well as widespread overseas operations. It is a company which enjoys a well-deserved reputation for progressive management and has never allowed industrial relations to deteriorate to a stage where a major dispute has occurred. It can afford to pay above-average wages and provides very good conditions of employment. The company counts itself among the best employers in British industry. With such a good record and well-deserved reputation, it is hardly surprising that headquarters personnel staff regularly pat themselves on the back – though this has never led to complacency.

One factory, at Loch Clearwater, manufactures bulk industrial chemicals and has a total workforce of 1,400 employees. The plant has only been established for 15 years, working conditions and pay are by far the best in the area and there has never been an industrial dispute involving a stoppage of work. Apart from minor individual grievances – which have always been dealt with quickly and effectively by the Personnel Department – union–management relations have always been cordial. All employees, regardless of status, are paid an annual salary with comparable fringe benefits. They are divided into three groups: the plant management and white-collar employees; the process staff, which includes the production workers (who actually make the chemicals) and all other indirect blue-collar workers such as scaffolders and our six laggers; and the maintenance staff, such as electricians, carpenters and engineers, who are all skilled craft workers. The salaries paid to all these employees are scaled according to a company-wide job evaluation scheme which had been negotiated some 8 years before. Job-evaluation is a method of comparing different jobs and occupations in order to rank them in terms of physical difficulty, training and skill so as to produce a salary structure which will be seen to be fair and equitable. Once a job has been rated it can be slotted into a pre-determined structure of grades or levels in the overall pay structure. The three groups of employees at the Loch Clearwater plant were paid according to the scales in table 1.1.

Table 1.1   Pay structure at the Loch Clearwater plant

Group 1 Staff employees	Group 2 Process employees		Group 3 Maintenance employees	
Grade 1 £12,000–20,000			Grade 1	£11,000
Grade 2 £ 9,000–12,000			Grade 2	£10,500
Grade 3 £ 6,800– 8000	Grade 1	£9,000		
Grade 4 £ 4,800– 7000	Grade 2	£8,500		
Grade 5 £ 3,800– 5000				
	Grade 3	£7,500		
	Grade 4	£5,500– 7,000		

These scales are in operation throughout the company so that pay is standardised. For example, shorthand typists (Group 1, Grade 4) will be paid approximately the same at Loch Clearwater as they would in the Hull plant. Similarly, laggers (Group 2, Grade 2) will be paid the same throughout the company. The total number of employees in Group 2 is 850, most of whom are represented by the General, Municipal, Boilermakers and Allied Trades Union (GMBTU).[1] The 350 maintenance workers, in Group 3, are all represented by the Amalgamated Union of Engineering Workers (AUEW). Some 85% of the process workers, including all the laggers, are members of the GMBTU while all the maintenance workers are members of the AUEW.

Well, the seemingly idyllic industrial relations of the Loch Clearwater plant were rudely shattered on 9 June 1973, when the six laggers, all of whom had been with the company for over 5 years, went on unofficial strike. The local newspaper, *The Clearwater Mail*, instantly reported the facts under the headline 'Six militants threaten 1,400 jobs'; an unnamed management spokesperson stated that 'their claim is exorbitant and we may have to shut down the plant'; while the laggers' representative, Mr S. Hardhead, was happy to have his photo on page three and be quoted as saying 'Our aspirations must be met before justice can be seen to be done'; and even the Group Personnel Director, on one of his rare days off, cancelled a golf match and flew up in the company jet to try to resolve the dispute.

What had occurred was that history had caught up with cosy Loch Clearwater. The dispute resulted from the unanticipated consequences of a routine management decision. Normally, the six semi-skilled laggers, whose job was to prepare and apply thermal insulation materials to pipes, boilers and any other plant as required according to the instructions of the chief engineer, could do all the lagging work that was necessary. However, on the few occasions when a new piece of processing plant was being installed, or a major overhaul of existing plant was in progress, the company had to employ outside contractors in order to complete the work on schedule. This occurred two or three times a year. The dispute centred on the fact that the contractor's laggers were being paid considerably more than the plant laggers. This occurred because the laggers working for the contractors enjoyed terms and conditions of employment determined by a separate agreement between the Thermal Insulation Contractors' Association (TICA) and the GMBTU. This agreement, called a 'national' agreement, states that laggers – or thermal insulation engineers as they are referred to in the document – are classified as skilled workers, specifies an apprenticeship of 4 years and further states that where laggers are employed on sites where skilled rates are being paid, that laggers will be paid at those rates. In other words, wherever laggers work alongside skilled workers they are to be paid the same money as the skilled men. In effect, this meant the contract laggers had to be paid at the same rate as the maintenance men at Loch Clearwater. The contractor,

4

being an honourable man, was merely abiding by the terms of the agreement signed by his association on his behalf. This national agreement, it must be remembered, is nothing to do with ChemTar International – they have not signed it and do not actually pay the wages of the laggers brought in by the outside contractors: they merely pay the contractors an agreed sum for the work done. Thus management at Loch Clearwater did not break any agreement with their own employees: it was events which had taken place elsewhere which were the source of the disruption to their tranquil industrial relations.

In June 1973, as was usual, the Loch Clearwater management employed a local firm of thermal insulation engineers to assist their own six laggers in refurbishing a sulphuric acid manufacturing unit and, as they say, it came to the attention of the six laggers that the five contractor's laggers working alongside them were being paid nearly 25% more for doing exactly the same work. The laggers, through the person of their shop steward, Sam Hardhead, made representations to management demanding, essentially, equal pay for equal work. It soon became clear this was a totally unacceptable demand and the laggers decided to walk off the job in protest. Not only were they being paid considerably less than the contractor's laggers but, to add insult to injury, as Sam Hardhead pointed out in explaining his aspirations, 'And what's more, since we know the job inside out, we have to supervise these cowboys. And where's the justice in that?' Patently, at least so far as the laggers were concerned, nowhere to be found.

At least two kinds of question can be asked about this dispute: how do we come to understand what has *caused* the dispute? and how do we reach a *solution* which will satisfy all those involved in it?

POSSIBLE CAUSES

At a rather superficial level, the strike was caused by our hothead, Hardhead, who led the six laggers out of the front gates having been told by the plant Personnel Manager, Mr Warmly, 'we cannot pay you the same as the contractor's men because they are not employees of this company. What the contractor pays in wages has got nothing to do with us; that's his responsibility.' But, as in all quarrels, it takes two to reach a disagreement. Just as the laggers refused to continue to work unless there was a change in their terms of employment, so too, management, through the Personnel Manager, refused to agree to any change. Hence, irrespective of the merits of the case, both sides may be regarded as having behaved in an intransigent or militant fashion. Thus, Peter Warmly's response to the demand for equal treatment might suggest that *he* caused the dispute. In refusing to remedy what seemed, at least for the laggers, a clear case of industrial injustice, he left them no option but to go on strike. So far as they were concerned there was no other way they could pursue what they regarded as a genuine and legitimate demand. Why should they work for so much less than other men doing exactly the same work? And why should the company not be prepared to pay out what would only have been a relatively small additional sum, given the total wage costs? More significantly, what led ChemTar International to accept the much greater financial losses resulting from lost production rather than incur the marginal costs of paying the six laggers what they saw as a 'fair' wage? Unless we are prepared to accept the rather banal conclusion that Sam Hardhead and Peter Warmly had simultaneously been stricken with brain-fever which caused them to become totally uncooperative, we have to look elsewhere for the real sources of the dispute.

In this case, as with the vast majority of industrial relations problems, it is not what individuals do which really cause a dispute, but conflict results from the organisational structures which constrain or limit the choices of action which are possible in the circumstances. Such structural constraints are not easily visible to the casual observer, may not always be apparent even to those directly involved and, invariably, are too complicated for journalists to explain when reporting industrial relations. Hence the widespread belief that strikes are caused or called by particular individuals, such as shop stewards, or specific institutions, such as trade unions.

In the case of the Loch Clearwater laggers' dispute, there are two particular structural features which need to be considered in coming to an understanding of the 'cause' of the dispute. Firstly, there is the job-evaluated pay structure of ChemTar International. This *internal* system of rewards is designed to provide a coherent and meaningful structure to which all employees can relate themselves and their jobs to all other employees. They know what grade their work has been allotted and how it compares to other jobs, and they can locate themselves in the overall company hierarchy. It tells them how far up the ladder they are, how much higher they can rise and what is the maximum they (or anybody else) can earn. As a system it possesses its own internal logic and, indeed, its own internal measures of 'justice' and 'fairness': it is based on an agreed set of measurement criteria and took a long time to work out and negotiate with the various unions. From the mangement's point of view, it is a structure which is designed not only to ensure peace, but also as a device to ensure centralised financial control over wage and salary costs. It was company policy, for example, to instruct local plant managers on the approximate number of employees to be employed in each grade in each of the three groups of employees. In this way head office accountants could more easily control and predict the actual labour costs at any one time and thus provide more accurate cost data – the latter are needed so that another set of management accountants in some other office can provide estimates of the prices ChemTar International needs to charge its customers in order to maintain a profit margin which will keep the shareholders' dividends at a level which will ensure confidence and future investment. Only thus do we begin to grasp the impossibility of Mr Warmly, smiling broadly and saying to the laggers, 'but of course you're being done down; leave it to me and I'll adjust the rates at once so that you will be paid the same as the contractor's men'. Not only would this have been deeply upsetting to the management accountants tapping in standard costs to their desk computers, but one of the major sources of managerial control over the *total* workforce would be put in jeopardy, for to permit the grading of the laggers to be altered on the basis of some arbitrary and *external* criterion would undermine, perhaps terminally, the whole delicate balance of the job-evaluated structure. This brings us to the second significant structural feature: the trade unions involved.

In general, British trade unions, unlike those in some other advanced industrial societies, are not industrial unions. Thus, as at Loch Clearwater, there was not one single union which all the workers in that sector of industry could join if they so wished. There were two unions which recruited from different categories of employee depending on the different skill levels of the various jobs. The GMBTU recruited process or semi-skilled workers, while the AUEW organised all the craft or skilled maintenance workers. When the six laggers went on strike the local full-time official of the GMBTU, Mr Golightly, refused, at first, to endorse their action and tried to persuade the men to return to work while he negotiated with the company. He had never been called in before, was unfamiliar with the pay system and, in any case, liked a quiet life. Once the 'full facts' of the case had been forcefully explained to him, however, he accepted the laggers' account and informed the company that the only solution would be to re-classify the laggers' work as skilled, thus permitting them to be paid at the appropriate rate. The problem faced by Mr Golightly was not one of his own making nor, indeed, the sort of problem he or his union would have gone looking for. Some 8 years before, as noted earlier, his union, the GMBTU had signed an agreement with ChemTar International on the job-evaluated pay structure which had defined lagging as semi-skilled work for which the appropriate pay would be Group 2, Grade 2. At a later date, in a quite different and separate organisational context – that which exists between the GMBTU and the Thermal Insulation Contractors' Association (TICA), the employers' 'trade union' for all the independent thermal insulation contract firms – the same union had signed another agreement in which it had been agreed that laggers (now called thermal insulation engineers) are skilled operatives and should therefore be paid at skilled rates. The logic of this seemingly anomalous situation so far as the laggers were concerned was quite simple: they were all doing the same job and therefore must be paid the 'going' rate; and, since trade unions rarely insist on their members being paid less than they are currently receiving, the operative 'going' rate in the Loch Clearwater case, and the obvious solution, was to upgrade the company laggers so they could be paid the same rate as the contract laggers.

It does not take a great deal of reflection to appreciate that this was the *only* choice of action available to Mr Golightly. If he had refused to give official backing to the laggers he would have risked being accused of not representing their interests, and, perhaps, of siding with management. Given the very strong feelings generated, the laggers might well have decided to leave the union in protest. While such action is rare, Mr Golightly could not afford to take the chance: the other GMBTU members at the plant and, perhaps, others throughout the company might follow suit. Only three years previously, during a strike at Pilkingtons glassworks in St Helens, his union had endured the public ignominy of having a large proportion of their members accuse it of complacency and neglect before leaving the union and setting up their own breakaway trade union.[2] Both he and his superiors in the union organisation were acutely sensitive to any possibility of a repeat performance of the Pilkington debacle. This aside, there was a more compelling logic for GMBTU support of the laggers' case: having negotiated skilled status for lagging with TICA the union could not continue to support the position at Loch Clearwater where laggers, performing similar operations, were defined as semi-skilled. The GMBTU, just as much as the company, was caught up and trapped in a process of change.

The position of the AUEW, representing the skilled men, is also relevant to the dispute. Their local official, a certain Mr Aaron Ratchett, was placed in a far less invidious position than his GMBTU colleague. On the afternoon the strike was called, Mr Warmly had phoned the district office of the AUEW to tell them he had a definite answer to the AUEW's suggestion that maintenance engineers should be given company cars and, in the course of the conversation, he mentioned he would be having his usual drink in the saloon bar of the 'Laggers Retreat' on his way home that evening. In the event, while sipping his campari and soda, Mr Ratchett happened by and they fell into a discussion about the strike. After listening to each other's problems, Ratchett explained that while he couldn't make any official comment, he thought that his union wouldn't want to interfere in the affairs of the GMBTU and, should pickets be at the gates in the morning, his members would be honour-bound not to cross them. Then he added, seemingly as an afterthought, 'of course, I doubt if my blokes would agree that those six loafers really are skilled men, but then that's not our problem. All I can say is that we won't back the strike officially, we won't try to influence the company's decision but, of course, we'll have to reserve our position.'

This amiable chat had confirmed all of Peter Warmly's worst fears, for Aaron Ratchett had told him three things: firstly, that the AUEW was not prepared to endanger its relationship with the GMBTU in order to maintain the job-evaluated structure – while they wouldn't actively support the strike, they wouldn't oppose it either by, for example, crossing the picket lines; secondly, that the AUEW did not consider lagging to be an activity of equivalent skill to that of time-served maintenance engineers; and thirdly, there was the chilling remark that the AUEW would 'reserve its position'. Translated, this meant that should the company agree to the laggers' request for upgrading, then the AUEW would respond by insisting that the differential between their members and the laggers would have to be restored, thus setting off a chain-reaction of leap-frog claims. Peter Warmly had another drink.

Pay differentials between different categories of worker were, at one time, considered by *both* employers and trade unions to be almost untouchable: they symbolised the craftsman's status and clearly marked his superior position in the labour market; for the employer they meant he could be assured of high-quality work for, in the past, the unions of skilled men, often with seven-year apprenticeships and rigidly maintained demarcation lines, were jealous guardians of the standards of craftsmanship. In the years after World War 1, however, with the increase in mechanisation of productive work activities, the category of 'semi-skilled' worker became more widespread. While historic rearguard actions are still occasionally fought to preserve the traditional demarcations – especially in printing and ship-building – it is now the case that the conventional distinctions between craft, semi-skilled and unskilled work have become increasingly difficult to sustain. As at Loch Clearwater, the separation of process from maintenance workers – while it reflected presumed skill differences – was made on the basis of the worker's *function* in the overall organisation of work activities. Not only have the technical skills required of craft work gradually been eroded over time – and there are many instances where semi-skilled process or production workers require high levels of skill – but the traditional earnings differential which reflected this hierarchy of skills has also become far less clear-cut. Nonetheless, as Aaron Ratchett indicated in his chat with Peter Warmly, that differential remains a potent indicator or symbol of the historic value attached to nominally craft work and, invariably, it is fiercely defended. The personnel staff would not have expected any other response from the AUEW and a major reason for management to resist the laggers' demands was the attempt to maintain the integrity of the existing structure of pay differentials: it had worked very effectively for 8 years and establishing a 'new' pay structure can be not only an extremely tortuous process but also an expensive one.

While these structural elements – the job-evaluated pay structure and the collaborative but also competitive relationship between the unions involved at Loch Clearwater – are critical in coming to a causal analysis of the laggers' dispute, they are by no means the only salient factors. As noted at the beginning of this chapter, the laggers are a rather distinctive occupational group in that they have established themselves as a skilled category; and this dispute was merely one step in that historic process.

THE PROBLEM WITH SOLUTIONS

In speaking of 'solutions' in industrial relations – or any other sphere of social life for that matter – care must be taken in order to avoid assuming that this refers to a *definitive* solution. Put at its simplest, an arrangement which suits one person may be totally unacceptable to the other. For example, an employer may conclude that the solution to her industrial relations problems is to ban trade union membership – as occurred in January 1984 when the government decided to insist that employees at GCHQ (the government top secret communications centre at Cheltenham) should give up trade union membership. Such a solution may, in turn, become a *new* problem for the employees. Their alternative solution may be to propose the retention of union membership rights and to suggest that the industrial relations problems be resolved through negotiations. In other words, one proposed solution may come into direct conflict with another acceptable solution. In many instances what is proposed by one party may be no more than a solution to his or her particular problem, and may be suggested either in ignorance of what the other party would find acceptable or perhaps in clear defiance of what the other party is seeking to secure. It is for this reason that the representatives of the various parties in industrial relations expend a great deal of time and energy in talking to each other and negotiating acceptable solutions. However, it would be naive to assume that such discussions are conducted solely on the basis of rational argument: each party, having proposed their preferred solution, may, if they do not get the desired response, choose to exert pressure by imposing sanctions.

What this suggests is that, at best, most solutions in industrial relations should be seen as no more than temporary arrangements or accommodations in the relationship between employer and employee. Indeed, this relationship is best thought of as one in which there is a *permanent* potential for differences of opinion and conflict and, as will be shown later, such potential for conflict is both a normal and predictable characteristic feature of the employment relationship.

More specifically, when we come to consider the possible solutions in the laggers' dispute, we seem to be faced with an impossible situation for no matter what happens it seems that someone must lose. Our problem is complicated by the fact that all those involved seem to have a good case. This may seem paradoxical but it is not uncommon: the frequency with which agreements break down is evidence of the extent to which people feel they still have a good case even after they have reached some temporary accommodation.

In the case of the Loch Clearwater dispute, management are right to refuse the laggers' demand for parity with the contract laggers because, so far as they are concerned, the price of such an arrangement is too exorbitant: it will destroy the painfully worked out pay scheme and, in all likelihood, lead to a series of counter-claims by the maintenance workers and, perhaps, other process workers such as scaffolders.

Once the established ranking of the various groups of jobs within the job-evaluated structure is undermined it may also take a very long time to re-establish the stability of the pay structure. To take one example, on what grounds can it be reasoned that lagging work has, virtually overnight, become more valuable and more skilled than that of scaffolders? Even more difficult in this case is the problem of persuading the scaffolders that their work – which is crucial to the process of lagging – is to be paid at a lower rate than lagging. But, if management have a good set of reasons for defending the present arrangement, the laggers also have a compelling case: it seems manifestly unjust for them to be paid almost 25% less than the contractors' men for doing more or less identical work. Their position is considerably reinforced by the arguments of Mr Golightly that his union, the GMBTU, in recognition of the increased technical complexity of lagging and the extensive training that is now necessary in order to become an effective lagger, have formally endorsed their new-found skilled status. Indeed, says Mr Golightly, even the independent contractors' association, TICA, have recently agreed that thermal insulation engineers, as they are now known, should henceforth be regarded as enjoying craft status. Similarly, the AUEW members who, for longer than anyone can remember, have always been paid a higher rate than laggers, also seem to have right on their side: why should they be paid no more than, in their view, the far less skilled and less valuable laggers? They fought hard to establish proper recognition for their undoubted skills, and if they agree to this then what will be the next category which will claim equal status with them? They too wish to retain the existing set of arrangements. Well, almost: they are happy for the laggers to get more, but only on condition that the differential between engineers and laggers is maintained.

Even if all these actors are not deemed to be right then, at the least, any fair-minded outside observer could do no less than appreciate the justice of their respective cases and recognise that each may have a point. But how do we reach a judgement on who, so to speak, has the 'most' just case? How can a practical solution be reached given such incompatible demands? How do we explain the 'fact' that these various groups, who have worked together on a seemingly quite cordial basis for 15 years, suddenly take up such aggressive stances towards each other? Such issues are not uncommon: they are raised every time we open our copy of the *Clearwater Mail* and read of yet another group of loyal employees who've caught the social disease of mindless militancy and are holding the country to ransom. Sadly, such continual and frequently ill-informed public criticism does little to assist in the resolution of industrial disputes and, for reasons we shall come to in chapter 6, the media treatment of industrial relations in general rarely raises the level of public understanding regarding the complexity of the issues involved. In virtually every industrial dispute the question addressed by the media is not 'how do we understand this problem?' but 'who's to blame?'.

SOME MORE ABOUT SOLUTIONS

There are three initial issues in coming to a fuller understanding of the Loch Clearwater dispute. What *criteria* do we, and should we, employ in trying to assess such conflicting claims to social justice? What is the optimum *practical solution* to the dispute and how do we secure it? How, in terms of social science, can we analyse these *competing definitions* of social justice and social reality? None of these questions have definitive answers and each is very complex. But some grasp of them is essential in order to begin to comprehend the murky undergrowth of the practice of industrial relations and the analytical uncertainties in the study of industrial relations.

When we talk of the criteria of social justice we talk of moral and political values. Anyone assessing the merits of the laggers' claim against the claim of management and the potential claim of the maintenance workers must refer to his or her own beliefs in order to reach a conclusion. That process, whether we like it or not, involves us in 'taking sides'. The side we take will depend, in this case, whether our sympathies lie with the management position or that of the laggers. If we believe that management ought to have a right to determine how much their employees should be paid and that this right takes precedence over what the representatives of the employees – in this case Messrs Hardhead and Golightly – say, then we will conclude that the laggers ought to go back to work on whatever terms management deem suitable in the circumstances. In adopting such a view we are saying that the social legitimacy of management's claim to social justice is greater than that of the laggers. Alternatively, if our sympathies lie with the laggers' claim to 'equal pay for equal work', then we are saying that, in a 'just society', such a moral principle should take priority over the managerial protest that such a course of action will force them to revise and reconstruct their pay structure. It is not difficult to see why the Conservative Party tends to be seen as the political representative of employers and why the Labour Party is regarded as the champion of the workers. It is important to remember that behind many, if not the majority, of industrial disputes lies a substratum of moral incompatibilities such as those in the Loch Clearwater affair – and the 'side' we choose to support will tend to reflect our own political preferences.

But the practice of industrial relations is not conducted

through the medium of a rarefied debate on moral philosophy, and this brings us to the question of the optimum
practical solution to the problem in question. Given what has
just been suggested about the critical impact of our social
values and beliefs on how we see fairness or justice, you will
not be surprised to read that what we think of as the optimum
practical solution is similarly 'contaminated' by our values.
Sadly, it is only politicians with their eternal promises who
can always be relied upon to claim knowledge of the
'optimum practical solution' to each and every problem.

Fortunately, we can lay the question of values aside for the
moment because there is no such thing as the optimum
practical solution. Whatever solution is arrived at, whatever
management decides to do, involves a *choice* between alternative 'benefits' and 'costs'. Similar choices face trade unions
and workers. For example, some years ago a large car
manufacturing company, which had experienced a series of
unofficial strikes, decided to deal with this 'problem' by
sacking all the shop stewards it thought were responsible for
the disputes. This had the 'benefit' of eliminating the
unofficial strikes but it also had a 'cost': for about 9 months
following sackings *other* symptoms of industrial discontent
increased dramatically: the remainder of the workforce
became sullen and uncooperative, productivity declined and
the turnover of staff (i.e. the numbers of employees leaving)
increased. What is significant about this example for present
purposes is that there is no way of knowing whether the
sacking of the stewards *was* the best or 'optimum' solution.
Did the company lose more production through the consequences of their action than they would have lost through
additional strikes had they not sacked the stewards? Since the
stewards were sacked there was no way of knowing.
Management made a choice between alternative courses of
action and bore the consequences of that decision. No doubt
they comforted themselves with the belief that their action
was 'in the best interests of the company in the longer term',
and this became a justification for the 'costs' of the sackings
but – fortunately for those who made the decision – there
really is no way of establishing whether this is or is not an

accurate conclusion. In this respect managerial decisions, however well-informed and professional, are just as fragile and as fallible as those we all make going about our daily lives.

Whatever strategy we select from those available we can always find a way of rationalising and justifying the choice no matter what the outcome. The more optimistic among us may, without any way of really knowing, conclude that: 'I did the best thing at the time' while others, perhaps more sanguine, might say, 'Well, it could have been worse.' Managers and trade union leaders, if they want to keep their jobs, cannot resort to such common-sense notions and they hide, instead, behind such notions as 'rational decision-making' or the idea that 'it was the optimum practical solution'. The difficulty is not that the available choices cannot be rationally analysed – there are shelves of managerial textbooks and tomes of learned articles devoted to the detailed explanation of how to go about it – it is, as young Peter Warmly and his head-office masters discovered, that the behaviour of people and the way in which they perceive the social world around them does not always conform to the *rules* of rational decision-making. People do not behave in a consistently rational fashion; they do not always do what is in their own 'best interests'; and often they do not even think clearly about the consequences of their action. This is compounded in the laggers' dispute by the fact that each of those involved saw the situation differently: each, in other words, could provide a clear, if different, *rationale* to what they saw as the 'optimum practical solution'.

Thus, in thinking about the 'optimum practical solution' or the 'best solution' to any industrial relations problem there are always imponderables and uncertainties. Not only are there competing conceptions of what the solution might be, but those involved may also make errors of judgement in selecting the appropriate strategy. And once launched on a particular 'optimum solution' it is often very difficult to turn back to a safer choice without incurring an irreversible loss of face. For example, Mr Warmly could have decided to sack the six laggers and put all the lagging work out to outside contractors. This would have solved his immediate problems by protecting the pay structure and also getting the lagging work completed. But the remainder of the GMBTU workers, perhaps backed by their AUEW comrades, in the face of such heavy-handed arbitrary action, might have decided to strike in protest, and this might then have spread to all the other ChemTar International plants. Head Office would not have been happy with such an escalation of the dispute and, undoubtedly, any 'optimum solution' to this new problem might have included the removal, if not the sacking, of Peter Warmly. He, in turn, with his wife, two children, a maximum mortgage on their new bungalow and hire-purchase commitments would, to say the least, have made the wrong choice. Similarly, the employees also have personal responsibilities and they might have decided that the six laggers – who, after all, 'aren't really skilled workers and don't really deserve to be paid that much more than us – can fight their own battles. School holidays will be here in 4 weeks and I need all the overtime I can get between now and then to make sure we all have a really good 2 weeks in Whitley Bay this year.' In this latter scenario, Peter's decision to sack the laggers could prove to be an important plus factor the next time he applies for promotion to Head Office.

Hence, in many situations the 'optimum practical solution' for those involved is any solution which produces a return to 'normal working', whatever the actual terms of the outcome. In practice, this means that most solutions are best regarded as 'partial' solutions: it is rare for both sides to come out of a dispute feeling perfectly content with the new arrangement. The pragmatic and inevitably partial character of the solutions to industrial relations disputes reflects not only the constant underlying tension between employer and employee but also the methods usually employed to secure desired outcomes. These are many and varied, ranging from contented cooperation, through hard bargaining to social coercion. All three are to be found, with varying degrees of visibility, in all industrial relations. They will be discussed in detail in later chapters. For the present their significance lies in the way they permit us to reformulate the difficulties arising from the different views of social justice held by our central actors. One way of explaining their differences is to say they have different *interests* and that these interests are expressed and reflected in their different views of what the solution *ought* to be. Sam Hardhead, for example, knows if the company agree, or can be persuaded to agree, that the principle of 'equal pay for equal work' is a fair basis on which employees will be paid, the result of such a happy meeting of minds would be that he and the other five laggers will be paid more and will enjoy craft status. The fact that this will require what he sees as merely a 'marginal adjustment' to the pay structure and might, but only might, generate feelings of deprivation among the maintenance workers, is not his problem. His responsibility is to represent the interests and views of the laggers; no-one else. Similarly, Peter Warmly's conversation with Aaron Ratchett clearly suggested that Ratchett's sole concern was with the specific interests of the AUEW membership. In turn, Warmly saw his role as promoting and defending the interests of company policy. Since the success of any one of these three interests automatically means that one or both of the other sets of interests must suffer, it follows that industrial relations are normally and naturally characterised by competing and conflicting interests.

This realisation that the different conceptions of social justice held by our protagonists are related to their different interests provides a basis for addressing the third critical issue noted earlier: the problem of how, as social scientists, we can proceed to an understanding of the competing definitions of social justice and social reality. The problem, in this instance, is that each of the main characters in the laggers' tale selected out certain 'facts' from the range of possible 'facts'. For Sam Hardhead the most important 'fact' was the discrepancy between what the company laggers were paid in comparison to the contract laggers: all the other possible facts were deemed to be of subordinate significance. The 'fact' which was most important to Peter Warmly – that the granting of such an increase would have destroyed the logic of the company wage structure – was seen by Hardhead and his fellow-laggers as something to worry about after their major injustice had been remedied. Similarly, Aaron Ratchett, in his role as AUEW District Officer, saw the issue in such a way that both the laggers' problem and management's problem faded into obscurity given the 'fact' that craftsmen have always enjoyed a pay differential over all other manual workers.

It is important to recognise that our participants are not deliberately or even consciously deciding to emphasise one 'fact' as opposed to another: their perceptions are directly related to the roles they occupy and the interests they represent. More generally, what this suggests is that all of us may be regarded as having a *frame of reference* through which we come to an understanding of the social world around us. What this means is that each and every one of us, metaphorically, wears a pair of rose (or blue) tinted glasses which colour what we see. Such glasses do not distort the world so much as highlight certain features and make them more significant for us. Our glasses permit us to be selective about what we see and focus our attention on those elements we think are more important.

This process of selection is something which pervades our social lives and can be shown to influence just about everything from the most trivial to the most important. Indeed, in many cases it seems to be a necessary process. For example, when we forget where we have parked the car, we do not carefully examine every car in the car park to establish which is the decrepit old red banger with a black roof and severe damage to one wing which resulted from a minor error of judgement when backing into the garage. What we do is to scan the car park, scarcely seeing all those cars which do not have any of the salient identifying marks. In this way we selectively attribute far greater significance to some elements or cues within our vision. What this means is that what we actually see is what *we were looking for in the first place*. We do not see everything that is available to see – merely what we *choose* to see. Similarly, when considering important social issues, such as whether to bring back capital punishment for murder or what might be the most effective solution to increasing unemployment, our initial frame of reference will be all-important in arriving at our chosen conclusion. If, for example, we believe that the increased provision of social welfare benefits inhibits individuals from really trying to find employment then we are likely to conclude that the 'fact' of a reduction in such benefits will, eventually, lead to a decrease in the number of people without jobs. Or we might support the return of hanging because we believe that the fear of such punishment will deter others from committing the same crime. Such assumptions and beliefs are constituent elements of our frame of reference and thus go to make up our conceptions of social reality and of how the social world operates.

Thus, the concept of frame of reference is vital in coming to an understanding of *any* social behaviour, not merely that of industrial relations. It helps to account for the 'fact' that every father's daughter is 'the most beautiful girl in the world'; the 'fact' that Chelsea football supporters think their club 'is the best in the league'; the 'fact' that, for some newspaper editors, the mention of an industrial relations problem automatically makes them pen the headline: 'Nation held to ransom again', irrespective of the particular circumstances; and the 'fact' that some groups of employees, on occasion, behave in what seems to be a non-rational and self-destructive fashion. On rare occasions, for example, strikes have occurred because a foreman has sworn at an employee or because management have sacked an employee caught stealing. Such events can hardly inspire support from those who are not involved in the situation but, without a fuller knowledge of the particular context in which the events took place and an understanding of the frames of reference of those involved, it is very difficult to grasp the logic of such behaviour: the way in which we see 'the facts' is all-important.

What lies behind all these 'facts' – or alternative perceptions of social reality – is a social process through which certain features, attitudes and opinions come to be seen as far more critical and significant than others: in other words, in coming to an understanding of social reality, we have a tendency to weight the evidence – or 'facts' – in favour of what we want to see. In any social scientific attempt to grasp social reality we have to recognise that anything which purports to be knowledge about the world around us is always constructed from a particular frame of reference. This is an intrinsic limitation not only of social science but of *all* kinds of science.

A frame of reference is a 'way of seeing', no more, and certainly no less. It is no more than a way of seeing because once we put our ways of seeing to the test they come into competition with other views of the world and, what is more important, once put to the test may then become nothing more than empty dreams. The world is not flat simply because we believe it to be flat. Similarly the laggers will not be paid the same as the contractors' men simply because they believe such an arrangement to be fair: they will have to succeed in their conflict with management in order to impose – or superimpose – their view of social justice on that held by management and the maintenance men. This raises an issue which is central to a fuller understanding of the mechanics of industrial relations: the distribution of power between the various participants in any particular situation (see chapter 8). For the present, the key point is that the laggers' power resources, relative to those of management, may be insufficient for them to be able to secure what they see as a fair solution. Hence, when it comes to the optimum practical solution, having right on one's side may be less important than having the necessary might. This link between the actors' frame of reference and power resources suggests that those with greater power, if they so choose, may be able to impose their preferred solution irrespective of any consideration of social justice. Just as management may be forced to take back a sacked shop steward, so too employees may be forced to accept a cut in wages.

In the course of discussing the Laggers' tale, the objective has been to establish a number of themes and concepts which will run as a sort of scaffolding throughout the remainder of the book. There are three major points which are important for any attempt to come to a dispassionate and disciplined understanding of the politically contentious issues which are at the centre of industrial relations.

Firstly, a clear distinction must be drawn between what

managers, shop stewards and governments actually do, or appear to be doing, in their triangular relationship and the contexts in which such actions take place or appear to take place. The term *process* or *social process* is used to refer to a wide variety of social practices which take place in industrial relations. Bargaining, working, going on strike, sacking someone, closing down a factory, disciplining an employee or passing laws regulating trade unions and employers are all examples of social processes. The contexts in which these actions take place are referred to as *structures* or *social structures*. Organisations such as trade unions, hospitals, insurance offices, local authorities, government bureaucracies, schools, universities and factories are all examples of social structures. They, in turn, may be located within grander structures such as the Trades Union Congress (TUC), the Confederation of British Industry (CBI), Regional Health Authorities, the Greater London Council, and so on.

The central *analytical* point is that social processes never take place in a vacuum: they are always performed – done and undone – within social structures. Such structures are usually established with certain purposes in mind – such as providing health care, defending the interests of union members, making motor-cars, generating profits, or collecting taxes – and the activities required to achieve these purposes operate as constraints on the range of behaviour which is possible, desirable and appropriate. A great deal of the argument, dispute and conflict which typically characterises industrial relations reflects different views of what is possible, desirable and appropriate. Management may feel a particular shop steward is causing too much disruption to the production schedules and therefore dismiss him; an office manager may decide that there are too many typists and not enough filing clerks, and re-allocate work accordingly; a union safety representative may conclude that a particular machine is too dangerous and must be shut down, or a government may decide that, for efficiency, the collection of motor vehicle tax be centralised and re-located in Swansea. Any and all of these decisions – which are attempts to achieve certain purposes within specific social structures – may have significant consequences for the character and quality of industrial relations.

The second important theme which was briefly introduced was the suggestion that industrial relations cannot be grasped without some attempt to identify the role of *social power*. The way this is distributed between actors, the kind and scale of resources they can draw upon and the possibility that power resources may be employed to shape the way in which we 'see' social reality have all been noted in the account of the Loch Clearwater dispute. Concerning social power, the most important point to recognise is that, fundamentally, the power to do something or to prevent someone or some group from doing what they want to do, resides in the capacity to exert real influence and not in mere threat. Capacity refers to the various resources that can be drawn on and utilised in any conflict. For example, those mythical shop stewards who threaten to 'take the lads out the door until we get our rise' can only succeed, if their bluff is called, provided they have persuaded the 'lads' that this is a wise course of action and they have the necessary financial resources to be able to sustain a strike of the required length. Without such resources no amount of militant rhetoric will make any real difference to the outcome. Generally speaking, employer resources tend to be both greater and more flexible than those of the employees. In recent years, for example, several large employers have, in the course of a dispute, spent large sums of money on adverts in local and national newspapers appealing to the workforce to accept the deal being offered. This tactic may be more expensive than sending individual letters but has the added potential of turning public opinion against the strikers. The relative financial outlay may, in practice, be irrelevant because whatever the cost it can be off-set against tax liabilities. There are very few trade unions which could afford to mount a comparable exercise.

Thirdly, considerable emphasis has been placed on the analytical value of the notion of a *frame of reference* in the interpretation and assessment of the significance of different 'facts'. This concept has two important implications which, thus far, have not been admitted. As members of families, schools, churches, work organisations, political parties and social clubs we both act on the social world and are acted upon by others engaged in similar activities. Our individual frames of reference – those constellations of values, beliefs and ideas which constitute our windows on social realities – also operate as a kind of sounding board against which we measure, test and make sense of whatever circumstances we find ourselves: this sounding board, of whatever moral, political, artistic or religious complexion, provides us with a barely articulated model of society. This model consists of certain assumptions about how people 'tick' and of how society 'works'. When we make remarks like 'its only human nature' or 'you've got to work the system' or 'all politicians are in it for what they can get' or make any such 'common-sense' statement, we are expressing what we take to be almost universal truisms about how people 'work' and how society is organised and constructed.

What this means is that we are *all* social scientists: it is, in fact, the only part-time occupation that all members of society, irrespective of their location in the social world, have no choice in refusing. In so far as we employ, albeit perhaps unconsciously, a frame of reference to comprehend our place in society – and we all do this – we are also in the process of analysing and making sense of how the social world operates; in this respect we are all social scientists. Some of us, by dint of education, training and mostly by simply having read more books than other people, may lay a claim to be better and more 'professional' than, for example, those for whom this book is intended, but that does not necessarily give us any greater insight into what *ought* to be done. Just as the best car mechanic at Silverstone is not always the best person to drive the racing car so the best person to run the economy is not necessarily an economist. The vision of the social scientist – amongst whom there is as much disagreement as one finds in any professional group – is also constrained by his or her frame of reference.

The second important implication concerns the notion of 'fact'. We are accustomed to talk about 'the facts' of any particular situation as if those 'facts', once established through a process of observation, are concrete indisputable realities with which no one can argue. We even say 'the facts speak for themselves'. But in social science nothing could be further from the truth. Facts *never* speak for themselves. As the laggers' tale demonstrated, where there did seem to be a number of 'indisputable facts', four people who were acutely aware of those facts – Warmly, Hardhead, Golightly and Ratchett (who now sound like a thriving firm of solicitors) could not come to any agreement about the meaning of those facts. Each placed a different interpretation on the same set of facts; each saw them as having a different impact on the organisation and each used the facts to draw quite different conclusions about their significance for social justice. Meaning and knowledge do not reside in the facts, but in the way we *choose* to see those 'facts'.

Finally, in attempting to sketch a preliminary basis for coming to a disciplined understanding of the 'facts' of industrial relations and the sometimes fierce political apoplexy such a discussion often generates, it should be clear that the first priority, if we are to avoid self-deception, is to be aware of our own 'way of seeing'. The implications of this can be profound: it can lead to a radical reassessment in our 'common-sense' grasp of social reality and to an ability to see far beyond the daily expressed truisms which are trotted out as solutions to our industrial relations problems.

2

Who's Got an Industrial Relation?

At the mention of industrial relations we are accustomed to think of trade unions, strikes and a shop steward pointing his finger blasphemously at the sky. The instant recall of the television camera permits us dramatic images of angry pickets, workers being prevented from attending their jobs, six-foot mounds of rat-infested garbage, empty railway tracks criss-crossing into the distance, and patients being turned away from hospitals. But such drama, while it captures a moment of social energy, is a grotesque parody of the daily reality of industrial relations which, like the England football team, is a busy affair of standard routines with the occasional rush of blood to the head. For all that some 60% of the working population are members of employee organis-ations, strikes are an aberration and occur, relatively speak-ing, about as frequently as aeroplane crashes; and that's what makes them dramatic: they are rare events which nobody – least of all those involved – wants, everybody criticises and, after a settlement or an inquiry, promises to avoid in the future.

But industrial relations is not about strikes, nor, indeed, is it just about trade unions – though they are deeply involved in the matter – for there are at least 40% of the working population who are not members of trade unions or other kinds of employee organisation. Anyone who is employed by someone else enjoys having an industrial relation. Conventionally, the term 'industrial relations' is used to encompass a wide range of relationships which occur in the world of work and work organisations. However, the employment relationship between an employer and an employee may be regarded as the core industrial relation. Hence, the study of industrial relations focuses on the different historical and cultural forms this relationship takes, the variety of social mechanisms, laws and social institutions which regulate and control this relationship and the possible futures for the industrial relations of tomorrow. The industrial relation is always to be found in work settings and is best understood as a form of socio-economic exchange. But first, some examples of the employment relationship.

THE EMPLOYMENT RELATIONSHIP

Mohammed Khan is 9 years old. His father, from Bangladesh, makes a precarious living as a Muslim butcher. Mohammed works in the shop every morning from 7 a.m. until 9 a.m. – he's always late for school – and from 4 p.m. until 6 p.m. every evening. He also helps out most Saturdays. It is illegal for him to work so many hours but, since there are too few inspectors, it is impossible to prevent it. Not that he is complaining; what he does is normal in his family and his father does pay him £1.50 a week. Down in the High Street, Rachel Lewis, who has just left university with a very good degree but can't find a job to match her qualifications, is working as a cashier in a supermarket. Her problem, apart from trying to manage on the £53.00 she earns each week, is the manager. At 41, he's thinning on top and seemingly at a difficult age, for he is constantly making suggestive remarks and keeps touching Rachel and the other female employees. But she needs the job, only four of the twenty-three employees are members of the shop-workers' union and, if she made his behaviour a real issue, she expects to be dismissed. She wonders if it is worth talking to Mrs Adam, the area personnel manager, if only to find out whether a transfer to another store could be arranged. Barbara Adam, now 58 and approaching retirement, remains an energetic and assertive member of the management team. Her husband died some 20 years before and she returned to work as a clerk in the personnel department of the supermarket. She became very interested in the work, took the Institute of Personnel Management diploma and, eventually, was promoted to her present post. Now that both her children are married her major interest is her work.

Meanwhile, Rachel is serving Simon Crowther with tins of cat food. This 33-year-old, a slight figure in oily overalls, works at a small garage alongside four other car mechanics and their boss, an expert engine tuner. Simon really likes his work and, now that the boss has managed to secure a contract with a local plastics manufacturing firm to service their fleet of company cars, feels secure for the first time in 6 years. He joined the AUEW when he was 15 at the start of his apprenticeship, and has been a member ever since. While he never goes to union meetings and has never been on strike, he pays his dues and would never think of leaving. He's rushing back to finish off servicing a Ford Sierra: with the new contract all the mechanics are now paid a bonus if the fleet cars are returned within 24 hours. The car is one used by Raymond Fullair, a top salesman at Plas-o-Pac, the local plastics company. He has been selling plastic packaging to fresh food wholesalers for the past 3 years during which time his gross sales have increased over 250%. Apart from the company car, with commission, Ray clears about £18,000 a year. (You'll not be surprised to learn that some of the plastic bags he sells can be found wrapping up cheese in Rachel's supermarket.) He reads the *Daily Mail*, thinks trade unions should be abolished and plays squash twice a week. He used to sell rat poison to West Country farmers – an experience which taught him all he knows. The only other car on Simon's work schedule for that afternoon is a 4-year-old Marina in for its regular service. It belongs to Arthur Grimace; a careful man with an eye on depreciation. At 43 he has reached the top of the promotion ladder as a senior accountant employed by the local council. He left school at 15, got a job in the finance office as an office junior, struggled through night-school and eventually qualified as a cost accountant 12 years later. These days he is almost exclusively concerned with monitoring the overall costings for council building programmes. He's now a little grey of face but owns a caravan on the Gower coast where the family goes three weekends out of four. At one time he was a member of NALGO, the trade union for local government employees, but allowed his membership to lapse when he was given his first supervisory appointment 15 years ago. He thinks trade unions have their place in society but feels they are out of touch with the realities of economic life: he's seen restrictive working practices add thousands to the cost of building council houses and holds that strikes are a ridiculously inefficient way of resolving differences of opinion. Looking at the figures, he knows that strikes cost the employees more than they ever cost management.

What all these people have in common is that they are all employed by someone else to carry out certain tasks in exchange for some package of rewards. In contemporary society, money is the most direct and, for most people, the most significant element of the exchange. Financial considerations tend to be seen and valued as the central reward or price given for work performed. However, they are by no means the only factor determining what work we choose, nor the only source of satisfaction which can result from employment. Rachel has taken the only employment she could find while Simon Crowther decided to work for a small concern at lower wages than he could have obtained at the local munitions factory because he prefers some variety in his work and enjoys the personal element in servicing cars for particular individuals. Arthur Grimace stays with the local authority because of the job-security: he has had opportunities to go into business on his own account but never felt sufficiently self-confident to take the risk. Even the egregious Fullair turned down a promotion because it would have meant his children moving schools.

Just as money is not the only factor governing whether we decide to take or stay in a particular job, so too it is not the only source of satisfaction. Sometimes the work itself – such as nursing or social work – may endow a desirable social status or be intrinsically satisfying in ways which outweigh the loss of financial reward incurred by not doing something else. Some academics, for example, earn considerably below what they could obtain in industry or government service. In many cases this is not only because they place great value on the kind of work they do but also because of the relative freedom they enjoy in deciding for themselves what work they will pursue.

Another important generalisation can be made about all these characters. Each of these employees occupies a position or role in the complex mosaic of jobs which comprise the *occupational structure* of a modern industrial society. This structure is not static and it is important to recognise that the individuals within it are all at different points in their work careers, are paid in a variety of ways, and do not work the same pattern of hours or enjoy the same terms and conditions of employment. Not all are equally secure in their employment; some derive greater job satisfaction from what they do and all are at different points in the life-cycle. While no employer would – or, indeed, could – take account of such diverse circumstances, they do have important consequences for the quality and character of particular kinds of employment relationship. This means that, depending on the character of the labour force, there is likely to be considerable variation not only in what individual employees put into their work and what they expect from work, but also in what they need by way of financial return from employment.

There is one other general point that is illustrated by our collection of employees. Despite the diversity of their situations and in their expectations, they can all be seen to be linked, more or less closely, through a series of distinctive socio-economic exchange relationships with others in society: cooperating in work, making products, buying, selling and providing particular goods and services for each other. Such activities always take place in the context of *social* relationships between individuals or groups and involve exchanges between them that reflect the *economic* traffic within society. At the heart of these socio-economic exchanges is the 'industrial relation', the employment relationship. This is the medium through which a person's labour is translated, through the exchange of work, for money; and money is the medium through which most of the other exchanges take place. Hence the idea that the employment relationship is best regarded as a socio-economic exchange between employer and employee.

WORK AND THE EMPLOYMENT RELATIONSHIP

These days, most of us perform some highly specialised task in the overall socio-economic structure – like selling the plastic wrapping for cheese or manufacturing steel or processing insurance claim forms or reading gas meters – and this has increased the degree of interdependence between individuals in society. As the kind of work we perform has become more specialised, often requiring technical training or a long period of education, so we have come to rely more and more upon others to provide for the variety of our individual needs.

This increasing interdependence is seen most dramatically wherever there is a breakdown or stoppage in the production of particular goods or services. A cut in the supply of electricity, for example, not only closes all the factories in the affected area but also dramatically disrupts domestic routines: cooking facilities, heating and lighting may all be instantly cut and, even if we decide to do the cleaning to take our minds off being hungry, there would be no electricity for the Hoover. Similarly, if bakers stop making bread, panic-buying sets in – not because anyone would starve – but because so few of us now make our own bread. With increased specialisation in our work has come a progressive reduction in our general skills; and this increasing interdependence is also evident within the production process itself: if the people who manufacture carburettors go on strike, the factories where car engines are assembled may also be forced to cease production.

The character of the occupational structure at any point in time reflects the way in which work activities have come to be segregated and split up – a process usually described as the *division of labour*. It is a process which has had both positive and negative consequences on the employment relationship. Indeed, one of the reasons why the character and quality of industrial relations in general has become more critical over time – and especially since 1945 – has been the increasing degree of specialisation in the provision of goods and services. Under seemingly constant competitive pressure to increase efficiency, in the extreme case, individual workers – such as those working on assembly lines – are required to perform very simple, highly repetitive tasks. While such production techniques make for much higher levels of labour productivity, they have had a negative impact on employee involvement in their work: the elimination of skill, variety and responsibility has facilitated a greater degree of control over what the individual employee actually does but has also reduced their commitment to that of the proverbial cog in the machine. At the same time the interdependence within the production process has been intensified to the point where even a minor disruption to the process can have considerable repercussions throughout the whole process. Such sensitivity, combined with an apathetic or even hostile workforce – whose only possible reward from the employment relationship is money – means management are likely to find it very difficult indeed to maintain uninterrupted production. It is little surprise that car manufacturing tends to be characterised by volatile, conflict-prone employment relationships.

While the intense division of labour commonly found in car manufacture is not typical of all production processes, the principles which lie behind it underpin and inform the way most work is organised in modern industrial societies. It illustrates the kind of tensions that can develop within the socio-economic exchange of the employment relationships. On the one side there is the employer who, through management, is usually seeking to maximise efficiency, increase productivity and reduce costs. This is attempted through a variety of control mechanisms – such as supervision, different kinds of wage payment systems and – as in the case of the assembly line – sometimes through the production technology itself. In addition there are usually a range of organisational rules and, of course, there is the formal contract of employment which imposes certain legal obligations upon both employer and employee. On the other side there are the employees who, while they are usually prepared to accept most managerial directives in exchange for wages and work, sometimes attempt to resist what are perceived as unfair demands through whatever means are available. Some employees – like Ray Fullair – may be such good salesmen that, should they feel dissatisfied, they can take up employment elsewhere. Sam Hardhead and his noble band of laggers relied upon their union to produce the necessary changes in their employment relationship. Others, like Rachel Lewis or Mohammed Khan, may have nowhere else to go and either have to accept their terms and conditions of employment or forgo employment. In the relatively 'free' labour markets which characterise liberal democracies, our value as individuals depends not only on what we have to offer by way of skills and qualifications but also on whether anyone wants to buy us.

Primarily, employees have relied upon trade union membership to protect and advance their interests. Historically, such organisations began to develop in the 19th century in order to resist the often exploitative conditions imposed by the early industrial employers. In this they were given some protection by Parliament which, having declared trade unions subversive organisations in 1800, eventually granted them legal recognition by about 1875. In addition, there were numerous legislative attempts to create minimum standards of safety and to limit the number of working hours. In 1833, for example, a factory act sought to civilise the textile industry: children under 13 were limited to a 48-hour week and had to have 2 hours schooling every day – though this was to be after work; children between 13 and 18 years old were not to work more than 69 hours per week and, while on nightwork, they were prohibited from working before 8.15 p.m. and after 5.30 a.m.; and employers were prohibited altogether from employing children under 9 years old. Although at the time this act was regarded as a considerable

34

achievement, enforcement was minimal and, in practice, most manufacturers found it easy to evade. (In 1835, for example, one employer was fined 1 shilling for working boys 15 hours at a stretch.) While such conditions may no longer prevail today, a recent report of the Low Pay Unit found that, in 1982, some 3.2 million full-time adult workers could be defined as low-paid, earning less than £90 gross per week. With the inclusion of part-time employees the figure rose to 6 million or one-third of the adult workforce.[1] More recently, in 1984, it was reported that 7 million people, about one in eight of the population, are entitled to claim Social Security benefits, which are designed to ensure no-one goes without the minimum necessities of life.[2]

THE CONTEXT OF SOCIAL ACTION

As these last examples suggest, a grasp of the historical and social context of the situation can prove of considerable benefit to our understanding of why people behave in the way they do and why people hold the views they do. There is *always* a social, or, more precisely, a socio-historical, dimension to social behaviour. This can best be explained by way of some examples.

Any discussion of contemporary British industrial relations invariably includes some reference to the relatively trouble-free situations in West Germany and Japan, to their seemingly much higher rates of labour productivity and their coopera-tive rather than confrontational trade union organisations. While such statistical comparisons may leave all concerned shaking their heads in dismay, there is no small danger of ignoring the very factors which help to account for the difference between these societies. Any explanation of the current situations in West Germany and Japan must start from the post-war social, economic and political reforms which accompanied reconstruction in those societies: much of their present-day successes can be traced to that time. In contrast, in Britain, while the post-war period did see a radical restructuring of our economy through nationalisation, no significant changes took place in the attitudes of employers and employees with regard to each other: the old status differentiations and class attitudes simply reasserted themselves. In short, though this is somewhat of an oversimplification, since we had won the war, there was no need for us to change. In both West Germany and Japan, where the old political and economic elites had been swept away, the new order was informed by, amongst other innovations, new approaches to labour–management relations which laid the basis for the kind of collaborative relations in industry necessary to produce sustained economic growth in a period of rapid technological change.

The socio-historical context in Britain during the same period was quite different. British industrial relations – already burdened with the historical memory of all the social and economic hardships that accompanied the industrial revolution – were further disadvantaged by the failure of both managerial and trade union ideology to adapt to the new times. Ironically, the clearest evidence in support of such an argument comes from the way the 'problem' is usually formulated: employers and their organisations blame the trade unions, and the trade unions blame the employers.

Hence, one of the elements of the socio-historical context of British industrial relations is the persistent influence of the deeply rooted class attitudes forged during the industrial revolution. While the more obvious indicators of 'them' and 'us' have become blurred with increased affluence, the social and economic cleavage between employer and employee remains the most enduring distinctive feature of our industrial relations. For the present we are not concerned as to whether this is a 'good' or a 'bad' thing, nor with who is to blame and, far less, with what ought to be done about it: what is fundamentally important in this context is to recognise the impact 'class attitudes' have had in shaping contemporary attitudes in industrial relations. To insist, as many contemporary observers do, that 'class' is something of the past, is to miss the point that if we wish to *understand* industrial relations – rather than simply criticise workers for not doing what is 'self-evidently' in their best interests – it is necessary to grasp the historical context with all its emotional sinews, cultural modifications and folk-memories within which present employees come to comprehend their relationship with their employers. A 'rational' assessment of social reality is no substitute for a sociological evaluation of how those actively engaged in particular social situations come to define those experiences.

The social context of action is also important at the level of group and individual behaviour. Quite apart from the individuals' frame of reference – which will provide some indication of how people orient themselves to work and how they locate themselves in particular employment relationships – the brief sketches of our employees suggests that a myriad of factors – cultural, legal, economic, political and even psycho-sexual – may play a significant role in shaping the character, form and nature of specific employment relationships.

We might feel a sense of outrage at the situation of poor little Mohammed. But he himself might never question the seemingly exploitative character of the employment relationship with his father: what happens to him in that 'historical context' is, culturally, defined as normal. This does not, of course, make it 'right': indeed, it is – like race and sex discrimination in employment – illegal. But that does not prevent it happening nor, more importantly, does it make Mohammed experience that relationship as exploitative: it is, for him, the way of the world. In contrast, Rachel's deep resentment at being subjected to sexual harassment at work reflects the increasing social awareness and condemnation of the traditional discrimination practised against female employees. Thirty years ago she might not have become so offended by the seedy manager's chauvinistic tendencies: she might even have experienced it as 'normal' behaviour. As social values change, so too do the standards of conventionally acceptable behaviour.

One element of the social and historical context is the experience of work and employment in itself. Just as we each bring our own particular expectations to the workplace so too the work we are expected to do influences the way we react to

37

any new demand, moulds our social lives and informs our opinions.

For example, the occupational culture of 'salesmanship' places great store by the art of persuasion and, despite sometimes intensive training in 'hard-sell' techniques, it is generally regarded as a highly individualistic talent. Success in sales does not depend upon the adoption of set routines but, mostly, results from the cultivation of a particular style and set of tactics. In addition, having once captured a customer the next problem is to retain that business – nothing is more secure than a 'solid' customer; all the more so if, as in most sales organisations, individuals rely heavily, or even exclusively, upon commission for their earnings. All of this keeps the salesperson in constant competition with his or her fellow salespeople: individualism at work would seem to be the best policy. Not surprisingly, in such an occupational culture there is little room for the belief in collective action, and trade unions are regarded with deep and abiding distaste. It is just possible that had Ray Fullair not become a salesman – and had he not been emotionally scarred extolling the virtues of rat poison – he might not have become a saloon-bar union-basher.

Similarly, it is no mere accident that Arthur Grimace is a relatively predictable person: he conforms – more or less – to our expectations of how accountants think and behave. His training and education, the values which inform his work activities and his personal experience in that particular kind of career ladder all propel him towards certain kinds of conclusions. It would be a strange variety of accountant who did *not* tend to construe social relations in terms of 'efficiency' and 'inefficiency' and who did not occasionally reduce moral and political judgement to a sort of philosophical cost–benefit analysis.

Just as we must try to understand how Arthur comes to his understanding of the social world so too with others, such as miners, whose attitudes to work and employment have been and still are developed within a powerful social and cultural (or sub-cultural) tradition of militant trade unionism. The historical context of employment in the mines is one which reflects a long memory of extremely onerous and dangerous working conditions, countless bitter conflicts with the employers – many of which resulted in wage cuts – and a prolonged struggle to get the coal mines nationalised. It is this industrial memory, combined with the close-knit social relations of miners, which conditions contemporary industrial relations in the mining industry rather than the mild histrionics and loudly proclaimed class affiliation of an Arthur Scargill. All that the phrasemonger can do is articulate grievances and fears: he cannot create them. Nor can he proclaim solutions: these have to be worked out in conjunction with the other parties in the particular socio-historical context.

A DEFINITION OF INDUSTRIAL RELATIONS

Formally, industrial relations may be defined as *the administration and control of the employment relationship in industrial societies*. This may seem a somewhat pallid and bloodless label for a sphere of social life which is marked by a rich and colourful range of behaviour and which is fundamental for any society to sustain itself. Furthermore, like all general definitions in social science, it is not instantly very helpful or revealing. This is because its function is to do no more than mark out our analytical territory and provide an indication of the general focus of inquiry. It is what is usually called a *nominal* definition; that is, one which is quite general, singularly descriptive and sufficiently flexible to accommodate a broad range of material. Nonetheless, it does provide a clear starting point and constitutes a good basis for asking the deceptively simple question 'What are industrial relations?'.

Thus far, the concern has been to become familiar with some typical industrial relations situations and to establish some elements of the framework which is necessary in order to consider matters in a reasonably disciplined fashion. Industrial relations are found in the world of work and, in particular, concern the characteristic behaviour of people in an employment relationship. While the form such relationships take varies considerably the basic structure remains constant: one person exchanges his or her labour, time and freedom to act for the various rewards of being employed. For the most part, such relationships are reasonably congenial, though what are seen as excessive demands by the employer or the employee are frequently resisted. This is a constant source of tension and may, on occasion, lead to a temporary breakdown or even severing of the relationship. As in the laggers' tale, the administration and control of the employment relationships at ChemTar International was disrupted by the arrival of the contractor's thermal insulation engineers. In response, the company laggers dramatically revised their expectations of their employment relationship. This, in turn, proved to be unacceptable to the company. These changed circumstances produced a series of unanticipated consequences for all involved, the full effects of which we have yet to consider.

One important conclusion has already become apparent: the administration and control of those employment relationships was not the sole responsibility of any *one* of the interested parties. While the major parameters of the administration process were clearly delineated through company policy and management practice, neither the policy nor the practice could be sustained without the aquiescence of the two trade unions and the employees themselves. What this highlights, once again, is the *inter*dependence of managers and managed, of employers and employees. It reflects another facet of the tension common to all employment relationships: the managers' need to control the labour force has always to be tempered by the managers' parallel need to maintain an acceptable level of employee cooperation and commitment. Although, these days, the balance of control varies considerably from one situation to the next, it is uncommon for one actor to enjoy exclusive control over the administration and control process. Indeed, any attempt to exercise a much greater degree of control than is customary, or to radically readjust the existing balance of control, is likely to meet with disaffection, increasing employee alienation or even determined managerial resistance.

Nonetheless, in general, the employer is invariably the dominant partner. From the specific examples used at the beginning of this chapter it should be clear that none of these individual employees could exercise any real influence over their employers. However, some choices were available and, even in the case of Rachel Lewis, who was the most disadvantaged, she preferred to stay employed in the supermarket rather than opt for unemployment benefit. While the range of options available to Rachel in relation to her employer may be regarded as being so narrow as to reduce her freedom of choice to little but a semantic technicality, so long as there exists a minimum provision of welfare benefits, a society can maintain the illusion of individual freedom of choice.

CONCLUSION

In this chapter the more important general factors influencing behaviour in industrial relations have been briefly discussed. Emphasis has been placed on the intricate consequences of the division of labour in society, the impact of the experience of work in itself and on the significance of the socio-historical context in which behaviour takes place. The responses of employers and employees alike cannot be understood without some insight into such factors.

Employment and work are not merely part of a process of simple economic exchange in which political, social and moral considerations play a subordinate and insignificant role. Ironically, the division of labour among social scientists themselves – which has given us economists, sociologists, psychologists and political scientists, all, ostensibly, operating in distinctive disciplines – has contributed to and reinforced this simplistic and deeply misleading conception of how we should understand the employment relationship. It is only when we ignore such artificial barriers that we can begin to grasp the character of industrial relations and the nature of the employment relationship in a more meaningful fashion. To regard the employment relationship solely or primarily as a means of economic exchange is to miss the point that work and employment are critical to the creation of our social identities and fundamental to the overall development, growth and decline of societies. An understanding of industrial relations is therefore central to understanding society.

3

Mobilising Your Interests

Now we can recognise our industrial relations and have some idea about what it is they are trying to do to each other, it is possible to examine how they organise themselves and how they relate to each other. This chapter is focused on the various organisations which are directly involved in the control and administration of the employment relationship.

For simplicity, the analysis of industrial relations is often conducted in terms of the *actors* involved, the social *processes*, such as bargaining, conciliation and arbitration, which typically characterise their relationships, and the various *structures* which operate as constraints on what they can do. As we have seen, the actors – employers, employees, governments and various state agencies – all have interests which may, from time to time, come into conflict with each other and they mobilise themselves in various ways to more effectively pursue these interests. While it is not always easy to see how such organisations operate to encroach on the control of the other actors, almost any daily newspaper provides a clear indication of all the huffing and puffing, charge and counter-charge flying back and forth between the major actors. Such public and often highly publicised differences of opinion should not be construed as evidence of irreconcilable conflict or fundamental breakdown in their relations. These high-profile histrionics which often accompany disagreement between employer and employees reflect one element of the mobilisation of interests in the attempt to persuade public opinion that what you are engaged in doing, or trying to do, to the other actor is justified.

In this seemingly constant war of attrition conducted through the media, governments occupy the most favoured position: they deal the cards and can always claim they are the honest broker acting on behalf of the national economic interest. This would be fine if only there was some agreement as to what *is* the national interest. Difficulties arise because the election of a new government is invariably accompanied by a complete re-definition of what the national interest is and how we should go about achieving it. Politicians, of course, may operate with quite different frames of reference, and while they may agree, for example, that unemployment is a major problem which must be tackled, the proposed solutions may be based on diametrically opposed assumptions about how the world works. One says increased public expenditure will create new jobs while the other insists it is only through reducing public expenditure that new employment can be generated.

Meanwhile, employers – almost irrespective of the government in power – tend to insist their hands are tied by economic necessity: pressures of competition, increase in national insurance or VAT (Value Added Tax), and the taken-for-granted need to increase productivity and reduce labour costs all combine to make it impossible for them to offer more than a 2% increase on basic rates of pay. Indeed, they can't really afford this. In reply, trade unions insist labour productivity has seen a dramatic increase, jobs have been lost, inflation and VAT have effectively reduced real earnings and they are actually 5% worse off than a year ago. All they are asking is to maintain their hardly extravagant standard of living.

Behind all this surface posturing lies a complex structure of institutions, public relations officers, research workers, trade union officials, Treasury accountants, parliamentary lawyers, civil servants and managers all beavering away to present their case in the best light. And all claim to be acting in the best interests of the nation, the company, the economy, the employees or whatever. In trying to make some assessment of this bewildering array of competing claims to social justice, it is all too easy to forget the consequences for those on the receiving end of the victorious claim: it may result in lower wages, unsocial working hours, more tedious or less skilled work or even redundancy and unemployment. Such prospects are one of the primary motivations which have generated trade unions, professional associations and employers' organisations of various kinds.

In any specific industrial relations issue, the number and complexity of the organisations, actors, laws or other relevant elements will vary considerably from one situation to the next. Nevertheless, whatever the degree of complexity, the fundamental industrial relation, the employment relation – which may be regarded as the core structure – remains invariant; for without this, no industrial relations can take place. A simple example is the relationship between Mohammed and his father. Despite the absence of any formal contract of employment, that relationship could be depicted as shown in figure 3.1.

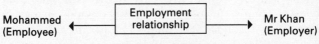

Figure 3.1   A simple employment relation

An analysis of this simple employment relation could be accomplished by examining the interests of the two actors, by identifying any differences in their frame of reference and by assessing their relative control. This could be used as a basis for explaining how *both* actors are involved in the administration and control of the employment relationship. In practice, of course, it is much more complex than this suggests, but this basic approach can be applied to all the various situations we have encountered so far to provide an insightful account of what happens. All employees are engaged in exchanging work or labour for a wage or salary. They do not act autonomously but within the context of a dynamic relationship with their employer and within the constraints of their respective work organisations and other institutions, such as trade unions and State agencies, which may also have an interest in regulating the employment relation and, thus, effectively limit the range of options available to actors. Trade unions, for example, through the bargaining process, seek to influence the level of wages for particular occupational groups; where the individual employee is not represented by a trade union he or she can bargain on his or her own behalf, often in competition with other individual employees or potential employees. Trade unions are often directly opposed by countervailing organisations of employers – such as the Thermal Insulation Contractors' Association (TICA) which appeared in the laggers' tale. These operate as umbrella organisations to represent employer interests; and government has always played a significant role in regulating the employment relation.

The major actors and institutions which have an interest in the administration and control of the employment relationship are presented diagramatically in figure 3.2. This, it must be stressed, is no more than a very simple image of the basic skeletal structure of industrial relations. It is simple, firstly, because it only includes the most obvious actors and institutions; secondly, and more importantly, it is simple because it tells us nothing about the relative significance of the various actors: some, depending on the circumstances, will be far more influential and powerful than others. Thirdly, it presents such a generalised image of those involved it could easily be forgotten that large numbers of employers – in particular those with a workforce of less than 100 – will never encounter an angry union member, far less be faced with an overworked union official. Provided such limitations are recognised – and all diagrams are potentially deceptive – it does provide a useful check-list of the various actors and interests which need to be considered when attempting to understand the factors and social forces which operate to maintain daily industrial relations.

EMPLOYEE ORGANISATIONS

The natural focus for collective employee organisation is the work-group and the immediate place of employment,

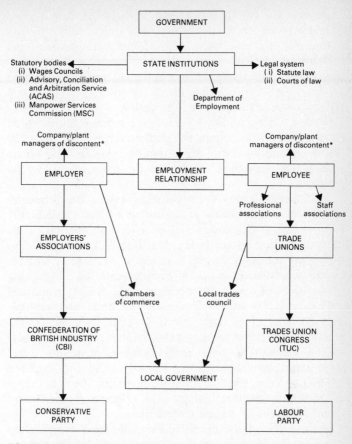

* See chapter 4.

Figure 3.2   The structure of industrial relations

whether this be a workshop, office or any other place where employees with similar terms and conditions of employment come into immediate contact with each other. Early trade union organisation was built from such interactions and, these days, despite the existence of formal bureaucratic union structures, the real strength of employee organisation remains anchored in the degree of employee cohesion and solidarity found at the level of the workplace. As the National Union of

Mineworkers (NUM) discovered in 1984, in their dispute over proposed pit closures, even the most well-organised union can do little when faced with an obdurate and determined employer unless the whole membership is prepared to act collectively. If those at the point of production do not feel a sense of collective identity then the most colourful rabble-rouser in the country is powerless to generate effective collective action. At this level it is the much-misunderstood shop steward – to whom we shall return – who bears the prime responsibility for organising membership and representing the views of employees to management or the employer.

The form employee organisation takes, the strategies employed and the *density* of organisation varies considerably from industry to industry and from one occupation to the next, depending on a complex set of factors. Density refers to the proportion of employees in an industry or factory who are members of the trade union. For example, in coal-mining nearly 100% of miners are members of the NUM; in contrast only about 5% of employees in the hotel and catering industry have joined trade unions. Overall, some 60% of the working population are members of some employee organisation – the vast majority being members of unions. Total trade union membership reached a peak of about 13.4 million in 1979 and, largely as a result of unemployment, has since declined to about 10 million by 1985. Of these, some 60% are members of the 10 largest trade unions.[1]

Historically, as the overall density of union membership among the working population has increased, so the number of individual trade unions has decreased. In 1920 there were 1,384 trade unions; this figure has dropped year by year ever since and now there are about 430 individual trade unions.[2] Trade unions have not simply disappeared, but have amalgamated to form larger and more appropriate units of organisation. This process reflects not only technological changes in the nature of work, which had the effect of eliminating certain craft skills and thus the rationale for a large number of craft trade unions, but also, and more importantly, changes in the sheer size and scope of activity in the major employing organisations. Hence the creation and growth of 'big' employers – such as the major motor-car manufacturers, the larger chemical and consumer goods companies, the nationalised industries, the National Health Service and the Civil Service – also provided the stimulus to 'big' unionism. Just as economic power has become increasingly concentrated since 1945, so too trade unionism has become increasingly monolithic.

The next logical phase would be for trade unions to attempt to establish international organisation to negotiate effectively with multi-national companies. However, this involves overcoming formidable problems: not only are there simple language barriers and marked differences in the cultural traditions and forms of trade union organisation, but, in addition, there are much greater difficulties in identifying a collective interest across national borders. Why, for example, should employees in a Ford assembly plant in Germany or Belgium see it as in their interest to argue for more investment in Britain or Spain in order to maintain the overall levels of employment of car-workers in those countries? If the result is fewer jobs for German or Belgian car workers, they are unlikely to see beyond their immediate work interests, far less their national boundaries. Just as employees may have collective interests in one situation, so too they may have conflicting interests in another. Thus far, Karl Marx's famous injunction, 'Workers of the world, unite!' has proved to be little but empty rhetoric.

The character of unions has also been very significantly shaped by the changing nature of work itself. At one time there was a clear distinction between skilled and unskilled work. This was reflected in the existence of craft unions which were exclusively composed of skilled workers. The AUEW, for example, was originally established in 1851 with relatively high union dues and membership strictly limited to those who had served the appropriate apprenticeship. This remained almost unchanged until 1926 when the AUEW opened its doors to non-craft workers employed in the engineering industry. Now it also has a white-collar section which, primarily, recruits from among the technical and supervisory staff in that industry.

Such policies, which have effectively transformed the union from a craft union into a general union, reflect not only the increasingly nebulous distinction between skilled and non-skilled work, but also attempts by the full-time trade union officials to maintain the financial health of the union as an organisation. With a declining or stagnating membership the union cannot develop or expand the services it provides nor, for that matter, maintain the existing employees of the union. The employment security of union officers ultimately depends on them increasing the membership. Since 1979, for example, those unions most affected by the loss of members due to unemployment have reacted by not replacing union employees who leave. A dramatic reduction in membership would undoubtedly produce unemployed trade union officials.

More generally, while there remain many skilled occupations, unions which seek to maintain an exclusively craft membership are in decline and face a bleak future. Some, unable to accommodate the technological changes which eliminate their skill-base, simply disappear. Others forgo their autonomous occupational identity and merge with another union in an attempt to sustain their bargaining power. In 1983, for example, the Boilermakers' Union – a once proud, financially secure and somewhat august craft union – amalgamated with the GMWU, a general union. A few craft organisations have become embroiled in sometimes desperate defensive action to fend off such changes. Some of the most bitter disputes of recent years involved long-established craft traditions now in decline or under severe pressure from technological advance. ASLEF, the Associated Society of Locomotive Engineers and Firemen – as its very name suggests – draws on a tradition which was laid down before the era of diesel engines and has been fighting a rearguard action against the new employment demands of advancing railway technology while at the same time trying to ward off progressive financial deterioration resulting from the absolute decline in the number of train drivers and footplatemen. Logic impels them toward merger with the

NUR (National Union of Railwaymen) but, thus far, this has been defied by an historical 'craft-consciousness' and pre-empted by periodic rivalry between the two unions.

Another exclusive craft union, the print workers' NGA (National Graphical Association), is facing historical oblivion in the wake of technological change in newspaper production. The 'hot metal' print composing process is rapidly becoming outmoded with the advance of photographic computer-controlled production technologies. This means their work can now be performed by non-skilled print workers and even journalists. The NGA was created in 1964 through the amalgamation of two ancient craft print unions and subsequently incorporated five other small but similar unions in order to create a more secure financial and organisational base. As such, despite very considerable pressure from the print and newspaper employers, it was able, through the closed shop and the vulnerability of newspapers to strike action, to maintain exclusive control over entry to jobs in the composing rooms and exercise considerable control over the terms under which newer technologies were introduced.

This long historical process of change erupted into the public limelight in 1983 with the very bitter dispute between the NGA and Shah Newspapers over the sacking of six printers who had gone on strike rather than work with non-union printers. The brief public infamy enjoyed by the NGA at that time probably marks the beginning of the end for the remarkable degree of control the NGA has been able to exercise in the employment relationship. In that dispute the employers, through the particular employer concerned, Mr Shah, have finally established a significant breach in the closed shop. So what was at stake was far more than merely the sacking of a small number of craft print workers: the whole basis of NGA influence throughout the industry is now in question.

Once a group of skilled workers lose the right to define who shall be employed to do their kind of work the essential prop of their economic leverage is undermined. In the case of the NGA the technical basis of their claim to specify who should be employed had long since been overtaken by technological innovation. However, since the NGA was able, through the closed shop, to ensure all employees were members of the NGA, it could effectively maintain control over jobs and keep earnings high in exchange for agreeing to some of the new technology. Now the closed-shop principle has been breached the NGA can no longer be sure such policies will continue to be effective. While it is most unlikely the significance of the NGA will decline overnight, the 1983 dispute is likely to prove to be an historical turning point in the fortunes of the union. Such conservatism may be viewed as stubborn, blind and even self-destructive, but can only be understood in the particular historical contexts in which it is found.

In contrast to the now declining craft unions, which are organised around a particular set of marketable skills, general unions – such as the TGWU (Transport and General Workers' Union) – draw their strength almost entirely from the extensiveness of their recruitment of employees into membership. After unsuccessful attempts to set up general unions for unskilled workers in the 1830s, the first permanent trade unions for unskilled employees were established in the 1880s. These unions, initially created by dockers and gas workers, are now among the largest in Britain and have continued to base their bargaining strength on large numbers and a high density of membership.

The largest of all British trade unions, the TGWU, is a general union. It has members among trawlermen, agricultural workers, transport drivers, dockers, car workers and hotel and catering employees. Gas workers, the original core of the GMBTU, are now greatly outnumbered by GMBTU members in the engineering and food and drink industries. General unions, though less successfully than craft workers, also try to establish closed-shop agreements with the employer. Membership of such unions is not confined to unskilled workers – the laggers, for example, with their new-found skilled status, were members of the GMBTU and the AUEW, as noted above, is now more accurately regarded as a general union.

Another frequently mentioned category of trade union is

the industrial union: a union which organises all the employees in a particular industry irrespective of skill or occupational category. In Britain there are no such unions, though the NUM is often suggested as the nearest approximation we have. This is because the NUM organises nearly all of the manual workers in mining; the 'foremen' are members of NACODS while managerial personnel may join BACM, both of which came to public attention during the 1984–5 mining dispute. Members of NACODS (National Association of Colliery Overmen, Deputies and Shotfirers) oversee the daily operations underground and have a major concern with safety: legally, no mining can take place without their approval. They signed a separate agreement with the NCB during the strike and this dashed the hopes of the NUM for, had the NACODS men also stopped work, this would have closed down the whole of the British coal-mining industry. BACM (British Association of Colliery Management) briefly hit the headlines when they expressed concern about the way the strike was being handled by senior management at the NCB.

The distinctive character of mining work is one of the major reasons why the NUM is the only trade union which resembles an industrial union. Mining can only take place in particular geological locations where the required minerals are to be found. This is one of the factors which helps to account for the particular kind of cohesiveness which characterises miners and their trade unions. Whole communities spring up around the mines and virtually everyone is dependent upon the mine for his or her livelihood: the fate of the mine determines the fate of the local shops, schools, pubs, banks, churches and other mining service businesses. In the absence of alternative sources of employment such communities are likely to develop into much more close-knit and cohesive social settings than would be found in, for example, a large town or city where the collective interests of the community are far less visible. In the early days of extensive coal-mining, the dependence of mineworkers was even greater than today because it was usual for the mine owner to own all the housing and, in some areas, even the shops. In the event of a dispute, the miners and their families could be thrown out of their homes and denied access to food. There were countless disputes, often violence and considerable hardship quite apart from the dangers of the work itself.

In addition to the almost unique character of mining work, the fact the industry is nationalised means there is only one employer and relatively uniform terms and conditions of employment. It is only by appreciating these factors in conjunction with the powerful 'historical memory' and culture of miners that the contemporary behaviour and policies of the NUM can be grasped with any degree of security.

Mining also illustrates why we have so few industrial unions. Every few years some eminent politician will point to West Germany which, in the complete reconstruction which took place after World War II, established a structure of industrial trade unions,[3] and claim their better record of industrial sense and cooperation and higher levels of labour productivity can be accounted for by the much more rational basis of trade union organisation in West Germany. There are sagacious nods of approval from the back benches and *The Times* leader column writer oozes sympathy for employers and managers faced with our seemingly archaic pattern of unionisation with competing trade unions, demarcation lines and inter-union disputes. Everyone agrees the industrial union structure is a better way and, as usual, nothing is done. There are very good reasons for this.

Existing trade union leaders – fearful of the consequences to their own particular organisation (and their own employment prospects) – voice well-rehearsed objections concerning the difficulties of actually reorganising trade unionism on such a basis. Like all long-established organisations, such as the House of Lords or the legal system, unions tend to react in a conservative fashion when reform is canvassed. Their objections, however, are not without some merit: while it is relatively easy to see who are the employees of the mining industry or the railways system, it is by no means a simple task to clearly identify where the boundaries between other industries should be drawn. For example, who should be included in the car-manufacturing industry? The employees who work on the assembly lines are easily identified, but should we also include all those who supply components to the industry, those who make the steel from which car bodies are pressed, those who are employed by rubber companies to make, among other things, tyres for cars, and those who sell and market cars? Even if we overcome this issue which, like all such issues, is only capable of being resolved in some arbitrary fashion, there remain formidable problems in persuading individual occupational groups to join with others in the same industrial union. Leaving aside the obvious reluctance of craft workers (such as those in the NGA) to be subsumed in a union organisation which contains a majority of unskilled or semi-skilled workers, let us examine a less obvious but more instructive example.

The National Health Service seems to be a reasonably coherent industry comprising all those people in society who are employed in caring for the sick and disabled. Like mining, there is one employer and the NHS is a seemingly obvious candidate to provide the first of our new industrial unions. But the thought of doctors, nurses, hospital administrators, porters, ambulance drivers, domestics and catering staff all joining together in one large 'certified' trade union is hardly a suggestion which would draw much support from even the most fanatical trade union reformer. Indeed, the image of members of the Royal College of Surgeons agreeing to sit down hand in hand with hospital cleaners to negotiate the next year's annual wage increase is, in present times, little short of ludicrous. The differences in interest between medical staff and ancillary staff may, in practice, be perceived as being far greater than any collective interest they might have in relation to the employer. On sober reflection, good ideas such as the creation of an industrial union for the NHS staff may prove to be no more than the blind ideology of ambitious politicians or the product of a naive idealism.

Employers too, on sober reflection, are likely to step back from any really positive actions designed to reorganise our trade unions along industrial lines no matter what the alleged long-term benefits. As hinted above, the successful creation of such structures would be an extraordinarily complex and long-winded process. Months would be spent defining the industrial sectors and arguing about which categories of employee went into which unions; it would take years to reconstruct the existing bargaining structures in both private and public industries, and, in spite of a Royal Commission to determine the shape and composition of the new NHS industrial union, the doctors would still refuse to sit down with the ancillary grades.

More fundamentally, apart from such practical difficulties, the faint-hearted enthusiasm of employers for industrial unions reflects their well-founded suspicion that any such restructuring – while it just might, in the long term, reduce some of the more tiresome and irritating sources of industrial conflicts – would almost certainly increase the coherence and improve the operating efficiency of trade unionism. In short, by eliminating the competition for membership and provid-ing a comprehensive industrial base for their activities, industrial unionism could, potentially, provide for an increase in the bargaining power of trade unions. Hence there are very good reasons why employers, in general, while paying lip-service to demands for industrial unions, remain extremely reluctant to do anything concrete to establish such institutions.

There are also white-collar, occupational and managerial trade unions. The variation in size, organisational structure, composition of membership and policy among these unions is just as great as, if not greater than, it is within the ranks of the longer-established, 'blue-collar' unions. It is important to recognise that, since 1945, the absolute growth in trade union membership is accounted for by the dramatic expansion in white-collar trade unionism. Membership of these unions increased by nearly 80% between 1949 and 1970. Initially this growth reflected no more than the increase in the number of white-collar jobs within the economy, but since about 1964 the density of membership (that is, the proportion of the total white-collar workforce which is unionised) has also increased from about 30% to 40%. Although white-collar employees remain more reluctant to join unions than traditional manual workers, this sector has continued to be the only one where real advances in unionisation are apparent.

It is also important to remember this growth in membership is uneven. Membership is much higher in the public sector – where about seven out of every ten white-collar employees are members of unions – than in the private sector where only one in ten is a member. This reflects not only the greater scale of operations in the public sector with its highly efficient sprawling bureaucratic agencies, but also the increasingly routine character of administrative work and, at least until 1979, the relatively benign attitudes of successive governments to trade unionism in public service. Until recently, for example, governmental employers abided by what were called 'Fair Wages Resolutions' passed from time to time by Parliament. These insisted that people employed directly or indirectly by State agencies should not be paid less than the rates prevailing for comparable work in the private sector. Similarly, the enabling legislation through which the major nationalised industries were created included provisions for bargaining and consultation with the relevant trade unions. Such relatively positive attitudes have undoubtedly assisted the faster growth of white-collar trade unionism in the public sector. In contrast, the conditions under which white-collar trade unionism was established and developed within the private sector of the economy were far more hostile and – in some enterprises, such as banking and insurance – remain so. Governmental economic and industrial relations policies – such as incomes policy in the 1960s and pro-trade union legislation in the 1970s – have also stimulated the growth of white-collar trade unionism in those times.

Not surprisingly, the pattern of white-collar unionisation reflects all these factors. For example, the largest white-collar union NALGO (National and Local Government Officers' Association), is a public-sector trade union. While it is the major white-collar trade union in local government, it also negotiates for office employees in the NHS and several nationalised industries. Second in size is ASTMS (Association of Scientific, Technical and Managerial Staffs) whose general secretary, Clive Jenkins, is probably the best known among the leaders of white-collar unions. The public notoriety he enjoys reflects his accomplishments in developing ASTMS from two small specialised trade unions of technical employees into the fastest-growing union in Britain. ASTMS membership has expanded by about 800% since 1960 and, while such labels can be deceptive, it is the nearest we have in Britain to a *general* white-collar trade union. There are few other white-collar unions which will recruit almost any grade of white-collar employee in almost any sector of employment. The majority, like the NUT (National Union of Teachers) or the RCN (Royal College of Nursing) are more accurately described as occupational unions since they only recruit from one specific occupational group. The most well-organised managerial trade unions, such as BACM (British Association of Colliery Management) and the Engineers' and Managers' Association in the electricity supply industry, could also be regarded as occupational trade unions.

In addition to independent trade unions, employees organise themselves into two other significant forms of organisation: professional associations and staff associations. The former are a focus of organisation for individuals employed in occupations which enjoy or, more often, aspire to professional status in the world of work. In terms of both structure and functions they vary much more than do conventional trade unions. More specifically, there are wide differences between professional associations in the degree to which they can actively control the employment relationships of their members.

At one end of the spectrum are organisations such as the BIM (British Institute of Management). This is open to anyone employed in a managerial role and others, such as academics, who work in the field of management education. It holds conferences, supports research into management and provides certain kinds of information and advice to members. Membership is voluntary and has no direct bearing on the employment of members – though one might join so as to make friends and influence the right kinds of people. Another, more specific professional managerial association is the IPM (Institute of Personnel Management) which, in addition to the kinds of activities pursued by the BIM, also provides what might be called a certificate of competence – the Diploma in Personnel Management. This examination, for the most part, is taken by aspiring young personnel staff, for whom the diploma is an indication of their familiarity with the body of knowledge deemed necessary to be regarded as a suitably trained personnel officer. Unfortunately, such a qualification is not regarded by employers as being essential and, while possession of the IPM diploma does provide a useful edge in the job market and may be a requisite to promotion in some companies, personnel management has yet to achieve a secure professional status.

In the longer term, the objective of the IPM is for the diploma to become like the apprenticeship served by craft workers: a prerequisite to employment. But there still seems to be a long way to go before employers will be persuaded the personnel function is of such a highly specialised variety that no-one but fully trained and qualified people should be let loose on it. Until that changes the IPM will remain unable to exercise any significant influence in the employment relationships of personnel staff.

Doubtless the IPM might suggest this is over-simple and perhaps too cynical an interpretation of the functional objective of professional associations, and it would be pointed out their primary purpose is to maintain and improve the working environment of all employees by establishing appropriate professional standards – to which end, for example, there have been proposals concerning a code of ethics for personnel management. Such a position is both responsible and laudable. However, precisely the same kinds of arguments have been put forward in recent times by solicitors to preserve their near-monopoly of house conveyancing, and by dentists in defence of their monopoly in fitting dentures. In this respect the functional problem faced by professional associations is how to create – and, indeed, maintain – a climate of social opinion which legitimises the claim that only they should be allowed to decide who shall be employed in a particular kind of work. Professional associations, at their best, enjoy exclusive 'job property rights' to certain kinds of employment and, as such, may be regarded as closed shops for the middle classes.

By far the two most effective such organisations are the Law Society and the BMA (British Medical Association): the models to which all present professional occupations aspire. Both exercise extensive and intensive controls over the employment relationships of doctors and lawyers. Entry to these ancient trades is strictly circumscribed by a lengthy process of socialisation and education. All examinations have to be approved by the respective professional associations which, for this reason, are often referred to as 'qualifying associations' rather than trade unions. Such control over training ensures the standards of craftsmanship are maintained and improved, but also prevents potential competitors – such as homeopathic practitioners, acupuncturists, estate agents, building societies and the like – from making significant inroads into the available markets of clients. The salaries of medical staff and the fees paid to lawyers are also, more or less, directly regulated by the two professional associations; this aspect of their activities is so successful that doctors rarely resort to industrial action for better wages and it is unknown for lawyers to work to rule. In addition, and of critical significance to the intensive controls exercised in the employment relationship, these two professional associations also have – outside of criminal or civil proceedings – almost exclusive jurisdiction in the event of any complaint from clients about the standards or quality of work performed by these professionals. In the extreme cases a doctor may be 'struck off' or a lawyer 'debarred', actions which, in effect, mean he or she can no long practise and, in addition to the social stigma attached to such sanctions, there is the loss of livelihood.

While such professional controls are seen to be necessary in order to protect clients from abuse, malpractice and incompetence and, for the most part, are socially endorsed, their significance in the present context lies in their impact on the employment relationship. Qualifying associations, like the Law Society and the BMA, in that they exercise extensive control over who shall be allowed to practise, can be seen as exercising intensive control over individual doctors and lawyers. At the same time, such controls also permit these occupational groups a remarkable degree of independence in regulating their own affairs in relation to their employers, whether these be institutions, such as the NHS, or individual private clients. Such control over both the labour market and the product or service also facilitates maintenance of relatively high levels of remuneration and there are few who, once admitted to the profession, complain about the restrictions on their freedom. It is no small irony that among critics of the conventional trade union enforcement of closed shop provisions are to be found some MPs who earn sufficient from their legal practices to be able to devote the greater part of their time of professional politics. As members of the most effective closed shop in Britain – the legal profession – we might expect them to have a greater understanding of why others, like the NGA printers or railwaymen, should seek to maintain a similar degree of protection in their respective labour markets.

In contrast to professional associations, staff associations are often the weakest form of employee organisation. Many employers – especially in the white-collar sector – have sought to pre-empt the growth of trade union membership among their employees by actively encouraging or even establishing an in-house staff association. Membership is invariably confined to the employees of the particular company with the employer providing the necessary facilities, often financing and, perhaps, even staffing the organisation. Such organisations are an alternative to independent unions and have proved to be a stubborn obstacle in the way of any union seeking formal recognition from the company. They often provide good channels of communication and, while it would be mistaken to see them as no more than creatures of managerial interests, there is precious little evidence to suggest they ever come into serious conflict with the employer. With no independent organisational base, no significant financial resources and no independent full-time officers, it is hardly surprising they are unable to bargain effectively on behalf of employee interests. Such associations are much beloved in banks and insurance companies and viewed with considerable contempt by trade union official-dom.

TRADE UNION COOPERATION

Most trade unions maintain strong links with other unions. At the workshop and company level of organisation, committees of shop stewards from several unions often exist – if only informally – to coordinate policy as far as possible. More formal relationships are frowned upon by trade union officialdom because it undermines the authority of individual unions and may result in local policies which go against the official union line. This does not, of course, prevent such links being forged, though even the most coherent, such as the committees of shop stewards in car-manufacturing, have proved difficult to sustain in the face of pallid support from union officials and determined employer resistance.

The more visible forms of union collaboration are to be found in joint negotiating committees where several unions representing the diverse employees of a single employer agree to cooperate and bargain together. This is most common in the public sector where there is an extensive formal structure of bargaining institutions to regulate employment relations between public employees of all kinds and the variety of government, local government and nationalised industry employers. Similar arrangements exist in some parts of the private sector, notably in the engineering industry, where the CSEU (Confederation of Shipbuilding and Engineering Unions) coordinates and conducts collective bargaining with the Engineering Employers' Federation (EEF).

At national level the Trades Union Congress (TUC), originally established in 1868, is regarded – sometimes mistakenly – as the official voice of British trade unionism. In simple statistical terms, the TUC appears to be a powerful institution: in 1980 just under 90% of all trade unionists were affiliated to the TUC and of the 27 union organisations with over 100,000 members only the RCN (Royal College of

Nursing) and the Police Federation were not members of the TUC.[4] Nonetheless, the TUC, with its own General Secretary, administrative, education and research staff is only as strong as the degree of cohesion among the unions which are affiliated to it and provide the necessary finance. And unions, over the years, have jealously guarded their independence and autonomy. The TUC only really coordinates trade unionism when it is empowered to do so by the member unions, and this has varied considerably over time, depending on the circumstances. This somewhat fragile status of the TUC was highlighted during the course of the 1984–85 mining dispute. At the TUC Congress in September 1984 a strongly worded resolution of support for the miners was passed to widespread acclaim and the Congress was regarded by some as a triumph for the NUM. But the TUC could not deliver: key unions in the electricity and steel industries, both members of the TUC, simply ignored the resolution and there was nothing the TUC could or would do to persuade them otherwise. Later, towards the end of the strike in February 1985, a high-level TUC group, including the General Secretary, met the NCB to produce a formula to resolve the dispute. This was rejected out of hand by the NUM. But the fundamental weakness of the TUC is best illustrated by the way it has been treated by recent governments.

After years of gradually accumulating influence with and representation to governments, the TUC experienced a seemingly dramatic increase in influence during the 1960s, when a Labour government sought to implement national economic planning and an effective incomes policy; and 1970s, when a subsequent Labour government was reelected in part on the claim that it was the only party which could persuade the trade unions to cooperate with government. This latter administration, during 1974–79, created the Social Contract: ostensibly a new form of collaboration between the trades unions, as represented by the TUC, and government. Social and economic policy was to be formulated in conjunction with unions in exchange for income regulation. In practice, largely because of the deteriorating economic situation, the Social Contract tended to be little more than an euphemism for incomes policy and it – and the government – foundered in that 'winter of discontent' in 1978–79. The election of 1979 was held in a public climate deeply hostile to trade unionism and since then we have seen the emergence of a radical alternative to collaboration with unions. The Conservative administration of 1979, re-elected in 1983, has virtually ignored the TUC, and a hobnailed boot has not scratched the polished corridors of power since Mr Callaghan was defeated in 1979.

The seemingly catatonic response of the TUC to the loss of political influence reflects not only the bewilderment total exclusion and the transformation in the political climate brought, but also the essentially democratic principles of British trade unionism. The TUC can only do what the member unions permit it to do and, particularly in times of economic recession, the TUC and trade unions are only as influential as governments allow them to be.

Nonetheless, the TUC is not unimportant for it performs two major related functions. It is the public voice articulating the general interests of employees and unions and it coordinates national trade union policy and action. Both these functions have increased in scale and scope over time in response to industrial development and the legal regulation of both trade unionism and the employment relationship itself.

As the major representative of employee interests, it has institutional membership on a variety of tripartite committees and statutory bodies. The most notable are NEDC (National Economic Development Council) and ACAS (Advisory, Conciliation and Arbitration Service). Whether being courted or rejected, the TUC continues to regard the representations it makes to all governments as of central importance. In the role of 'executive manager' of trade union policy and action, it facilitates amalgamations between unions; adjudicates disputes where unions are seeking to organise the same group of employees; provides education and training for, in particular, shop stewards; and conducts research. The latter is often used in the formulation of trade union policy documents – such as the annual TUC Economic Review – which are published by the TUC, as are a wide range of publicity, information and educational materials. If coordinated action is required – such as lobbying for or protesting against legislative change – the TUC invariably takes the leading role.

At regional level there are intermediate organisational structures, the most well-known being the Scottish TUC and the Wales TUC, both of which hold an annual conference and seek, with far fewer resources, to fulfil the same functions for unions in those parts of the United Kingdom. More locally, at the base of the TUC, are the Trades Councils. These are to be found in cities and most large towns functioning as mini-TUCs coordinating local union interests and action. They are composed of representatives from trade union branches in the area and, overall, represent about one-third of the total union membership. As ever with such union organisations, membership is voluntary and union branches in the locality are expected to affiliate directly to their Trades Council. Although largely unnoticed, such Councils can often mobilise effective union support around local issues – such as campaigning against the closure of hospitals – and lobbying local authorities. Trade unionists who are also local councillors often provide an important link in articulating the interests of local trade unions.

EMPLOYER ORGANISATION

Employers have a history of mobilising their interests which goes back as far as, if not further than, the emergence of trade unions. Just as employees associated to exercise some control over the price paid for their labour, so too employers formed alliances to reduce competition between themselves. They got together to fix wages or establish a united front in the face of union demands. Like the early trade unions, the first *employers' associations* were often temporary affairs lasting only so long as necessary to achieve some immediate aim; and when unions became stable and financially secure organisations so employers created more permanent organisations to combat them.

Compared to employee organisations we know far less about, and hear far less from, the organisations set up by employers to facilitate their control of the employment relationship. There are two main reasons why this is so. Firstly, employers' associations tend to conduct their business in private, avoid publicity and, because many of them have commercial as well as industrial relations functions, operate in a relatively secretive fashion. The vast majority do not hold public annual conferences and, in general, they are not open to the same kind of public scrutiny and criticism as unions. Secondly, the *collective* organisation of employers, as compared to those of employees, has never been quite so fundamental to the protection and furtherance of employer interests. This is because employers have always enjoyed two critical advantages over employees: they have always had greater legal standing and it is always the employer who decides whether or not there will be any employment in the first place.

This latter point requires emphasis, for it is so obvious we often overlook it. Historically, it has meant employers have always established the initial terms and conditions of employment and these have constituted the ground rules of the employment relationship. To stress such inbuilt employer advantages may seem, at first, to be no more than to adopt a political or partisan position. This is not the case, for such advantages flow naturally from the employment relationship: it is in the nature of that socio-economic exchange for the actor doing the employing to specify the critical elements – and this appears to be so in both capitalist and non-capitalist economic systems. Thus the employer, by definition, possesses important organisational resources prior to any collective mobilisation of employers in the same or similar labour market; unlike individual employees, individual employers can, almost invariably, stand alone. For example, many employers have never felt the need to join any employers' association while others have been able to leave such associations without having to worry about the consequences.

One measure of our incomplete knowledge about

employers' associations is the fact that accurate figures on the number of active associations are hard to come by. In 1968[5] it was estimated there were about 1,350; in 1979 one introductory text suggested a figure of 1,000, though this included 'a proportion of trade associations which are not involved in any industrial relations activities',[6] while another, in 1983, is adamant there are 481 together with another 1,000 or so which are concerned with matters of trade rather than labour;[7] and a more recent study[8] indicates there are now about 300 officially registered employers' associations. Such uncertainty reflects not only ambiguities as to what kinds of organisation ought to be included and considerable variation in the degree to which different employers' associations are involved in regulating the employment relationships, but also an understandable reticence amongst employers to advertise their activities. Nevertheless, it has been estimated[9] that about 60% of employers are members of some association, a figure suggesting that, at least statistically in terms of density, they are better organised than are employees.

The structure, functions and prime activities of employers' associations vary more than among employee organisations. The most well-known, the Engineering Employers' Federation (EEF), has a federal structure with individual regional associations affiliating to the national body. A similar pattern is found in the National Federation of Building Trades Employers which is comprised of over 200 local associations organised into 10 regional associations. The degree of centralised control over bargaining is less in these federal structures than in, for example, the Electrical Contractors' Association. The latter, which represents about 80% of the employers in the industry, has both branch and regional groupings but also more centralised policy-making. In many associations there is no intermediate tier of organisation between the member companies and the national organisation. Examples of the latter would include the Multiple Shoe Retailers' Association, the Newspaper Publishers' Association and, curious as it may seem, the Test and County Cricket Board. Such variation reflects not only the history of employer collaboration in particular industries, but the size of the industry, the size and profitability of the member firms, the scope of their activities and whether the industry is privately or publicly owned.

Leaving aside the commercial aspects of employers' association activities – which may from time to time significantly affect their industrial relations policies – employers' associations have engaged in four relatively distinctive strategies in their effort to administer and control the employment relationship: bargaining, dispute-resolution, providing advice and pressure-group activity.[10]

In general, the major contribution of employers' associations to British industrial relations has been the establishment of multi-employer collective bargaining and the creation of industry-wide disputes procedures (see chapter 5). Since the late 1960s, particularly in the private sector, the operational significance of these functions has declined in relation to the extent to which companies have opted to develop their own tailor-made industrial relations policies and agreements. However, this latter development, combined with a significant extension in both the amount and scope of legislation regulating unions and the employment relationship, has led to an expansion in the advisory function. Members have significantly increased their demands for advice on a variety of legal issues, how to cope with incomes policy restrictions, and what sort of bargaining structures, disputes procedures, and wage-payment systems to establish. There is also a high demand for information on local labour market prices.

Employers have always engaged in pressure-group activities, seeking to represent their interests through various forms of organisation – such as employers' associations, local, regional and national Chambers of Commerce and a succession of allegedly national federations and associations of employers. Such influence has been exercised both locally and nationally. However, it was not until 1965, with the formation of the Confederation of British Industry (CBI) that a single, clearly acknowledged national employers' interest grouping emerged. Just as employers' associations tend to be regarded as the equivalent of trade unions in function, so too the CBI is viewed as the parallel institution to the TUC.

Although there had been pressure for many years to establish a single representative voice for employers, the critical stimulus to the formation of the CBI came, somewhat ironically, from the Labour government of 1964 which was determined to institute some form of national economic planning. Despite dogged resistance from some major employers and their associations, the CBI has, since that time, grown in membership, stature and influence and is now widely recognised as the authoritative voice of British industrialists and manufacturers. As one analyst has remarked, 'There can be little doubt that the performance of the representative function lies behind the very considerable increase in the membership of the CBI in recent years. Indeed, there is little else to explain it.'[11] Membership extends across the whole range of enterprise – large and small companies, both public and private sector employers, employers' and commercial associations. Indeed, the CBI has claimed to represent more employees than does the TUC, since the employers affiliated to it account for some 75% of the working population.

On the surface it functions in fashion similar to the TUC: there is regional organisation; an annual conference to decide policy (since 1977); it publishes an Industrial Trends Survey; sits on numerous tripartite bodies such as ACAS and the NEDC; has a structure of specialist committees dealing with various aspects of employer interests and, like the TUC, makes representations to government and is, from time to time, consulted by governments. Again somewhat ironically, just as the TUC and the unions are prone to come into conflict with their natural political ally, Labour governments, so the CBI has, on occasion, not always approved of the policies pursued by Conservative governments.

Employers have also mobilised their interests through a variety of other institutions and associations, the most notable being the Chambers of Commerce and the Institute of Directors (IOD) which are powerful pressure-group organisations. The Chambers of Commerce can be regarded as the functional equivalents of Trades Councils for they coordinate local business and employer interests, represent them to local authorities and are rarely directly involved in employment relationship as such. They enjoy their greatest influence at local levels, but also have some very articulate regional associations as well as a national association. In 1980, for example, the West Midlands Chambers of Commerce published a report which was highly critical of the Conservative administration's economic policy and demanded changes to protect their interests.[12]

In the past five years the IOD has been, as one observer put it, 'transformed from a rather seedy dining club for old buffers into a highly visible pressure group'.[13] If the CBI is regarded as the 'responsible' voice of employer views, then the IOD, if such a parallel is permissible, could be seen as the 'militant tendency' in the employers' camp. It has mounted a series of powerfully sustained campaigns in favour of drastic reductions in trade union powers and a more extensive denationalisation programme. It is one of the most outspoken advocates of legally restricting trade union activity and, in this respect, has not been unsuccessful. How far such aggressive and drastic reforms are supported by the majority of employers is difficult to gauge, though the views of the IOD have not always found favour with the CBI.

GOVERNMENT ORGANISATION

All modern governments, regardless of their political ideologies, are deeply involved in the regulation of the employment relationship. Indeed, they occupy such a centrifugal position they may be regarded as the most influential of the three major actors. This is not a commonly held view and it will be elaborated in some detail in following chapters.

In brief, governments and the State agencies they control have an almost all-pervasive influence because they perform three critical and interdependent functions. As legislator, they determine the ground rules under which employers and employees interact – and there is now legislation covering almost every aspect of employment. As the largest employer, any government decision to increase or decrease public expenditure can have far-reaching effects on the labour market. And, as the general manager of the economy, the content and direction of economic and fiscal policy can have an instantly sobering impact on the interests of both employers and employees. As noted above, there is not necessarily a consistent identity of interests between Labour governments and unions nor between Conservative governments and employers. Governments may have their own interests – like getting re-elected – or may regard themselves as 'balancing' the interests of labour and capital. For these and other reasons, governments may come into conflict with their apparently natural constituencies of interest-groups.

In pursuing their chosen policy with regard to administering and controlling the employment relationship, governments have a wide range of State institutions and resources at their disposal. These include the law itself – which only governments may change; the civil service to administer government policies through Whitehall; control over all decisions on public expenditure, taxation and general economic policy; direction of the nationalised industries and public services; and, not to be forgotten, the forces of law and order. More specifically, there are a variety of statutory bodies, such as ACAS, the Manpower Services Commission (MSC), Wages Councils and any others they choose to set up, which are directly responsible for regulating different aspects of the employment relationship. For example, the MSC was created to assist in alleviating the problem of rising unemployment and has been particularly active in trying to ensure young people do not face immediate unemployment on leaving school. These have included a variety of youth training and community work schemes designed to educate such potential employees in the ways of work and, where possible, find real employment. It is a measure of the scale of this enterprise that the MSC budget is now greater than the total expenditure on all forms of conventional education.

In contrast, Wages Councils have been with us for over 70 years. They were set up in low-paid industries – such as hairdressing, hotel and catering, clothing and footwear and agriculture – where the trade union organisation was regarded as being too weak to bargain effectively with employers. They are tripartite committees of trade unions, employers and independent members appointed by the Department of Employment charged with establishing minimum wages and conditions of employment. The largest proportion of Wages Council workers (42%) are to be found in the hotel and catering business, while the lowest-paid Wages Council workers are to be found in hairdressing. The Wages Council system has not been very effective despite the existence of a wages inspectorate – which is grossly understaffed – and the potential legal penalties for failing to pay the statutory minima. In 1982, for example, employees and their unions made over 10,000 complaints and 40% of employers in the Wages Council industries were found to be making illegal underpayments.[14] There are some who think Wages Councils keep wages artificially high, and the present government is considering their abolition in order to stop people being priced out of jobs.

CONCLUSION

This chapter has considered the major organisations created and controlled by the three actors to pursue their interests in the employment relation. All must be understood in the social, political and economic contexts in which they emerge, develop and are superseded.

4

Employment Managers

In all the advanced industrial societies the dominant social process which regulates, controls and, on occasion, afflicts our existence is the process of management. It impinges on almost every facet of social life and it is this all-pervasiveness which has helped to make it an accepted, if not always acceptable, feature of contemporary society. The 20th century, as the German sociologist, Max Weber, observed, has been typified by the insidious spread of the bureaucratic mind and the relentless expansion of bureaucratic modes of control. Rules are the essence of such controls, managers are the handmaidens of bureaucracies and management has become the euphemism to describe all forms of control, bureaucratic or otherwise.

Given our almost unthinking acceptance and endorsement of management as a social process, it has become a notoriously difficult term to define. In the context of industrial relations it can be used to describe almost any aspect of regulation in the employment relationship. Even if the half a dozen or more common-sense meanings are ignored, it remains an intractably ambiguous term for it is used to refer not only to the *process* of controlling and directing employees but also as a catch-all label to describe those *actors* who carry out such tasks. However, undaunted by this definitional swamp, in this chapter we will be concerned to identify who are the managers of employment and to outline their role in the management process. The major methods used by such managers will be considered in the next chapter.

WHO ARE THE MANAGERS?

Among the wholesome collection of employees encountered in previous chapters – at first sight – only three appear to be directly concerned with the management of employment: the personnel experts, Peter Warmly and Barbara Adam, and the supermarket manager who makes Rachel's life a misery. The former two work at a specific 'management function', personnel, which is centred on the creation and maintenance of good industrial or employee relations. The latter, the manager of the supermarket, is responsible for a spectrum of activities apart from the employment relationship. He has to maintain adequate stock levels, re-order goods, ensure that products are correctly priced, mount advertising campaigns, meet certain profit and turnover targets and, generally, organise and control the whole range of activities necessary for the supermarket to function. In short, he is a general manager.

In broad terms, anyone whose job includes supervising the work of other employees or is concerned with monitoring the use of labour as an economic resource can be seen as being involved in the management of employment. This includes a very wide range of people and they can be directly – as in the case of a foreman – or indirectly – as in the case of a management accountant calculating the labour cost of a particular product – involved in this management process. Each of them plays a more or less significant role in determining the overall character and temper of industrial relations. For our present analytical purposes, three kinds of employment manager can be identified: the immediate boss, the managers of discontent, and those who both provide and regulate employment opportunities.

The immediate boss

Our immediate boss is the person who directly supervises our work. It may be a chargehand, a ward sister, a maintenance engineer, an office manager, an executive officer in the civil

74

service, a solicitor, the mate on a ship or even a Prime Minister. Everyone who is employed works within the confines of an authority structure involving formal subordination and supervision which will be more or less congenial. The immediate boss, whoever it is, directs and seeks to control our behaviour at work. This inevitably personal relationship, not surprisingly, is likely to be very important in influencing the character of our immediate work environment, the amount of work we are expected to do and the quality of our working life. Bosses come in all shapes and styles, may be good, bad or indifferent, and the quality of our working day may reflect no more than their personality defects and what they had for breakfast.

Of course much also depends on the particular kind of work we do and whether or not it is directly supervised – assembly-line workers, long-distance lorry drivers and milkmen may only see their immediate boss intermittently. Nonetheless, for most individual employees the character of their immediate supervisor may be the single most important factor in their particular employment relationship. Despite this, our immediate bosses – even though they may be the cause of interpersonal tension and conflict from time to time – are far less significant for the general tenor of industrial relations than the other two types of employment manager.

The managers of discontent

The phrase 'managers of discontent' was coined by C. Wright-Mills in a now famous study of trade union officials.[1] He used it to highlight the function of trade unions in the management of the employment relationship. What Wright-Mills suggested was that, in the process of mobilising employees to join trade unions, trade union officials took the lead in identifying grievances, presented demands to the employers and generally made a nuisance of themselves in the pursuit of social justice for working people. However, as he also observed, having generated such discontent, they then promptly sat on it, organised it and, through bargaining, came to arrangements with the employers on behalf of the disaffected employees. Thus, he suggested, while union officers and activists brought the underlying conflict of interests between employer and employee into the open they also, at the same time, channelled it in such a way that it became more predictable, more controllable and therefore more manageable. Hence the idea that trade union officials should be seen as managers of discontent or, in more conventional language, managers of industrial conflict. In effect, trade unions, through their persistent demands for formal recognition by the employers and their insistence on the use of collective bargaining, joint consultation and other formalised means of discussing and temporarily resolving matters of dispute, have greatly assisted in institutionalising conflict within tolerable and, for the most part, acceptable limits.

The responses of Messrs Golightly and Ratchett in the laggers' dispute can best be understood in these terms. Both opted for strategies which, while designed to reflect the interest of their respective membership and protect themselves from reproach, were calculated to contain the dispute within manageable limits and minimise disruption. Indeed, as we shall see below, the eventual resolution of the dispute was achieved by one of them accepting a relative deterioration in the position of one set of employees in order to achieve a quick return to work.

Given the endemic conflict of interests which characterises the employment relationship, the process of managing discontent in a constructive fashion is a continuous endeavour. But it is not only trade union officials who may be regarded as industrial relations social workers. As we saw in the last chapter, there are a wide range of people and institutions which are engaged in similar activity. Employers' associations bargain on behalf of members, have established disputes procedures to process conflicts in an orderly fashion and provide advice and help on industrial relations problems.

The Donovan Report[2] placed considerable emphasis on the need to create and maintain adequate procedures for the efficient resolution of disputes. The absence of such mechanisms was seen to be a major cause of the increase in unofficial strikes in the early 1960s and employers' associations, in particular, were criticised for not taking a sufficiently active role in the management of discontent.

More obviously, perhaps, many employing organisations – and virtually all the larger ones – now have specialist personnel and industrial relations staff who are directly concerned on a daily basis with the maintenance and improvement of harmonious work relations and, where possible, pre-empting the emergence of discontent. Managerial activity to motivate, cajole and persuade employees to remain happy at work and even increase their effort has become a major feature of organisational life in Britain since 1945. The job of generating loyalty to the organisation and producing a more enduring basis for employee commitment beyond the simple but also fragile 'cash nexus' has taken a variety of forms reflecting several fashions in managerial thinking.

In the late 1940s and 1950s there was widespread enthusiasm for 'human relations', an approach which highlighted the social character of work and emphasised the beneficial consequences for productivity if the social needs of employees were accommodated in the design of production systems. Advocates of this frame of reference insisted that authoritarian management be replaced by a managerial style which included improving communications, creating socially gratifying work groups and the training of first line supervisors to understand individual and group motivation. The growth in use of such techniques coincided with the growth in employment which accompanied post-war reconstruction: in effect, this meant that the pre-war stick of unemployment was replaced by the carrot of being made to feel a valued member of the organisation. It is vital to remember that the high level of trust which is a pre-requisite to the success of human relations can only be built slowly through the continual reinforcement of mutually satisfying experiences. In the context of the employment relationship – where the demands for subordination to efficiency and productivity goals are always likely to ride roughshod over the demand for positive social experiences – such trust is ever fragile and can be destroyed overnight. And, as suggested earlier, the folk memories of employees are deeply embedded and often unforgiving: at the same time as they were being wooed by the new caring converts to human relations so too trade union membership was rapidly growing.

Alongside the short-lived enthusiasm for human relations came a parallel – and more sustained – preoccupation with new forms of wage payment. Some, like the widespread adoption of individual payment-by-results schemes in the engineering industry, rely almost entirely upon a simplistic conception of the worker as an economic maximiser. Pay is directly related to the amount of work completed: the more 'pieces' of work an employee makes the more pay earned. Such systems are expensive to install and require continual maintenance. Each element of the job must be measured and priced in order to establish the 'piece-rates'. Once established these prices must be continually monitored by time-and-motion officers in order to sustain the integrity of the system and, since the employee is only paid for the *quantity* produced, it is invariably necessary to have some back-up system to ensure that the work completed is of an acceptable *quality*. Over time, such systems tend to break down for a variety of related reasons. Workers learn how to manipulate the system to ensure that they only do the jobs which are 'over-priced'; jobs which are 'under-priced' become a source of continual bickering – both between workers themselves over who shall do them and between workers and supervisors. Since all new jobs have to be rated and priced, bargaining between rate-fixers and workers or shop stewards becomes an almost daily occurrence and much otherwise productive time may be lost. This process of continual updating eventually distorts the overall system beyond redemption. When this happens disputes occur with increasing frequency. By the early 1960s the vast majority of unofficial strikes arose out of discontent over piece-rates.

This is not to imply that piecework pay systems are necessarily a managerial nightmare nor that British industry in the 1960s was a horror story of decaying piecework rates, but to illustrate two points. Firstly, that all wage-payment systems are subject to very considerable internal sources of breakdown. Simple piecework schemes are particularly prone to develop anomalies though, with a standard product, a stable market, a well-established set of routine tasks and careful monitoring, they can and do operate to everyone's satisfaction. Secondly, when breakdown does occur – and an unofficial strike is the result – we should not be too quick to condemn the employees involved, for they are on the receiving end of what might be a deeply frustrating system.

In part as a reaction to managerial dissatisfaction with such systems, the 1960s saw a new fashion in wage-payment systems. It was both a more sophisticated and more integrative approach to the management of discontent. Tactically, the objective was to minimise individual differences in wages and to increase income security by reducing the direct relationship between effort and reward. This was accomplished by using some form of group bonus scheme – which meant that should one individual in the group have a bad week he or she would be carried by the remainder of the group – or by introducing some form of measured day-work system (MDW). The latter involves individuals choosing a particular level of performance at which they contract to operate. Provided the individual meets the prespecified target performance most of the time there is no variation in wages. Should the individual consistently perform above or below the contracted level, the wages, accordingly, also go up or down. Measured day-work systems are designed so that short-term variations in performance which result from factors outside the control of the individual operator – such as a temporary shortage of material or machine breakdown – are not reflected in the wage packet. It is a more flexible and, some would say, fairer means of relating effort to reward. In many cases these new forms of wage-payment system were accompanied by the parallel introduction of a job-evaluated wage structure of the kind we encountered in the Loch Clearwater dispute. Strategically, the objective of such reforms was to provide a platform to ensure a more secure and enduring structure of rewards and, at the same time, increase company control over labour costs.

Job-evaluation is most common in the more technologically advanced enterprises – such as chemical manufacturing, oil refining and electricity generation – where the nature of the production process is such that there is no clear-cut relationship between effort and output. It is also found, often under other labels, in the larger seemingly non-productive work organisations such as the BBC, the civil service and local government where one's 'grade' appears to determine everything. The 1960s vogue saw it extended, usually in combination with some form of MDW, to more product-oriented enterprises with more traditional work technologies. The adoption of a job-evaluated basis to employee relations usually reflects a long-term positive managerial commitment to minimising employee discontent for, apart from its vital contribution to maintaining greater control of labour costs, it is often the result of a determination to create a perceptibly fairer, more just and more permanent structure of rewards within the organisation. The constant frictional back-biting which tends to accompany piecework systems is eliminated, employees usually have a clear idea of where they slot into the structure and some knowledge – though often illusory – of how far they can progress within it; and, while there are disputes over individual gradings, there are invariably well-respected appeals procedures through which such conflicts are processed.

But job-evaluation is not all sweetness and light. As the Loch Clearwater case illustrated, there are circumstances where the internal integrity of the wage-payment structure can be seriously and, perhaps, terminally undermined by forces external to the organisation and beyond the control of the managers of discontent. This should not be regarded as a source of regret since – unless we are prepared to accept the bureaucratic and social nightmare of some national job-evaluated wage structure covering *all* jobs – wage-payment structures will always proceed through cycles of decline and decay in a socially natural response to change. All such systems and structures wear out, come into conflict with others and are replaced by new devices. This constant process of renewal keeps large numbers of people off the streets. One such group are the management consultants.

Although many of the larger organisations maintain small numbers of organisational development (OD) personnel whose brief includes thinking about and working on plans for the medium- to long-term future of the management of discontent, the people who actually develop and market the new blue whiteners are usually independent firms of management consultants. There is no standard model management consultancy: some companies specialise in particular kinds of activity, such as recruiting staff or installing new salary or wage-payment systems, or in the design of computer-controlled information systems. The range of advice given is only limited by what is required: if a company identifies an organisational problem which is deemed to require the services of an outside consultant, the Yellow Pages will always provide one.

There are a small number of large well-established consultancy firms but many are very small, often selling only one product and being composed of one or two specialists. In so far as consultants possess clearly identifiable characteristics these tend to be limited to the outward signs of professional competence: they always travel first class, are immaculately tailored, type their reports on the most modern typewriters and always present them in plastic folders. The quality of the service and advice given varies considerably but tends, predictably, to reflect the length of time spent researching the problem and the specialised experience of the consultants. While some concerns offer off-the-shelf solutions to particular problems, the safest solutions are invariably those which are specifically designed to meet the needs of a particular enterprise. Changing the organisation – especially if it involves restructuring departments, reorganising work patterns and disrupting the life of large numbers of employees – is always a very sensitive and delicate process. In times of such uncertainty people invariably become very defensive, are reluctant to give up established routines and may take a long time to settle down to normal levels of productivity after the change. Outside management consultants are sometimes used to effect such changes and the instant solutions sometimes imported by them invariably create as many new problems as they resolve. This, of course, is not always the case and they are by no means the only source of such problems. In some situations – especially if it is designed to produce savings through redundancy – management may deliberately decide to use outside consultants as the 'hatchet-men' to avoid long-term resentment. Once the change has been effected everyone left – including the management – can blame the outside management consultants for all that has occurred. Functionally, it permits all the bad feeling to be displaced onto the outsiders who, of course, have departed from the scene.

The most recent products of the OD departments and the management consultants have been the introduction of job-rotation, job-enrichment and – in the wake of inter-national euphoria at the Japanese 'economic miracle' – quality-control circles. All three innovations seek to enlist or reactivate employee interest and increase job-satisfaction by making changes in job-content.

Job-rotation is almost self-explanatory. It involves employees – mostly at the lower end of the organisation – moving round from one job to the next in order to stimulate their motivation to work. And, particularly if the job is tedious and repetitive, a change of scene with different social contacts and a different work-rhythm may well have this effect. Similarly, job-enrichment schemes are also designed to increase the variety and scope of a particular task: this may involve an additional set of routines, changes in working hours, increased responsibility and more autonomy at work. While the creators of such changes are often well-meaning, their success in producing real improvements in the quality of working life depends on the extent to which the changes represent genuine enrichment of the job and the extent to which any improvements in productivity or increases in responsibility are properly rewarded. Increased autonomy might mean no more than no longer having to clock-in at work, and extended responsibility might result in the employee having to sign for goods as well as unloading them from the lorry. Otherwise, as one study showed,[3] the reaction might be that of one chemical worker who drily observed, 'you move from one boring, dirty, monotonous job to another boring, dirty, monotonous job. And somehow you're supposed to come out of it all "enriched". But I never feel "enriched" – I just feel knackered.'

Quality circles are something else. As the current fashion, hot from Japan, quite remarkable benefits are reported following their introduction. Increased productivity, better quality of work, a greater awareness of safety and a reduction in the 'them–us' feeling are the most commonly claimed consequences. A quality circle is formed from the work group and includes immediate supervisors. They meet frequently to discuss each and every work-related problem and to receive information. They might discuss how best to reduce wastage in a particular process or receive information about current sales and market prospects. Each group is encouraged to define its own responsibilities and to set achievable targets for better performance. Success seems to lie in providing the employees with a genuine forum to discuss issues and problems, providing them with much better information as to where they fit into the overall organisation and ensuring that where group members do make positive suggestions that these are fully considered – especially if they are to be rejected. While quality circles seem like an updated variation on human relations thinking, they have undoubtedly enjoyed no small success, especially in Japan. In Britain, one recent study[4] of 25 firms which introduced quality control circles found that less than half were successful, and concluded that success depends mostly on an enduring managerial commitment, managers with appropriate skills and a capacity not only to give genuine support to the groups but to accept the implications for change in their own behaviour.

Much of the innovative thinking which lies behind such devices as quality circles or the practice of job-rotation comes from the work of academic social scientists. Some, who are actively concerned to improve managerial practice in employment relations, work as part-time consultants, while the research findings of others are taken up and applied or become material for inclusion in training and management education. On occasion, seemingly disinterested research provides a very important stimulus to change in management practice. The human relations school of thought emerged, almost by accident, out of a series of studies by American industrial psychologists in the 1930s. Initially they set out to study the effect of different levels of illumination on productivity but, by the end of the study, they had produced considerable evidence of the independent impact of group norms on the rate of output. One group of female employees – assembling telephone relays – increased their productivity no matter what changes were made to their working conditions. They felt they had been singled out by management for special treatment. Another group of male employees, who wired up telephone exchange equipment, managed to continue to produce at much the same level no matter what changes were introduced to the lighting or the number of breaks they had during the working day. In contrast to the first group they seemed to feel that, since the country was in a very deep recession, any increase in output might result in some of them being sacked. Hence social norms can operate either positively or negatively depending on the circumstances.[5]

Another important set of academic managers of discontent are those who advise government departments and politicians on the formulation of social and economic policy. For example, leading British industrial relations academics provided the most influential evidence which shaped the conclusion of the Donovan Report in 1968. It is likely that it was their arguments which persuaded the Commission against advocating the legal control of collective bargaining and who were responsible for the Report stressing the need for management and trade unions to set up proper procedures to process disagreements. Some among these academics were also not only powerful advocates of incomes policy but were also actively engaged in running the prices and incomes policy of Harold Wilson in the mid-1960s.

The mention of incomes policy – which is invariably an attempt to control the rate of increase in earnings through governmental action – brings us to the final set of actors who may be described as managers of discontent: the government and its agencies. We will come to the most influential aspects of government action in the next section; in this we are only concerned with direct intervention in the regulation of the employment relationship and the regulation of industrial conflict. In these respects British governments have stepped up their activities since the 1960s with, in general terms, two objectives in mind.[6]

Firstly, to provide the employee with a basic set of rights – thus we have laws governing what an employee must be told by his or her employer when he or she is taken on, laws against race, religious and sex discrimination in employment and laws against unfair dismissal. Such provisions are, in part, an attempt to prevent such issues from becoming full-blown industrial disputes. At one time, for example, if an employee was dismissed for some action or misdemeanour which the work group and the shop steward did not think warranted such drastic punishment it might have led to a strike because the employee had been 'victimised'. Even in those situations where the individual did not enjoy a great deal of sympathy the resident shop steward might feel it a duty to take up the case since the local trade union was the only source of protection. Since the legislation governing unfair dismissal such disputes have been considerably reduced since the aggrieved individual can process the issue, with trade union help, through an Industrial Tribunal.

The second objective was to improve the tenor and character of trade union–management relations and to provide more constructive assistance from various government agencies. For the most part this took the form of passing laws which increased the security and rights of trade unions and trade unionists. In the 1970s trade unions had a legal right to claim recognition from employers once they had organised a majority of the work-force; under certain conditions closed shops became legally enforceable; trade unions had a right to ask for certain kinds of management information for use in collective bargaining and trade unionists could, as of right, get time off for trade union activities and training in industrial relations. It was a time when even Conservative governments sought to control trade unions through improving the management of conflict rather than attempting to subdue them through use of the law. Mr Heath's 1971 Industrial Relations Act was ill-conceived, but the Code of Practice that came with it – which attempted to spell out good industrial relations practice – had a much more substantial and longer-lasting impact on the management of discontent.

Alongside this floor of employee and trade union rights came a series of new government agencies the function of which was to improve industrial relations by providing advice and assistance. Of these the three most important were the National Board for Prices and Incomes (NBPI), the Commission on Industrial Relations (CIR) and the Advisory, Conciliation and Arbitration Service (ACAS). The first of these, the NBPI, was responsible not only for running the incomes policy of 1964–69 but also for producing more general advice on such topics as measured daywork, job evaluation and productivity bargaining. In concept the object of productivity bargaining was to increase real wages through reducing inefficient practices and thus achieve increased earnings without increasing costs. In practice, many managements – in collusion with their trade unions– faked productivity deals simply to get round the incomes policy but, nonetheless, the experience did force both sides to investigate all the possible sources of inefficiency and, in many other cases, considerable savings were made.

The CIR, originally set up in 1969, was given a statutory role under the 1971 Industrial Relations Act and disappeared when that Act was repealed in 1974. However, before departing it conducted a wide range of studies – some into particular companies with industrial relations problems and some of a more general nature into the conduct of industrial relations. All were designed to improve the methods of managing industrial relations.

Of the three institutions only ACAS is still with us. It was established in 1974 specifically entrusted with providing conciliators and arbitrators for the speedy resolution of industrial disputes and with the duty to work for the improvement of industrial relations. It carries out this latter function by providing any advice and help it can in response to employers and trade unions, and by publishing a series of codes of practice which spell out how, for example, to draw up a disciplinary procedure.

Conciliation and arbitration involves ACAS much more directly in everyday industrial relations. In the event of negotiations becoming deadlocked, where neither side can see their way clear to making a concession, they might decide to call on the services of an ACAS conciliator whose role is to talk to both sides separately to see if any common ground can be found. In many cases it goes beyond this and the conciliator will try to find a new and perhaps unthought-of route to a solution. It is a role which relies upon persuasion and, in total contrast to the arbitration role, the conciliator is not directly involved in the outcome. Many agreements between employers and trade unions contain a clause which states that, in the event of an unresolved issue, provided both sides agree to it, they will call in an arbitrator. The Loch Clearwater dispute provides an interesting example of the benefits of having such a provision.

In that case, at least according to our story, the laggers stayed on strike for 5 days, after which they agreed to return to work pending negotiations. These lasted for 3 weeks going on every day with none of our happy band giving an inch. Then, with a sigh of relief, they agreed to call in an arbitrator to whom they all presented their case. He, for reasons which he did not disclose, decided the laggers had a good case and should be upgraded and given the money.

Two final points are worth thinking about before we consign the laggers' victory to the annals of labour history. Firstly, the practice of arbitrators not giving the reasons for their decision, although not universal, is thought to have the merit of not giving either side any arguments which could be used to rub in the 'victory' and, in addition, it prevents the dispute breaking out with renewed vigour. The act of calling in an arbitrator reflects the recognition that a decision has to be made and that the two sides are not likely to reach that decision by themselves. It is usually tacitly understood that whatever the arbitrator decides both sides will accept it. Hence, once the decision is made, everyone wants to get back to business as usual as quickly as possible.

Secondly, the function of arbitration may sometimes be to save-everybody-from-themselves. In many cases the arbitrator – for the sake of re-establishing peace and goodwill – will try to split the difference between the two sides. This is relatively easy in the case of a deadlocked wage-claim. However, in the Loch Clearwater dispute there was no difference to split: it was all or nothing for there was no readily available compromise or partial solution: the laggers either were or were not skilled men. None of the protagonists could afford to concede: calling in an 'outsider' to decide the issue permitted those who had to 'lose' to do so without losing face publicly. Once this issue was decided everyone went back to work, picked up the remnants of the job-evaluated wage structure and started afresh content in the knowledge that all their problems were caused by that idiot of an arbitrator. Golightly, Ratchett and Warmly are not to blame and everybody is again producing chemicals.

Finally, it should by now be clear that all these multi-coloured managers of discontent play a vital role in maintaining compliance in the employment relationship. This involves two things: establishing and re-establishing managerial authority to direct employees, and securing and re-securing employee agreement to willingly participate on terms which are acceptable to the employer. This endorses the analytical point made earlier, that the employment relationship is one which inevitably involves the *coordination* of different interests: each side, almost literally, is seeking to profit from the other but, in order to do so, has to concede something to the other. Indeed, the variety and number of actors who are directly or indirectly involved in this process – shop stewards; trade union officials; personnel, industrial relations and employee relations managers; management consultants; academics; legislators and arbitrators – stands testimony not only to the permanent difficulty and sensitivity of this task but also, of course, to its social, political and economic significance.

In the analysis of a specific set of industrial relations issues or problems the managers of discontent are almost invariably more important than the immediate boss whose impact is personal and localised. The obnoxious or incompetent behaviour of the latter may, on occasion, provide the instant stimulus to strike action – such as when a foreman swears at a worker and the resident militant shop steward seemingly over-reacts and leads the lads through the factory gate – but the more important causes of that action are likely to be found in inadequate management of discontent. The local full-time trade union official may have failed or refused to take up a grievance the week before – thus leaving workers disaffected with management and disillusioned with the union; the personnel department may have been too slow in considering the re-grading of certain jobs; or management may have ignored signs of worker frustration and disenchantment with a new bonus scheme.

The providers of employment

Finally, we come to the third type of manager: those whose decisions as to where to locate private capital and public finance have a critical impact on the levels of employment and unemployment. It is the behaviour of these managers – who are both the least obvious and, often, the most significant actors in industrial relations – which must be examined when it comes to explaining the general character, quality and temper of relations between employers and employees. Analysing the relationship between the level of employment and the allocation of investment finance is an immensely complex exercise and, in the present context, can only be considered briefly by way of some examples.

When the owners and controllers of private capital decide on how to invest their money, they directly influence levels of employment. Such decisions may create new jobs as, for example, when company profits are re-invested or money is raised on the stock exchange to expand production. Sometimes such new investment is required simply to maintain the existing jobs. Alternatively, de-investment may reduce the numbers employed. This may be accomplished by running down one set of activities and re-investing in less labour-intensive operations, by reducing the total production capacity to accommodate a fall in demand for a product, or by closing down altogether in order to put the capital employed to more profitable use elsewhere. Such decisions may bear little or no relationship to the character of industrial relations or the levels of productivity: they may be taken simply because the financial return or profit from investing in property, a different product or keeping the money in the bank is greater than investing in manufacturing or service industries.

These days, those private capitalists with their top hats, Havana cigars and a bag of jingling cash are relatively insignificant. Occasionally, individual entrepreneurs – like Robert Maxwell, who bought the *Daily Mirror* in 1984, or the mysterious Al-Fayed brothers who, in 1985, paid £615 million for the privelege of owning Harrods – do enter the public arena. However, their impact on the provision of employment is unimportant when compared to the decisions of multi-national companies or nationalised industries. Just to take one example, the London-based Lonrho company has investments in Africa, Europe and the Americas and is engaged in an almost bewildering diversity of employment relationships. It mines and refines platinum, gold and other rare minerals, produces coal and is exploring for oil and natural gas. It grows tea, sugar, coffee, vegetables, has extensive dairy and beef farms and is the largest commercial food producer in Africa. It controls casinos and two luxury hotel chains; is a major distributor for a variety of motor car and commercial vehicles – including Rolls-Royce, BL, Volkswagen, Audi, Toyota and Massey-Ferguson; and owns a range of newspapers and printing operations. The latter include the *Observer*, 22 British provincial newspapers and Harrison and Sons, who produce postage stamps. Its engineering operations include the manufacture of stainless-steel sinks, engine components, buses and paints. On the drink front it distils whisky in Scotland, makes wine in France, brews beer and bottles soft drinks in Africa.

Household linens, textiles and clothing constitute another important interest, as do commercial freight, warehousing and transport. And there is more. The company is estimated to be worth over £2 billion and the decisions made with regard to the use of such assets can clearly have a phenomenal impact on the provision of employment.[7]

However, even the investment potential of Lonrho looks paltry compared to the sums of money available to the major institutional shareholders such as insurance companies, pension funds and investment companies. The financial managers of such concerns play a vital role in generating employment. In 1983, for example, British insurance companies had worldwide invested assets of £122.7 billion, of which over one-third is invested in industry through stocks and shares. In the same year the total premium income from conventional life assurance policies alone amounted to over £11.5 billion. Most of this is invested on behalf of policy-holders who leave the investment managers to decide what to do with it.[8]

Of equal, if not greater, significance to the provision of employment are the decisions made by government. This has been dramatically illustrated in Britain in recent years. Since 1979, with the persistent attempt to reduce public expenditure, cut back apparent losses in the nationalised industries (especially in steel and coal) and an almost exclusive concern with the rate of inflation, unemployment has come to be maintained at record levels and the impact of government in creating or reducing employment has become more or less self-evident. However, it should be noted that, these days, governments of any political complexion, whether they are pro- or anti-union, in the East or the West, are irretrievably involved in managing employment. The transnational character of trade and commerce, the high priority accorded to exchange rates, inflation and the balance of payments combine to make it impossible for governments to avoid being deeply involved. In consequence, nearly all the major policy decisions are likely to have powerful direct or indirect effects on employment levels. For example, government attempts to control public expenditure through cutting rate support grants to local councils – the so-called 'rate-capping' process – may force local authorities to try to raise money direct from ratepayers. Such increases can have a very harsh impact on small businesses which, if they do not go under, may be forced to make employees redundant. A local representative of the National Federation of Self Employed and Small Businesses, which has 5,000 members in Scotland, insisted that rate increases, resulting in part from government restrictions, were certain to cause between 3,000 and 4,000 redundancies in the small business sector.[9]

And governments cannot evade such responsibility; for the success or failure of governments in the modern era tends to be measured by their ability to manage the economy. This may or may not be the most desirable criterion of success, but now, it seems, it is the way of the world.

Although governments in Britain from the mid-1970s have retreated from the post-war policy of maintaining full employment, the government's role as the national general manager of the economy has, if anything, become more important. Some politicians see ₂ to think this job is not dissimilar to running a grocery business; but corner shops are rarely faced with the complex vicious circle of inflation, high interest rates, third world borrowing and rising unemployment, the control of which always lies tantalisingly out of reach of any national economic manager. Government economic policies are therefore addressed to those elements of the economic conundrum which can be influenced in the hope that, with luck, the worst effects can be avoided. Predictably, governments make choices between which problems they think are important. The primary efforts of the Conservative government since 1979 have been directed at reducing inflation and restricting the amount of money in circulation, both of which produce higher unemployment. Critics in the Labour opposition insist this is going the wrong way about it and claim that an increase – rather than a decrease – in public expenditure would have a much more positive effect on the economic problem. Nonsense, say the Conservative government, for that is precisely the policy which produced the problems we inherited in 1979. In truth, no-one really knows precisely what causes what, and the policies pursued by successive governments reflect a mixture of common-sense hunches, various untestable economic theories, political convictions and prejudices. We are back, of course, in the realm of frames of reference and competing value systems. And, not least because of this, no suggestions as to what we ought to be doing will be advanced here.

However, some of the more concrete elements of governmental options do need to be highlighted. For example, changes in taxation rates on company profits can have an important impact on employment decisions: if these tax rates are considered severe by a board of directors they might decide to re-invest the profit – thus creating new jobs – rather than pay out a dividend that would be highly taxed. Some taxes – like the National Insurance surcharge – are a direct tax on employment. Employers and, in particular, the CBI, were bitterly critical of this tax – which was an additional charge on all employees – until it was finally abolished in the 1984 Budget. They called it a tax on employment and said it operated as a direct disincentive to taking on new workers. Of far greater importance to those making investment decisions are bank interest rates since, in many cases, the level of interest is a critical factor in deciding whether or not a company will risk borrowing money in order to expand their activities and take on new staff. In Britain, which is, of course, a major financial centre for the Western world, governments are faced by an unavoidable double-bind when it comes to interest rates. In order to attract sufficient overseas funds to make 'invisible earnings' in the money markets – which are an important factor in our balance of payments – it is necessary to keep bank interest rates as high as, or higher than, elsewhere in the world. If this is done, however, it also means the interest rate industrialists have to pay to borrow money which might create new jobs becomes more expensive. Thus, although it is not as simple as this, governments have to make a choice between new jobs and profits for bankers. It is not as simple as this because bank interest rates are also linked to the exchange rate for the pound, and this varies according to how international financiers and money-dealers value the pound as a commodity. In short, if the oil sheiks can get a better return by switching their supernatural oil revenues from pounds to dollars, the price we have to pay for vital imports goes up because the value of the pound goes down. As suggested earlier, it is how one chooses to manage these vicious circles which tests the national manager; and the choices made have a very significant impact on the level of employment.

It is policy decisions on what to do with the level and direction of public expenditure which provide the clearest examples of the impact of government on the levels of employment. As an actual employer of labour the government and its agencies – such as the various ministries, the nationalised industries, local government, education, social services and the national health service – is without parallel. While exact figures are impossible,[10] it is estimated that at least 30% of all employed persons work directly or indirectly for the government. Although the actual figures are probably secret, the Ministry of Defence is estimated to be the largest single employer in Britain – this includes not only the armed forces themselves but all the servicing personnel and those employed to manufacture the vast range of goods and equipment required by modern armed forces.

In the hurly-burly of everyday industrial relations it is easy to forget that such an enormous proportion of the nation's employees can be directly influenced by government. A decision to cut back expenditure on the NHS can result in large numbers of jobs being lost; a decision to raise the school-leaving age to 16 will normally require an increase in the number of teachers; and a decision to reduce investment in council housing programmes means that large numbers of building workers remain unemployed. Energy policy decisions on the balance of nuclear power stations to coal-fired ones have a direct impact on the demand for coal and thus the number of pits that will be worked. The list is almost endless and the knock-on effects reverberate throughout the whole of the private sector since the goods and services provided can only be sold – and thus maintain employment levels in that sector – provided there is adequate demand for them from the public sector institutions as well as from public sector employees.

It might be objected that the inclusion of governmental decisions on the shape of economic policy and the investment decisions of the controllers of private capital are of only marginal relevance to industrial relations, and that it is mistaken to regard such actors as managers of employment. Industrial relations, after all, is what happens on the ground between employers and employees in the context of the both cooperative and conflictual employment relationship. The behaviour and action of ministers in Whitehall, investment advisers in the City of London, or corporate financial decision-makers in New York may seem far, far removed from the everyday bargaining of shop stewards in car-manufacturing or the leaders of the steelworkers union in 1980 who were powerless to prevent the total workforce in steel manufacturing being cut by almost one-third. Nonetheless, in any disciplined attempt to grasp the range of forces which influence the overall climate of industrial relations and the character of work itself, governments and the controllers of private capital have to be seen as playing by far the most critical role.

CONCLUSIONS

One of the objectives of the threefold classification of managers of employment outlined in this chapter has been to illustrate the various *levels* at which industrial relations must be understood. In the present context what this means is that if we confine our study to the behaviour of the actors directly involved in a particular issue – such as the immediate boss – this will only permit us to *describe* what is happening. In nearly all cases, if we wish to *analyse* that event it will also be necessary to examine what the managers of discontent are up to in order to grasp how the problem has been generated. Finally, if we want to *explain* why the problem has come about, it may be essential to reach an understanding of decisions taken by the providers of employment.

5

Regulating Employment

Work relations are managed through various management styles and methods. Since the nature of employment, the job-content of work, social values and expectations are in a constant state of change, it follows that there is not – and never can be – any one tried and trusted means or technique which could be adopted by all managers. This fact, one of the half dozen or so in which we can have complete confidence, does not prevent management thinkers from writing books on how best to do it. There is a new one just about every week.

In the industrial relations literature – which, until recently, tended to ignore the role of management and to focus instead on the doings of trade unions – management is usually discussed in terms of how the rules governing the employment relationship are established, enforced and changed. Three major methods have been identified: unilateral regulation, collective bargaining and State regulation. Of course, in any specific situation all three methods are likely to be found. University lecturers, for example, have their teaching loads determined unilaterally by their head of department: and such duties can be increased almost at will. It might not be a wise action – for there are norms relating to what is considered fair – but heads of department continue to enjoy such almost feudalistic authority. In contrast, wages are regulated by central government through a process of collective bargaining and individual universities have no say at all with regard to pay scales. Similarly, like all other employees, university lecturers, by law, have to be given a contract of employment and are protected by a wide range of employment legislation. Nevertheless, the threefold categorisation provides a useful means of illustrating the patterns of regulation that are typically encountered.

UNILATERAL REGULATION

Conceptually, unilateral regulation refers to those employment rules which are set solely through the authority or power of one of the actors or to those organisations where trade unions are either not recognised or play only a minimal role in the regulation of employment.

The newspaper and printing industry, for example, was, for many years, notorious for the number of work rules set unilaterally by workers through their trade unions: they managed to maintain strict rules about the number to be employed on particular machines long after management insisted they should be reduced. Similarly in ship-building, the workers, until fairly recently, enforced a series of demarcations between craftsmen which are usually referred to as 'outmoded working practices' and frequently cited as a major cause of the decline of British ship-building. These are, of course, not the only examples of unilateral regulation by workers but is should be noted that the power of employees to enforce such rules is rare and rapidly in the process of being eroded by economic decline, international competition and new technology. In any case, such examples are far outweighed in the overall balance of power by the extremely wide range of employer unilateral regulation and the relative ease with which even very small employers can sucessfully resist the demands of apparently powerful trade unions. In chapter 3 we encountered Mr Shah of Warrington in his dispute with the NGA: his was a firm with only a very small number of employees which managed, with the help of the law, to resist the collective muscle of the NGA and all the other unions which gave support.

Perhaps even more remarkable was the bitter Grunwick

dispute[1] of 1976 which also concerned a small firm run by one man, George Ward, whose workforce was composed of almost exclusively immigrant Asian labour, many of whom were women. The dispute was over trade union recognition: he refused to talk to the union and sacked all those who had joined. What followed was a strike which officially lasted for 2 years though, in the meantime, the business more or less continued to operate with the use of new non-union employees. During that 2 years an ACAS inquiry recommended recognition, there were periods of mass picketing, large numbers of arrests, demonstrations of support, a sympathy strike of postal workers, widespread support from other unions and the TUC, and a government-appointed Court of Inquiry under Lord Scarman which also recommended recognition and the reinstatement of the sacked workers. Nearly everyone it would seem – while disapproving of the sometimes violent nature of the course of the dispute – thought that the employees ought to be allowed to join a trade union (even the law said they could) and that the trade union ought to have the right to negotiate with the company. But not Mr Ward: he resisted all pressures and, after a series of legal battles, finally secured his position with a judgement from the House of Lords which was based on the letter but not the spirit of the law at that time.

But the cases of Mr Shah and Mr Ward are by no means typical, and most industrial relations observers, while recognising the social and political significance of their triumphs, would regard them as maverick employers. A much more representative example of unilateral regulation is reflected in the mangement style and techniques found at IBM, the multinational computer and business machine manufacturer.

Like Grunwicks, IBM is also a non-union company and was also subject to an ACAS inquiry to see if trade union recognition ought to be recommended. In the ballot of some 13,000 employees ACAS found that 95% did not wish to see any change in the existing system, 4.3% favoured recognition of trade unions and the remainder were 'don't knows'.[2] Given the sometimes highly conflictual industrial relations found elsewhere in Britain, what is it about the IBM system which seems to give its employees such a high degree of confidence in management? In part it reflects the market security of IBM itself – it is in the forefront of current technological developments and in an economic sector destined for continued growth and development. In addition its cost structure is such that it can afford to pay high wages – only 18% of total costs are spent on labour which means that even fairly large increases in remuneration do not, proportionately, add too much to the overall cost of operations. Of more immediate interest, however, is the character of its personnel policies and the way these are enforced throughout the company. There are six elements which, collectively, provide the basis of employee trust and loyalty. First – and probably most important – is a managerial commitment to 'full employment'. This means that if particular jobs disappear through technological change or the company wishes to shut down a particular plant and move elsewhere, it will offer alternative employment, even if this means moving house at the company's expense. This policy ensures a feeling of employment security which, in turn, promotes a willingness to change. Secondly, there is the policy of 'single status', which means that all employees enjoy more or less the same terms and conditions – there are no separate dining rooms for management, and all employees, from the chairman down, share the same sickness benefit scheme. The absence of status differentials common throughout other enterprises helps to pre-empt the development of 'them–us' attitudes and promotes the belief that all employees are part of a grand team in which reward is based on contribution.

Such beliefs are further reinforced by the third element: the use of merit pay. Predictably, IBM have long since abandoned the use of piecework systems and now have a sophisticated and flexible job-evaluated salary structure. Pay scales are systematically reviewed and increased in order to ensure that the company is always at the top end of the pay league for comparable jobs. There are no general 'once-a-year' pay increases: the performance of individuals is regularly reviewed by their immediate boss in consultation with the employee. At a previous meeting the employee will have agreed certain performance objectives, and merit increases depend on adequate progress towards these. While this system seems undoubtedly fair – since rewards reflect improved performance – it can also be seen as a technique which, perhaps insidiously, increases the degree of managerial surveillance and control over individual employees. Nonetheless, employees seem happy to operate under it and endorse its consequences.

All the other three elements reflect a strong managerial commitment to pre-empting employee frustration and dissatisfaction which, elsewhere, frequently develops unknown to management. There is the IBM Appraisal and Counselling system which provides, at least once a year, a statement of each employee's performance against set objectives. The employee and the immediate supervisor discuss the assessment, consider any possible job moves and career ambitions of the individual and, if necessary, make plans to acquire the appropriate training. Such discussions are, of course, not always the apogee of sweet reasonableness and there is provision for the employee to record his or her dissatisfaction with the appraisal. Managers are carefully trained for such tasks and their performance is, in turn, monitored by the Personnel Department. The cynic might add that it all seems as if everyone is watching everyone else to detect the first twitch but, in practice, the system is unlikely to be as oppressive as this suggests. In any case, relatively high pay and employment security might well prove to be perfectly adequate compensation.

This systematic care-taking of individual employees and monitoring of feelings and aspirations is matched by an intensive and extensive company-wide system of communications through which management can both inform and be informed of any change in the temperature of relations and – if necessary – take whatever action is deemed appropriate. Finally, as an additional safety valve, there are company-wide procedures through which individuals or groups can air grievances. The individual scheme – known, somewhat ingenuously, as the 'Open Door' scheme – permits an individual to take a grievance to the very highest level and, what is far more important, actually be taken seriously. (Peach estimated that 25% of such cases result in favour of the employee.) Alongside this procedure for specific individual grievances there exists the 'Speak Up' and 'Multiple Speak Up' programmes, through which individuals and groups can anonymously send in a question or grievance of any kind and, through a coordinator in the Personnel Department, receive a reply within 10 days.

It is easy to scoff at the quaintness of the labels used at IBM to describe their procedures but – since all these elements are part of a carefully formulated and organisationally significant policy for the management of discontent – the pragmatic measure of their usefulness is 'do they work? From the very small percentage of employees who wanted to see recognised trade unions, and from the comment of the ACAS investigator who suggested IBM had achieved 'a revolution in social thinking', clearly they do.

However, it would be mistaken to think the IBM system could be easily transplanted elsewhere to produce the same pattern of industrial harmony. Quite apart from the favourable circumstances in which the company operates, they are not burdened by any negative historical folk memories of the bad old days – since there were none – and, perhaps most important of all, the 'IBM way' is part and parcel of the mangement culture and managerial ideology. One factor which should be self-evident from the description is that IBM place a very high priority on a positive managerial attitude to what they call 'people-skills'. Such an approach does not mean they necessarily operate from any altruistic motives, for it can be highly cost-effective. Many of their employees require lengthy and expensive specialised training; their distinctive personnel policies have the effect of minimising turnover, promoting loyalty to the company and increasing productivity.

As one might expect, IBM has many critics who regard the strategy as one which is designed to prevent trade unions from encroaching on management authority and to surreptitiously increase managerial control over employee behaviour.

Maybe so; but, in the process, it also means that those employees enjoy a very high level of job security and can be assured of rewards at least as good as, if not better than, the average package of benefits available in comparable employment.

Finally on the question of unilateral regulation – where one side makes all or most of the rules – companies such as IBM, which are actively concerned to prevent trade unions from gaining recognition as the formal representatives of the workforce (other examples would be Marks and Spencer, Sainsbury's and Kodak) are often said to operate with a *unitary* frame of reference. What this means is that those in control of such organisations regard the enterprise as a unified hierarchy with one source of authority – management. Trade unions are seen as an unwholesome intrusion and industrial conflict as the product of agitators – usually of the politically motivated variety – or the result of personality clashes or poor communications. In short, the organisation is seen as one large family or team, all pulling in the same direction to achieve a set of agreed objectives. Within such a belief system the idea that the employment relationship is best conceived of as one involving different sets of competing interests – the view consistently argued throughout this book – is unthinkable. And, should the managerial staff of IBM be interviewed in order to establish whether or not they hold a unitary conception of the organisation, no doubt they would endorse at least some of the unitary features outlined above.

This appears to create a problem for our preferred conception: the management strategy of IBM is based on a unitary conception of the organisation; its managers operate as if it is a unitary structure; and its employees do not want trade unions to represent their views. What is more, the whole thing works: there are no enforced redundancies, there is low turnover of staff, good profits, high productivity and no example of a serious industrial dispute. Managers genuinely treat the employees as members of the team and they respond with loyalty and efficiency. Fortunately this does not mean that it *is* a unitary structure. The irony of the situation is that the managerial strategies used by IBM and, similarly, those of the other 'unitary' companies identified above, can be seen as being specifically designed to pre-empt the development of employee discontent. In managerial terms they are 'positive employment policies' based on a sophisticated, sociologically informed understanding of motivation and social behaviour. In other words, those who established the policies must have thought that, in order to *avoid* the typical conflict of interests which characterises employment relationships, it was necessary to spend a great deal of money, time, research and effort to establish a comprehensive and coherent strategy to pre-empt the usual disputes and grievances. Far from proving the organisation is a unitary structure, what the IBM case illustrates is the kind of managerial effort and commitment necessary to successfully manage the ever-present potential discontent. To describe the IBM management ideology as 'unitary' is to miss the point; for it was only through a realistic appreciation of the sources of conflict that they could actually construct a set of dykes to protect and nurture the belief that IBM is a unitary enterprise. This is not to suggest that IBM managers act in bad faith, but merely to make the very important point that simply believing something does not make it true.

COLLECTIVE BARGAINING

In 1966 Alan Fox, one of the most influential post-war industrial relations thinkers, stated that 'most social scientists have long since abandoned the unitary frame of reference as being incongruent with social reality and useless for the purposes of analysis'[3]. At that time, as an analytical alternative to the unitary conception of the organisation, he offered the *pluralistic* frame of reference. A manager holding such a view would see the enterprise as a coalition of competing interest groups which cooperate for mutual benefit; trade unions would be accepted as quite legitimate representatives of employee interests and conflict in the organisation regarded as a normal and predictable phenomenon of organisational life. Within this approach the key to successful management of discontent lies in establishing flexible and efficient procedures for the rapid resolution of any issue which becomes a matter of dispute. The principal method through which the competing interests of the various actors are reconciled is collective bargaining. This is often described as a process of joint regulation and, where trade unions are fully recognised by the employer, is the most common method used to establish and re-establish the rules governing the employment relationship.

The rules created through collective bargaining can relate to any aspect of the employment relationship although, in practice, they are usually confined to a very narrow range of topics. Employers invariably refuse to allow trade unions any say in those areas covered by what is called 'managerial prerogative'. For example, unions are almost never allowed a voice in who shall sit on the Board, on what production technology will be used, in pricing policy, or on how profits will be allocated between shareholders and re-investment.

Most rules fall into one of two categories. Firstly, there are *procedural* rules which cover how the two sides will go about conducting their relationship: in order for any worthwhile and meaningful bargaining to take place they must first agree to recognise each other as legitimate representatives and establish some procedure to be followed so that any disagreement between them can be resolved in an orderly fashion. The generic term for these is 'disputes procedures' and a variety of such procedures are usually set up. An individual with a complaint about his foreman would use a grievance procedure; the foreman, in turn, would wait until that individual had been late three times before using the disciplinary procedure in order to take revenge; and, in times of recession, many managements have recourse to a redundancy procedure.

Once a recognised procedure has been laid down, the two sides can get on with the major business of negotiating terms and conditions of employment for the employees. This creates what are referred to as *substantive* rules which govern the actual substance of the contract of employment and, as such, cover a very wide range of issues and practices. Most obviously they regulate wages, hours of work, overtime and shiftwork rates, sickness and pension provisions.

Despite the extensive use of collective bargaining through-out British employment relations – some 70% of employees are estimated to be covered by collectively bargained agreements – it remains a mysterious and deeply misunderstood feature of industrial relations, even to union members. In part this is because it is, for reasons we will come to, a secretive process and, in part, it results from the way it is presented to the public through the media. No one – least of all trade union officials and management negotiators – really takes the trouble to explain the process. At best such actors do no more than display their own sweet reasonableness in the face of the intransigence of the other party.

Media people and, in particular, television reporters, have great difficulty with collective bargaining because, as often as not, they have to create a news event out of something which is not happening and which they are not permitted to film. In consequence, collective bargaining is presented as a series of symbolic images, magic words and intonations and, predict-ably, has taken its place in popular mythology as a myste-rious, seemingly irrational process which adds £2 million a week to the balance of payments deficit. We see leading trade unionists, briefcases bulging under their arms, hurry into a building in the glare of the television arclights, pausing only briefly to mutter something about their aspirations and the cost of living. They are quickly followed by pin-striped management representatives who smile weakly in the harsh light and make no comment. And that is the end of the visible real action. The producer cuts to the industrial correspondent who appears, microphone in hand, his breath visible in the cold November evening air. It is explained that, after 7 days of all-night sittings, the 30 grown men we have just watched troop into the building have made very little progress; the trade union side will not settle for a penny less than 8%; and, with promises to return should anything happen before the end of the news bulletin, he ends with a darkly murmured reference to the possibility of deadlock by which, without actually saying so, we all know he means that the end of G.B. Ltd. is nigh. Well, with 2 minutes of prime time in front of the cameras you have to think of something to say even if no one will tell you what is happening.

Next, the Prime Minister refuses to intervene, the General Secretary of the TUC says he can't intervene but, after everyone has genuflected once again to their aspirations, the day is saved by Harold Wilson who sends in beer and sandwiches. And so it continues like some long-winded incomprehensible Wagnerian drama until 3 days later, all smiles, the union accepts 7½% and management claims the additional money will come from unspecified productivity increases. We are all left with the impression that it is more like grand farce than grand opera, for it has taken 10 days of apparently going round in circles to reach a figure which they all knew they were going to agree upon weeks or even months earlier.

Yet, as a method of managing discontent in a sensitive, flexible and effective manner, collective bargaining is regarded by most industrial relations experts as being without parallel. Despite how it seems, it resolves disputes at the point at which they arise in a remarkably harmonious fashion; and for some, is the institutional expression of democracy in action, for it ensures that employees have a voice in shaping the terms and conditions under which they will sell their labour. In order to try to demystify the surface imagery and symbolic baggage that has been erected to cloud our understanding of collective bargaining it is useful to start at square one.

The first simple point to grasp is that bargaining is not something confined to foggy November nights behind closed doors in London. It goes on daily at all levels of the industrial structure and in all kinds of organisations. A machine operator asks her forewoman if she can leave 15 minutes early to go to her children's school sports day and the answer is yes provided she works the afternoon teabreak in order to make up the lost production. Meanwhile, in the plastics factory down the road, a rate-fixer is engaged in heated conversation with the shop stewards: he finally agrees to increase the piecework rate on an urgent job since it is 18 months since the operation was last rated. Upstairs, in the office, the seven computer terminal operators have just agreed to work an additional hour every day next week in order to secure a day off for Christmas shopping. In all these examples of *informal* bargaining, the actors are engaged in negotiating deals and coming to mutually beneficial arrangements: the nature of the relationship is such that they have to accommodate each other – partly to get the work done effectively and on time, partly to meet each others' needs, and partly to retain a positive basis to the relationship itself. What the examples also illustrate is the similarity of these deals to those we make in all sorts of other social relations. We negotiate with our children – sweets often being the means of securing compliance; in our marriage relations – where the currency if often sex and emotional blackmail; and with our friends and neighbours, exchanging tools, garden equipment and cups of sugar to mutual benefit. Bargaining is thus a fundamental and all-pervasive social process oiling the wheels of our interactions with others. For most of us it is a familiar, natural process through which we maintain the working harmony of our social relationships. In this sense we are constantly doing deals, exchanging benefits and thus regulating our lives. That such behaviour should also come to characterise relations at work is entirely predictable.

Over time, with the emergence of trade unions, such bargaining between employer and employee has become formalised, more nationally based and highly structured. It suits both sides. For the employer, the task of negotiating individually with all the employees would be an extraordinarily wasteful exercise. In addition, if he bargains collectively with other employers he can be sure that they will not try to pinch his labour force by paying more. Similarly, by banding together in trade unions, individual employees protect themselves from the worst effects of competition in the labour market by establishing standard rates. Such deals not only provide security of income for the employee but also ensure predictability in labour costs for the employer; and, where collective bargaining is well-established, it has proved to be a means of stabilising the employer–employee relationship by permitting the endemic conflicting interests to be managed in an orderly and largely peaceful manner. Hence, despite the occasional rush of blood to the head from maverick employers and the odd example of excessive obduracy from a trade union, collective bargaining has evolved into the most socially acceptable method of institutionalising such conflict.

The pattern of collective bargaining varies considerably from one industry to the next with each employment sector having its own set of habits and arrangements. In most cases there are three levels at which bargaining takes place: the national or industry-wide level, the company or plant level and the workshop level. Different elements of the overall package of rewards are negotiated at each level and the key to stability lies in making sure that each level is confined to issues which are appropriate. Minimum rates of pay are often dealt with at the national level whereas piecework rates would invariably be negotiated at the level of the workshop. There are, inevitably, some problems of coordination – as we saw in the Loch Clearwater dispute – but, overall, there is sufficient flexibility to absorb such problems and adapt to changing circumstances. The most coherent and uniform structures and practices are found in the public sector where nearly all the most important negotiations are conducted through centralised national bargaining. Thus, in education, social services, the NHS, mining, gas and electricity, all the key decisions relating to terms and conditions of employment are settled by highly formalised once-a-year, set-piece joint negotiating committees. This is one of the reasons why public sector employees seem to be far more conflict-prone than those in the private sector where bargaining tends to be less rigid and where there is certainly more room for flexibility to meet particular, localised problems. Conflicts in the public sector are more visible – partly because governments sometimes need to use them as an excuse for failing yet again – on a grander scale, and can have a far more immediate disruptive impact on social life than, for example, a dispute in car-manufacture, glass-making or chemical production.

Alongside the development of these structures of formal bargaining institutions has come the emergence of specialised professional negotiators. Their codes of conduct, stylised language and secretive nature is often accompanied by certain patterns of ritual behaviour which often characterise the bargaining process. Such rituals – which we will return to in more detail below – function as smoke signals between respective negotiators and, in some cases, operate as symbolic gestures to reinforce the determination of the constituents. Once the deals have been done trade union officials have to answer to their members, and managements, though perhaps less obviously, have to face their shareholders.

Collective bargaining, with its often incomprehensible procedural mazes, its pregnant pauses for all-night sessions and its strikes, is the public face of industrial relations. It's the bit that we all see, are bemused by and sometimes wish would go away. It is where the action takes place but it is *not* where the outcome is necessarily determined. This point requires considerable emphasis for it is all too easy to assume that what takes place during the bargaining process determines the character and content of the agreement which is finally produced and waved in victory to the assembled onlookers. As ever with industrial relations, all is not what it seems and, in order to unravel this new puzzle, it is necessary to examine the context in which bargaining takes place before returning to the real-life action, the bargaining process.

THE CONTEXT OF BARGAINING

When negotiators face each other across the table they do not come as free agents with a blank sheet of paper on which, like gentlemen deciding on the order of play in a bridge match, they work out a deal to please the spectators. Behind each negotiator sit an array of eagle-eyed constituents watching every move to make sure no-one concedes too much; and behind the watchers lie a formidable range of factors and constraints which place very considerable limits on the options and choice of outcomes available to the bargainers. In the analytical language to which we have now become accustomed, these are the *contextual variables* which have a determining impact on the final agreement that emerges.

All the major variables are presented in a schematic fashion in figure 5.1. Although presented as a series of Chinese boxes which circumscribe the freedom available to negotiators, it should be clear that the variables do not operate as independent factors but interact with each other and, in any specific situation, some variables will be more pertinent than others. It should also be clear that, in previous examples, all these various influences have been illustrated – all the diagram does is to draw them together in a more systematic fashion. Nevertheless, some further examples should clarify how the diagram can be used as a check–list of factors to be considered when attempting to come to a more informed and disciplined understanding of industrial relations.

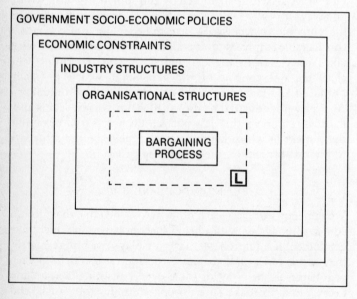

Figure 5.1   The context of collective bargaining

Government socio-economic policies

This refers to the nature and degree of governmental activity at any particular point in time. Quite apart from the legislative framework – which can operate to increase or decrease trade union and employer power by, for example, restricting picketing or making employers prove unfair dismissal before an industrial tribunal[4] – a most important consideration is how government decides to regulate the growth of incomes. If, as in the 1960s and 1970s, there exists a formal incomes policy, this may place statutory limits on the scope available to the bargainers. When there is a full pay-freeze it means that no increase at all is permitted. Price and dividend controls also existed for short periods, which gave employers additional reasons for refusing to consider any improvement in earnings. Governments can also directly influence the outcomes by placing limits on the increases allowed to public employees – either by imposing ceilings on public expenditure in such areas as education and health employment or through the 'advice' they give to the Chairmen of nationalised industries or, in the case of local government employees, through control of the rate support grants from central government. Indeed, governmental decisions on public expenditure can be of vital importance to the outcomes of collective bargaining since – as with increases or decreases on housing expenditure – a wide range of employee groups are affected. Just as legislative changes can significantly alter the tone of industrial relations so too can more concerted action as, for example, when the government took over British Leyland and installed Michael Edwardes as Chairman of BL. During his tenure, with an approach which gave rise to the term 'macho-management', he brought about a dramatic change in the character of industrial relations which involved a reassertion of unilateral management regulation over a wide range of issues which had previously been subject to joint control.

Other forms of seemingly less direct intervention can have a highly influential effect on the outcomes of bargaining and the general level of wages. Reducing the level of social security or unemployment benefits may have the effect of inducing more people into the labour market, thus increasing the overall degree of competition in the labour market and making it possible for employers to recruit staff at lower rates. Wage levels for young people in recent years have also been depressed by the advent of the Youth Training Scheme which, in effect, meant that employers could get all the youth labour they required for £25 per week.

Economic constraints

This set of variables includes all the 'national'-level economic conditions which, clearly, are often shaped by governmental decisions. Interest rates, the exchange rate, the level of unemployment and the level of demand for manufactured goods are all of particular importance to the demand for labour and the price that is likely to be paid for labour. High levels of unemployment and market recession invariably have the effect of reducing wage claims to minimal levels or even persuading employees to accept real reductions in wages.

Recent years have also witnessed the salutary effect of changes in the international economy on the livelihood of employees in a dozen or more British industries. The fate of steel, ship-building and textile workers has been singularly influenced by external factors: in steel it was world-wide over-production which forced the steelworkers to accept massive redundancies in 1980; the shipyards have died more as a result of better Japanese and European production technology than in consequence of the well-advertised craft demarcations among shipyard workers; and thousands of low-paid textile workers have lost their jobs because of thousands of even more low-paid workers elsewhere. But by far the most dramatic change of fortunes has occurred in the mining industry. In the 1960s, with oil relatively cheap, the industry lost over half its manpower through redundancies which were peacefully negotiated by the then leader of the mineworkers, Will Paynter, a lifelong member of the Communist Party. At that time there were still alternative employment opportunities, which meant that the reductions could be achieved without massive social dislocation. But the increases in world oil prices in the early 1970s produced a dramatic turnaround in the economic fortunes of the miners. Coal was again a highly competitive product in the inter-national energy market and, through two major strikes in

1972 and 1974, one of which saw the end of Edward Heath's Conservative government, they became reinstated at the top of the industrial wage-earners league. At that time there were many who felt the oil sheiks should be made honorary life members of the NUM. Since then, with North Sea oil, world recession and a glut of oil, their position has almost come full circle. By the onset of the bitter 1984 national strike, the unity which characterised the early 1970s had been dissipated, the demand for coal was less urgent and the NCB and the government had built up coal stocks at the power stations in anticipation of the confrontation.

The important conclusion from all these examples is that individual trade union leaders – no matter how aggressive or obdurate, no matter how florid their rhetoric – have a negligible impact on the outcomes of collective bargaining in comparison to the impact of prevailing economic realities. Economic realities, of course, do not occur autonomically but are the result of conscious human decision. In the examples above the key decision-makers were governments and employers in other countries and the Sheik Yamanis of the Middle East. While employees and their unions can and do have an important role in the regulation of the employment relationship, in most situations they are reacting to economic realities which are determined elsewhere.

Industrial structure

This refers to a wide range of industry-specific factors which significantly influence the outcome of collective bargaining. Of particular importance are the nature of the labour and product markets and the industrial bargaining structure.

In the civil engineering industry – which builds bridges, power stations and motorways – the nature of the product means that a highly mobile labour force is essential. So the reason why large numbers of Irish labourers work in construction is not because the Irish are particularly fond of digging holes, mixing concrete and laying tarmac. Large-scale civil engineering projects, often in isolated geographical locations, generate a high but temporary demand for labour which can only rarely be met from the local labour market. Because of this, the industry relies very heavily upon migrant labour to do the unskilled spade-work. Despite being unskilled, the geographical isolation and often primitive accommodation available means such work has to provide opportunities for, relatively, very high earnings. These are ideal conditions in which a tradition of migrant labour can be created and the Irish who, for geographical and historical reasons, have been forced to seek employment in mainland Britain, have filled the gap in this labour market. They come for short periods and, despite the stereotypes, take most of their earnings home with them. Predictably, such employees, since they are a floating, unstable population interested only in high wages, are very difficult to unionise. They are not interested in job security, safety is not a long-term consideration and, since each project throws up its own set of problems, local bargaining tends to predominate. This is not to say such workers do not organise themselves: they have become particularly adept at exploiting the fact that the contractors – if under pressure to get on with the job – have no other labour force to call on and the nature of the employment relationship is such that neither side has any real interest in building long-term harmonious industrial relations. The outcomes of bargaining will reflect the degree of isolation of the work and, often a critical factor in building and construction, the amount of time lost because of bad weather.

Product-markets can be equally significant. The level of demand for a particular product – and whether it is rising or falling – has an obvious long-term impact on the demand for labour and the price that will be paid for it. The significance of this simplistic economic truism for the outcome of collective bargaining only becomes apparent by examining the distinctive character of particular products. Much also depends on the nature of the product and the pattern of demand. For example, some products, like newspapers and fresh foods, are highly perishable and therefore particularly vulnerable to a stoppage of work. Unlike most manufactured goods, newspapers can never recoup lost production: if the paper is not published advertising revenue for that edition is lost for ever and, although it is a far less significant financial loss, the revenue from sales is similarly never recouped: no-one buys yesterday's news. This almost total product-vulnerability is one of the reasons why Fleet Street printers' unions have been able to exercise such control over their work and ensure such relatively high earnings.

Products may also be seasonal in character, which means the pattern of demand changes through the year. This in turn has a very significant impact on the relative power of the two sides. Car-manufacture provides the most well-known and well-researched example. Car sales enjoy two peak periods during the year: Spring, when every young man's fancy turns to a new car, and Autumn, when the new registration letter comes into operation. It is now well-established that most strikes in car production occur when demand for the product is lowest. Thus, when cars are not selling and stocks are high the motor manufacturing employers can afford to take a harder line with any demands from the employees because, if there is a strike, the income losses will be negligible since demand can be filled from existing stock. In effect, the nature of the product–market may determine when it is a good time to take on the union. This is one reason why there is sometimes considerable argument over when the annual negotiations actually take place – both sides want to ensure that bargaining takes place when the product–market is most favourable to their interests.

Finally, in this brief account of industry-wide variables, there is the impact of bargaining structure on the outcome of negotiations. The most obvious effects of this can be seen in the public sector where the government, in the form of the shadowy Treasury *apparatchiks* who hold hands with the employers' side of the joint negotiating bodies, can easily impose limits on the increases available because all the important decisions are taken at national level.

Among the most dispute-free sectors of British industry is the highly unionised electrical contracting industry which is comprised mainly of small to medium-size companies which carry out all kinds of electrical installation and maintenance work. Collective bargaining is highly centralised and conducted at national level between the EETPU (the Electrical, Electronic, Telecommunications and Plumbing Union) and the Electrical Contractors' employers' organisation. This union, which once went through a very embittered internal power-struggle to overcome communist control, is now somewhat of an embarrassment to other trade unions who regard it as over-centralised and rather right-wing politically. It is notorious for having negotiated private health care provisions for some electricians. Nonetheless, in its bargaining with the national employers' association in electrical contracting, the union has for many years now secured what are regarded as good terms and conditions of employment, and maintained a very consistent pattern of harmony within the employment relationship. Much of this is attributable to the centralised bargaining structure itself which, with its tightly enforced disputes procedure and high level of trust between national officials of both sides, has prevented any significant localised bargaining and thus pre-empted any significant wage-competition between the small firms. Efficient, well-respected procedures can, as the Donovan Report argued, ensure relatively peaceful negotiations but, as in the case of electrical contracting, this may only be achieved by an almost collusive relationship between the main negotiators.

Organisational structures

The structure of a work organisation refers to the pattern of roles and relationships between different types of employee and different departments. Organisations are invariably hierarchical in character although their precise structure will be the product of many varied influences – the history of the company, the work technology and the wage-payment system are three factors which have a singular impact on the organisational structure and, in turn, place considerable constraints on the pattern and choice of options available to those engaged in collective bargaining.

In recent decades the car-manufacturers have enjoyed the most unenviable record of industrial relations with, in some companies, very poor employee–management relations and an endless series of unofficial disputes – particularly in the 1960s. However, there were distinctive patterns associated with particular companies: the Ford Motor Company has, typically, always been much less conflict-prone than British Leyland. In part the explanation for the difference lies in the different company histories. Ford's have always been Ford's with fairly consistent policies, well-established bargaining and a uniform wage payment system throughout the years of operation. In contrast, it is easy to forget that British Leyland is the product of a grand merger between a number of long-established companies – Austin, Morris, Rover, Triumph, Jaguar and Leyland Buses were, at one time, individual companies each with their own particular practices and traditions, their own wage-payment structures and their own particular styles of management. All the major industrial relations problems of the past 20 years at British Leyland can be seen as a legacy of the original merger. The process of rationalising and standardising policy throughout the company took a very long time – and is still not complete.

Old habits die hard and were jealously guarded both by managers and employees, though the greatest difficulties stemmed from the inherited wage structures which meant, for example, that toolmakers in different parts of the company were still being paid quite different rates long after the new company had been established. And we should not be too quick to blame the new management or the trade unions involved for not trying to remedy such problems at an earlier stage than they eventually did – one of the management tasks when such a company is created is to minimise the degree of disruption in order to maintain output and productivity: too much change at too rapid a pace can have a traumatic effect on both managers and managed. Another important reason for not embarking on a company-wide reform of the wage system was the increased wage expenditure it would have involved: in order to secure agreement, the wages of all toolmakers or all engine-tuners would have had to be standardised at the highest rate currently being paid. Even if an agreement such as this had been reached there would have remained a legacy of problems from the old wage structures, for all the pre-existing wage differentials would have been seriously disturbed and those groups of employees who felt they had lost out in the rationalisation process would doubtless have continued to press their cause even after the new wage structure had been created. Sometimes history suggests that it is best left alone although, as the turbulent case of British Leyland illustrates, it always catches up in the end.

Work-technology and wage-payment systems are often closely interrelated though, with a little more help from the comparison between Ford's and BL, it can also be shown how they operate independently. One of the other reasons for the marked differences in the character and pattern of bargaining at these two concerns – despite both having comparable work technologies – was the differences in managerial choice of wage-payment system. Ever since Ford was first established by the American parent company at Dagenham they have always avoided any form of piecework, preferring, instead, to use a variety of measured daywork allied with careful supervision. In contrast, nearly all the various concerns which went into the pot to make BL had a variety of piecework systems. The distinctiveness of these protected the new organisation to some extent – in that direct comparisons of pay between similar operatives in different units was difficult to make. But, particularly in the 1960s, as these systems developed the deficiencies common to ageing piecework systems, there was a significant increase in the number of wildcat strikes and BL developed a deserved reputation as the running sore of British industrial relations. It was finally recognised that something had to be done and, after lengthy negotiations, BL bought out all the old decaying piecework systems and installed a form of measured daywork in 1972. This has been one of the factors contributing to the dramatic reduction in overt conflict at BL.

More generally, it should be clear that the kind of wage-payment system in operation will limit the range of options available and make some issues more important than others. Where there are simple time rates all the union's energies might focus on reducing the working week or increasing the premia rates for overtime. With piecework – which tends, in any case, to increase the range and scope of issues in such a way that extensive shop steward organisation develops – the major issues tend to be work measurement practices and rate-fixing. And, in the case of graded salary systems with annual increments, the central issues may centre on how the individual can become re-graded in order to get into the next salary band.

It is no accident that certain types of wage-payment systems tend to be associated with certain types of work-technology: the nature of a task may lend itself to a particular form of wage-payment. Sales people of all varieties, from retail shop girls to bread delivery men and from estate agents to insurance sellers, have invariably had some part of their earnings paid in the form of commission on sales achieved. Interestingly, nearly all the major chain stores have now reduced or eliminated this element in the wage packet, preferring, instead, to invest in marketing and advertising campaigns – this helps to account for the often sullen, uncooperative attitude on the part of salespeople now prevalent in such stores. One of the major exceptions are the staff who sell cosmetics and beauty renovation kits – many of whom remain employed by the manufacturers of the branded cosmetics – who are usually very active in their care and attention to potential customers.

Piecework is most frequently found where the relationship between effort and output is both direct and measurable. As noted earlier, it used to be used by BL and remains widespread among car component manufacturers and other companies which have mass assembly production techniques where the individuals' tasks are highly repetitive routines geared to some standard level of performance which is usually gauged in terms of the number of units produced. As soon as the production tasks involve active cooperation between individuals the attraction of the simple incentive of piecework begins to fade, for even with group bonus schemes geared to overall output, the rate of work of any individual is usually reduced to the slowest in the group and this becomes the norm. It is at this point that job evaluation, measured daywork, job enrichment and quality control circles begin to appear as viable alternatives in generating increased effort and, on occasion, increased reward.

Continuous process technology – such as oil refining, electricity generation, and chemical processing – is not appropriate for schemes which directly relate effort to output since the employee's task, for the most part, is to monitor the process to ensure it is operating effectively. Most employees in these industries – as at the Loch Clearwater plant – are paid on a salary basis with, perhaps, the kind of merit payment incentives like those of IBM, and, for the lower-level employees, payment for overtime.

The general proposition behind all these examples is that the nature of work and the kind of production technology used can have a direct bearing on the form of payment system and thus, in turn, constrain the choices available to negotiators.

Finally, it should also be clear that these four sets of contextual variables – which could be identified for almost every set of employment relationships – operate as constraints on the freedom available to negotiators of *both* sides. Although they have a differential impact at different levels in the bargaining structure, all levels are affected and, in some circumstances, when there is a pay-freeze, a drop in demand for the product or high unemployment in the industry, there may be very little room indeed for any improvements, and negotiators may be faced with little or no choice but to accept whatever is offered. This brings us to one reason why negotiations are sometimes unduly protracted: the union side has to demonstrate to the membership, even if no improvements are available, they have tried their best and, at the very least, given the other side a hard time. In this respect it has to be remembered that trade union negotiators are also employees who have to demonstrate they are doing the work for which they are employed. In some instances – as in the miners' strike of 1984–85 – the full-time officers secure their ties with the employees on strike by taking no pay during the course of the strike.

THE BARGAINING PROCESS

It is now possible to return to the live action – albeit in somewhat sober mood given the singular impact of all these contextual factors – and consider the innermost square of the diagram, the bargaining room. Perceptive readers will note that the walls of the room are indicated by a series of broken lines – to emphasise that even when the door is closed behind them, the bargainers cannot avoid government policies, economic realities, and the aspirations of their constituents. You will also note the little room in the corner. This is not what it may at first appear to be: it is the Learner Room; a place where pluralistic personnel managers keep their managing directors during the critical part of the negotiations. When not being used for that purpose it houses social psychologists and sociologists who are lucky enough to be allowed to observe the actors in order to try to unravel what goes on.

Firstly, some brief details about the bargainers. The major proportion of bargaining, as was illustrated earlier, does not take place in the smoke-filled rooms of the diagram – it occurs on the shop floor, in the foreman's office, in the Personnel Department, or in some informal setting. Apart from relevant managerial personnel it involves shop stewards, sometimes full-time, and committees of shop stewards representing all the various work groups which are involved in a particular issue. In some instances – such as in car-manufacture or the docks – even major negotiations will be conducted by a team or full committee of shop stewards. The range, scope and significance of stewards will be dependent on the salient contextual factors. In the public sector, in most cases, there is little for them to do except process individual grievances and worry about working conditions, whereas at a major construction site – where there are a range of bonus schemes because of the number of individual sub-contractors on site – the stewards are likely to enjoy a position of some influence.

On the management side, apart from rate-fixers and foremen engaged in minor negotiations on a daily basis, the role of personnel, production and industrial relations managers depends on their role in the bargaining structure. Peter Warmly – whom you should not yet have forgotten – was the Personnel Manager at the Loch Clearwater plant, but his role was merely to police the agreements and defend them as company policy. He worked in the context of a company-wide agreement which could not be varied except through the joint approval of the Group Personnel Manager at Head Office and the full-time union national officers.

When collective bargaining goes public courtesy of 'News at Nine', it is invariably some national-level negotiations involving a major employment sector – such as gas, electricity, the NHS or the mines – or some major public company – such as Ford's or British Leyland. While such occasions are often of considerable importance they represent only a tiny proportion of the total negotiations taking place in employment relations and – precisely because they are public, set-piece occasions – are unrepresentative of most collective bargaining which, for the most part, is an endless series of joint meetings at which patience, persistence and a capacity to discuss trivia for long periods in between the important issues are the prime qualifications.

The bargaining process is usually seen as involving three major stages: for present purposes they will be referred to as preparation, negotiation and settlement.

During the preparation period neither side actually talks to the other. It is a period when both parties collect their evidence, stir up confidence and solidarity among their constituents and fortify themselves with bottles of gin. A trade union preparing a wage claim might check on profits in the previous year, find out what comparable groups of employees are earning or what increases they have been granted, and establish their best figures for inflation. At the same time, management personnel will be engaged in a similar exercise. Similar but not the same, for they will be looking for reasons why last year's profits were the result of some very unexpected good fortune and why they are most unlikely to be repeated in the present year. They might even find a very impressive ten-page document detailing future plans for expansion – investments which would eat very deeply into last year's undistributed profits. They too will be looking for their own set of comparable employees which, for preference, will include at least some who have not done too well in the last wage-round. And if inflation has eaten into existing wages, they will be photocopying the latest CBI prediction that the rate is about to go down or – failing that – the most recent government statement about inflation which are always guaranteed to predict a dramatic fall in the rate. (Even in the most adverse times, governments invariably say that the rate of increase is slowing down.)

While all this rational data in support of why wages should go up and why they should stay exactly where they are is quietly being assembled, in public, our fortified bargainers are raising the aspirations of their constituents as far as they dare. This involves fine calculations, for if the employees come to believe that far more is available than the trade union negotiator privately expects is reasonable, then no matter what the final outcome it will look as if he has failed. Similar forces operate on the management negotiators who – particularly if they work in the personnel or industrial relations section – tend to be regarded with some suspicion by Boards of Directors. It is well known, for example, that all personnel staff are 'soft' on trade unions and that far too many of them have been contaminated by contact with sociologists during their training. Managing directors tend to know as little about the collective bargaining process as the employee on the shop floor and, like the latter, may harbour totally unrealistic ideas as to what is possible. The MD may well be under pressure from key shareholders who are threatening to sell their shares unless the rate of return improves; he, in turn, may feel that their threats can be bought off if the new wage agreement keeps labour cost increases below 2%. This message arrives on the desk of the management negotiator, who knows from experience that anything less than 5% will produce a strike. At about the same time the trade union negotiator hears that canteen rumour has it that the company is going to offer 11%. Both negotiators have to educate their constituents in the art of the possible. But not necessarily at this stage: during the preparation stage the object is to bolster the crowds for the struggle to come. (To this end, it is not unknown for MDs to threaten their negotiator with the sack if the final agreement costs more than a certain percentage increase in overall labour costs.) Sometimes, in order to generate the right thickness of backbone among the members, this preparation stage is characterised by what is called 'the Large Demand rule'; this states: ask for more than you really expect to get. This rule is frequently applied in the grand public confrontations where one of the objectives of the negotiators is to convince the other side that, unless a figure very close to what is being demanded is reached, the membership will refuse to accept the deal.

Hence to the second stage: the negotiations proper. These are held behind closed doors and secrecy is of the utmost importance throughout – the reason for this will become clear below. Before the negotiations proper can begin there is one vital issue to be agreed: the agenda. Where the ordering of items is of little consequence this may be agreed privately beforehand between the two main negotiators, but on many occasions the agenda is an issue in its own right since items can be interlinked and agreement on one might prevent agreement on another. The most common example of this is where management insist to changes in working practices to improve productivity before they will consider any wage improvements; in reply the union side might say that they cannot persuade the membership to agree to any such changes before there has been a 'substantial' increase in rates or before management can guarantee that there will be no redundancies as a result of such changes. Another reason why the agenda is important is that it shapes the pattern of the negotiations in important ways and is often designed so one side or the other can either put pressure on their opposite numbers or use a specious agenda item as a way of conceding something in order to induce a real concession from the other side.

For example, management might continue to insist that unless they get a firm agreement to change certain working practices they will not talk about any wage increase. If, at that time, there are strong indications that an incomes policy might be imposed at any moment, then the union side will be under very considerable pressure to agree for fear of having any wage increase strictly limited by the incomes policy. In the second situation the union side might insert an agenda item on reduction in working hours high on the list in order to be able to say: 'Well now, if we can reach agreement on a wage increase of 9% I feel sure we can persuade the employees to hold over the reduction in working hours to next time . . . perhaps we can leave the hours question to one side for the moment and come back to it later if necessary.'

Once the agenda is agreed, the negotiations proper begin. Each item is considered more or less contentiously depending on its significance to the respective parties. Each side presents its case, more or less rationally, with varying degrees of conviction, belligerence and goodwill. Pieces of paper are exchanged, figures are tabled and disputed, and, gradually, through a combined process of psychological warfare and communication they start to grasp what it is the other side really wants and might be prepared to settle for and what the other side won't or can't settle for.

All the two sides really know when they start is that they have to come to some agreement – but not at all costs. In so far as it is possible to rationally analyse the overall process, it is usually suggested that each side has certain target points – which represent their most optimistic expectations of what is possible; a resistance point – below which they will not settle; and a fall-back position which represents the least-acceptable terms they could consider. In that the bargaining process has a function in its own right, this is for the negotiators to discover the fall-back position of the other side and try to settle as close as possible to that point. This is why bluff and counter-bluff can be important, and one reason why negotiations are sometimes very protracted: it takes a lot of discussion and argument before each side feels sufficiently secure either to make an offer or to say 'we cannot agree to anything over 7%'. In effect, what both sides are doing is trying to discover 'good' information about the other side's fall-back position while providing a stream of misinformation about their own comparable position. This is one reason why secrecy is of the utmost importance and why television news industrial correspondents have such a hard time, for anything which is said publicly by one of the negotiators during the course of discussions might be used by the other side once they resume talks.

Another reason for the secrecy is mutual protection from their constituents: neither set of negotiators wishes to see the other suffer recriminations once the deal is signed and, even if one side knows it has achieved a singular victory, it is very rare for them to say so publicly.[5] Indeed to do so might jeopardise the third stage of the process, the settlement stage.

In this final phase, during which the agreement is eventually signed, both sides have to sell the terms agreed to their constituents. This is not always easy, especially if the proposed terms are far less than you had led them to expect at the outset. For this reason the actual terms are sometimes unclear or there is public disagreement as to what the terms actually add up to. One side might say that the new wage agreement means an overall increase of 7.2% on wages, while the management representative declares that the new agreement will amount to a 6.3% increase in wage costs. Both figures may be correct – the first being based on what might be expected should the employees work the same number of overtime hours as they did last year and the second figure being calculated solely on the predicted additional cost on basic rates of pay. At this point in the proceedings no-one wants to start the arguments all over again and, in any case, both sides know what the other is doing: the union negotiators are attempting to convince their members that they have achieved the best possible deal in the circumstances while the suspect personnel managers are seeking to reassure their employers and the shareholders that the new agreement will not be too expensive and is within the 6.5% ceiling which they were instructed, under no circumstances, to exceed.

Paradoxically, in practice, the actual figure is almost irrelevant. When the new rates become operative few employees can calculate accurately what the real increase amounts to – marginal increases in the deductions for income tax, national insurance or superannuation together with the fact that no overtime has been worked in the previous week makes such calculations very difficult. Similarly, on the management costs, it is an extremely complex process to work out exactly what the additional expenditure amounts to: changes in staff, in overall numbers, in the amount of overtime or bonus payments can all be used to demonstrate why the deal costs what the negotiators said it would cost. The critical point is that an agreement has been reached, and now both sets of negotiators need to come out of the talks looking as if they have successfully carried out what they boasted they could do. It is no accident that both sides invariably claim victory: it could even be said that both have to be able to convince their employers that they have won before they can actually lose. This game-like aspect of collective bargaining is important because it helps to maintain the unity and morale of the two sides and, especially if there has been a strike during the course of the negotiation, assists in the process of rebuilding relations once everyone is back at work.

Going on strike is one of the many tactics available to the two sides in their collective bargaining. It can occur at various points in the overall process. Sometimes a strike is necessary in order to persuade management to *start* bargaining. We frequently read that management refuse to open negotiations until the strike is called off – what we are not told is that it was management's refusal to negotiate in the first place which led to the strike. Everyone goes back to work having convinced management that they were serious about whatever issue is in dispute; or, in other instances, the strike is a result of management making what are deemed to be totally unacceptable proposals. Other times a strike may occur during the negotiations at that point where the term 'deadlock' is used to describe the state of play. This may result from the two sides making insufficient progress and the union negotiators decide to call a strike just to prove to the other side that they are serious about their demands. On yet other occasions there is too big a gap between the fall-back position of the two sides and neither side is prepared to make any further concessions.

In this situation it may take a strike to convince one side or the other that their position is unrealistic. What is common to all these strikes is that they are an integral element of the bargaining process – their function is to persuade one of the two sides to revise their expectations. Thus, even when a strike is taking place, the process of bargaining has not actually stopped: both sides have merely retreated to prepared positions from which they not only shout at each other – as Messrs Scargill and McGregor ably demonstrated – but attempt, through various offers and counter-offers, to persuade the other side to resume the employment relationship. Collective bargaining – in that it *necessarily* involves the actors in exercising their bargaining power – could not take place unless both sides are 'free', on occasion, to fully express that power.

THE SIGNIFICANCE OF BARGAINING

Finally, on collective bargaining, three concluding observations. The first relates to the economic impact of collective bargaining on the level of wages, an issue which is often a source of public controversy. It is also a major source of dispute between academic economists. On the one side there are those who say that wage increases lead to price increases and thus fuel the rate of inflation – this is the 'cost-push' theory favoured by Conservative politicians; this is opposed by the 'demand-pull' theory invariably argued by their Labour opponents which, simply stated, suggests that as demand for goods and services increases so the price goes up and, as price increases affect all employees, they demand increases in wages to maintain their standard of living. There is evidence to support both theories. In so far as it is possible to point to generally agreed conclusions, these would indicate two things: collective bargaining and trade unions have been far more successful at preventing wages from going down than they have at pushing up real earnings, and, if they have increased wage-levels by a greater degree than would have occurred without organised bargaining, then it is only by a relatively small amount.

This should not come as a surprise for, given the great importance that must be attached to the contextual variables constraining the bargainers, there is little scope for significant change and the best most employee groups can expect is to remain roughly on the same rung of the hierarchy of rewards in society.

This brings us to the second observation: that for all the huffing and puffing, for all the dire warnings from employers and governments as to catastrophic consequences for the company or the economy should wages increase by another 3% or 4%, and for all the bitter struggles by employees to assert the right to trade union representation; collective bargaining produces little but illusory gains and the bargaining process is no more than a self-deceptive symbolic exercise for *both* sides. A Marxist analysis of industrial relations would strongly endorse this conclusion and call for a social revolution to remedy the defects. Even Alan Fox, who was quoted earlier, later changed his mind about the practical results of collective bargaining and concluded that 'pluralism' was best seen as a social myth which gave the impression that the overall distribution of rewards could genuinely be altered through trade union action whereas, in reality, all they succeeded in doing was to produce insignificant changes at the margins of gross and stable inequalities in the distribution of rewards, power and privelege in society.[6] He is undoubtedly correct, but neither getting rid of collective bargaining nor having a social revolution would necessarily achieve very much. State regulation of wages – which typifies all those societies in Eastern Europe which have ostensibly experienced social revolutions – has demonstrated that the inequities remain and its use in social democratic societies – which we come to in the next section – has proved notoriously clumsy in operation and of little or no consequence in remedying inequality.

Even the pluralistic champions of collective bargaining recognise the weight of such criticisms. However, they suggest, the social benefits of collective bargaining – which permit socio-economic conflict to be regulated, institutionalised and processed in peaceful fashion – far outweigh its weaknesses as a method of redistributing wealth. In addition, such radical critiques of collective bargaining miss the point because bargaining is not a process which is designed to produce equality but one which functions to reflect pre-existing market inequalities in the distribution of power. In other words, collective bargaining is not some trade union technique for social reform – though it does have some defensive features – but the best means available to employees for organising their labour value in a free market society. This is a valid response to the critics who have confused the issue with all this talk about inequality. One final point in defence of collective bargaining-as-process is that some form of bargaining is inevitable. As suggested earlier, bargaining is a natural, spontaneous and taken-for-granted feature of social relations and – short of a police State or the use of forced labour – the employment relationship will naturally be characterised by bargaining even if this does not include formal collective bargaining.

The third observation concerns a major blindspot in many of the introductory texts on trade unionism and industrial relations. It is widely assumed that the heyday of unitary management is long past – it reached a peak when all the workers had to look forward to when they developed a bad back was destitution and the workhouse. But, so the story goes, once trade unions and collective bargaining became respectable and accepted as the normal means through which employers settled wages, the world of employment relations gradually became peopled with pluralistic managers who held hands with trade unionists in joint consultation and referred to their social conscience before sacking anyone. History is not so simplistic as this picture suggests.

While it is true that, in the 1970s, all the fashionable management journals had articles entitled: 'We are all pluralists now' and all management training in industrial relations included token lectures on 'pluralism in manage-ment', it would be grossly misleading to conclude that trade unions are wholeheartedly accepted in employment or that all employers and managers accept that they ought to consult and bargain with trade unions. Beliefs tend to reflect circumstances rather than convictions and the popularity of unitary and pluralistic approaches to the management of employment relations has tended to reflect economic circumstances. After the seemingly cosy pluralism of the 1970s, the 1980s have seen the rise of 'macho'-management – in which John Wayne takes on the bully-boys of the unions – and an aggressive rejection of unions by the government. Pluralism did not supplant unitarism, the latter simply retired hurt for a brief period awaiting the appropriate moment to re-emerge.

STATUTORY REGULATION

This is the third major avenue through which the rules regulating the employment relationship may be established, and there is now a wide range of legislation relating to all aspects of industrial relations. After the ambiguous complexities of unilateral and joint regulation, it might be thought that nothing could be more clear-cut, more straight-forward and, perhaps, more preferable than a well-intentioned and rationally constructed framework of statutory guidelines to take the heat out of the conflictual relationship between employer and employee.

Of the the advanced industrial societies, Britain probably still has the least degree of *direct* legal regulation of the employment relationship. It is comprised of three related strands of legislation covering individual rights, collective rights and legislative provisions to help resolve disputes. Among the individual rights are provisions detailing what must be contained in the individual contract of employment, a right to claim unfair dismissal, a right to certain minimum payments when made redundant, prohibitions on the various forms of discrimination in employment and provision for maternity leave and time off for some trade union activities. The principal collective rights refer to certain immunities from prosecution granted to trade unions in the event of a trade dispute – the legal euphemism for a strike. In contrast to many other nations, in Britain, employees have no legal right

131

to strike. Technically, employees on strike are in breach of their contracts of employment and can, legally, be dismissed. Provided *all* those who refuse to return to work by a specified date are sacked, the employer cannot be sued for unfair dismissal. In practice such extreme action is rare these days since the employer – apart from risking a Grunwick-type dispute which might be very disruptive – might find it very difficult to replace the sacked employees: the idea of looking for an entire new labour force of miners, for example, is preposterous. As suggested in the discussion of collective bargaining, strikes do not represent a total withdrawal of labour, merely a temporary stoppage or interruption in an ongoing relationship. Sacking employees on strike – even as a tactical device – would produce a smouldering legacy of bitterness and ill-will once work had been resumed. Thus it is only the small or foolhardy employer who takes advantage of the legal right to sack employees on strike.

At one time trade unions were also liable to be sued for inducing employees to break their contracts of employment and for causing financial losses by disrupting trade. In order to allow trade unions to represent their members, and for strikes to take place without fear of prosecution, trade unions have been granted certain immunities. After a century of uncertainty they were finally secured from such legal action in 1906. This protection remained much the same until the 1982 Employment Act which redefined a trade dispute to produce a significant increase in the range of unlawful actions. 'Political' strikes, demarcation strikes, where one group of workers takes action against another group, strikes in support of workers overseas and sympathy or secondary strikes are now, in most cases, unlawful.

Provisions relating to closed shops also reflect governmental attitudes to collective rights. Originally, they were created by craft unions and functioned not only to restrict numbers but also, and sometimes more importantly, to protect the standards of craftsmanship. The use of the closed shop was taken up, wherever possible, by non-craft unions. Most had management support and were established through custom and practice or collective bargaining and it was only in the

132

1970s that they were given a specific statutory basis. Since then, through the 1980 and 1982 Employment Acts, those collective rights have been significantly eroded. It is now – legally – much more difficult to establish a closed shop of any kind and, in some circumstances, individual employees, sacked for their refusal to join a union, can now claim considerable damages.

One area of collective rights – those relating to health and safety at work – have, primarily, always been regulated through statute law. Dozens of acts of parliament, from the 19th century onwards, were codified through the 1974 Health and Safety at Work Act. By that time about three-quarters of employees were covered by some form of statutory safety regulation and the 1974 Act extended such protective legislation to all but domestic employees. Although not a major source of contention – either politically or industrially – the health and safety provisions suffer more from a lack of commitment than conviction. Everyone stresses the utmost importance of such provisions, but employers and trade unions have, with notable exceptions, done little until a serious accident has occurred. Employees tend to find such rules tiresome and governments have never been prepared to maintain anything other than a token force of inspectors – a view for the most part underwritten by the courts where – with the exception of damages for personal injury – prosecutions for failing to adhere to safety regulations have usually amounted to no more than token fines.

With regard to legislative provision to assist the resolution of disputes, the most important statutory body is ACAS, the arbitration and conciliation service. In addition to its services to both sides in collective disputes, its officials also try to conciliate in individual disputes before an issue is taken before an industrial tribunal. These are perhaps best seen as an extension to the judicial system. Originally established in 1964, they were designed to operate informally to hear cases where individuals claim that their employment rights have been violated. These institutions, together with the legal limits that are placed on strikes and picketing, constitute the statutory procedural ground rules.

Despite its widespread use elsewhere, statutory regulation has never been popular in British industrial relations. It was not until the 1970s that any concerted effort was made to establish such a framework – at first, and in dramatically unsuccessful fashion, through the Conservative government's 1971 Industrial Relations Act and subsequently under a series of acts passed by the Labour administration between 1974 and 1979 which laid down individual employment rights and provided a legal endorsement of trade union rights and activity. Since the 1979 election, when the Conservative Party was returned to power, those rights – and especially the collective rights – have been seriously undermined.

It is very difficult to come to any concrete conclusions about the role and effectiveness of statutory regulation in British industrial relations. In comparison to unilateral and collective regulation, the ideological undergrowth is far more tangled and the use of statutory regulation cannot be divorced from the complex set of interlinked roles which governments and the agencies of the State play in the overall regulation of employment relations. In general – and this applies to *all* modern societies – governments occupy the most powerful position and must be regarded as the most influential actors. This is a contentious point and needs further clarification but, first, some comment about the British experience of statutory regulation.

EXPERIENCE WITH THE LAW

The lukewarm attitude to statutory regulation of trade unions, employers and most governments reflects not only ideological preferences but also a history of bad vibes. One simple reason for this is that our unique position as the first industrial society meant we were the first to develop trade unions and, for over a hundred years, they enjoyed a shadowy legal existence. Initially, they were viewed as distinctly dangerous, politically and socially subversive organisations and – following the uncomfortable precedent set by the French Revolution in 1789 in which the aristocracy was literally decapitated – their opposite numbers in Britain enacted the Combination Laws of 1799 and 1800 which totally prohibited trade unions. As noted earlier, it was not until 1906 that trade unions finally managed to feel they had achieved a secure legal existence and only then as a result of creating their own political voice, the Labour Party.[7] It is easy to regret such formative influences, to insist that trade unions and employees should enter the modern age and develop positive attitudes towards employers and the law, but – as the reversal of trade union legal fortunes since 1979 demonstrates – it is a battle that they can never put behind them.

For the most part it is a 'problem' of class attitudes which, on every occasion that it is economically possible, re-emerge to dominate social and political relations. Historically, the character of the law and the legal interpretations it has generated have only served to reinforce such attitudes. Even the most well-disposed law-makers have had their good intentions frustrated – either by the eagle eyes of those who draft the statute, whose legal training makes it possible for them to see a dangerous precedent behind every comma – or by the judges who have interpreted the law; those frail but bright-eyed old men who, for the most part, cannot tell a piece-rate from a shooting-stick and who, true to the heritage of British common law, have invariably favoured individual over collective rights. In consequence, trade union experience of the law and the courts is one long and almost uninterrupted experience of disaffection. Throughout the 19th century statutes designed to help them, once in the hands of judges, backfired and were used to declare one or other aspect of their activities illegal. More recently, the right to claim recognition from an employer – widely assumed to have been secured under the 1975 Employment Act – evaporated among the wigs of the House of Lords in the final act of the Grunwick dispute.[8]

But trade unions are not alone in having good reason to suspect the law and the real intentions of the law-makers. Employers too, on occasion, have had their freedoms curtailed or taken on new obligations. For example, in 1963, an Act was passed which, for the first time, legally obliged employers to provide their employees with a detail account of their terms and conditions of employment. This includes such items as pay, sickness benefits and holiday entitlement; the Act also introduced a provision which gave employees the right to certain minimum periods of notice should the employer decide to sack them. Two years later, and again for the first time, the Redundancy Payments Act provided employees with an entitlement to minimum redundancy payments related to their length of service.

However, the most instructive example is the 1971 legislation which – while providing dramatic evidence of the statutory swings-and-roundabouts principle – suffered from all the predictable weaknesses of a first attempt to create a comprehensive legal basis for regulating employment relations. Nonetheless, this attempt at a radical departure from existing practice taught politicians a great deal and was the model for all the subsequent legislation and the reform strategies that have been adopted since that time.

The political logic of the 1971 Industrial Relations Act lay in the reasoning that the law could improve the tone and quality of industrial relations by establishing clear standards of conduct and imposing reciprocal obligations on both employers and employees. Employees and trade unions were given a new range of statutory rights – the most important of which included the right not to be unfairly dismissed, the right to establish and enforce closed shops, the right for unions to claim recognition from an employer for the purpose of collective bargaining – and the Act introduced the concept of an unfair industrial practice which was backed by a code of good practice. Employers who infringed any of the new rights, or trade unions which were deemed to have committed an unfair industrial practice, could be taken to an Industrial Tribunal or hauled up before the newly created High Court, the National Industrial Relations Court (NIRC). The Act also created some new arbitration machinery and the Commission on Industrial Relations was to act as a wet-nurse to the new legal framework while everyone got used to it. In addition, collective bargaining agreements were to be legally enforceable unless they contained a clause stating that this was

136

not the case and the Act also included provision for a 'cooling-off' period. If the government decided that a particular dispute constituted an emergency it could ask the NIRC to issue a 60-day restraining order – which made a strike illegal – thus giving further time to find a peaceful solution to the dispute. If there was doubt concerning the degree of support for any such planned industrial action the NIRC could also order a ballot of employees. Finally, trade unions and employers' associations were granted special privileges and immunities from prosecution provided they submitted their constitutions and rule books for approval by the Registrar for trade unions. (To be accepted, such rules, for example, had to specify which trade union officers were authorised to call strikes.)

In the wake of the so-called 'winter of discontent' of 1978–79, the national steel strike of 1980 and the divisive strike in the mining industry of 1984–85, the proposals of the 1971 Act make wistful reading and appear to constitute an island of sensible rationality in the contemporary atmosphere of wilful confrontation. So what went wrong? There is no simple answer but, in brief, those who drew up the proposals completely ignored the lessons of history and refused to listen to the forebodings of the 'experts', such as academics who, for once, were right. In consequence, the Act was grossly over-ambitious in scope, politically naive in expecting support from employers and management, in part misconceived and – perhaps the greatest error – easily discredited and thus destroyed.

Both employers and trade unions were deeply reluctant to sign legally binding agreements – they had no experience of it and neither wished to be tied to something they might later regret or, worse still, end up employing lawyers to defend: throughout the lifetime of the Act only one concern – the Thanet and West Building Society – is known to have signed a legally enforceable collective agreement. Managements, fearful of creating a bad odour in industrial relations, were extremely reluctant to use the courts to penalise trade unionists for any unfair industrial practice: their concern, for the most part, is to manage discontent, not give it a sharper edge by taking shop stewards or union officials to court. The trade unions, for once coherently organised by the TUC, simply refused to register, making them all, technically, liable to prosecution should any industrial action take place. The government, having enacted the law, had to watch while the law, grinding mechanistically on its usual way, was applied and threw egg on their face: on the one occasion when the Secretary of State for Employment invoked the cooling-off procedure the strike they sought to stop – on the railways in 1972 – having been duly interrupted by 60 days, was conducted with increased solidarity after the break. On another occasion, the NIRC jailed five dockworkers for contempt of court for refusing to give an undertaking not to picket a container depot. Since nothing is more certain to guarantee a greater sense of outrage than the victimisation of workers' representatives, the government, in order to avoid a potentially damaging national dock strike – or worse – magically produced a figure known as the Official Solicitor who had the authority to release the dockers. He has never been seen again. The government, its law deeply opposed by the unions and studiously ignored by the employers, had little choice but to withdraw from the action in order to avoid further indignities and, subsequently, no serious effort was made to use the law.[9]

PONTIUS PILATE OR BIG BROTHER?

In order to grasp the deeper reasons why the 1971 Act was almost predestined to result in failure it is necessary to return to the contentious issue put on one side several pages back: the more general question of the role and power of modern governments and, closely related to this, the way in which we tend to regard such power.

There are many theories of the State – none of which will be considered in any detail here – but, roughly speaking, they tend towards one or two orientations: those which regard every additional law and every additional bureaucrat as another nail in the coffin of democracy, and those which regard the State as a sort of benevolent social worker which looks after all citizens regardless of their race, colour, creed and, sometimes, contribution to the common weal. There are all sorts of caveats and variations that can be added to modify these two polar positions but, in general, the British have tended to prefer the first of these two caricatures. While being sufficiently pragmatic to recognise the social and economic necessity of some state apparatus, we remain deeply suspicious of such machinery and, where possible, resist any extension. This may or may not be a good thing, but such social values play a key role in conditioning the responses to the statutory regulation of the employment relationship. Such responses can be translated into two quasi-theories: the Pontius Pilate theory and the 'Big-Brother-is-bad-for-you-even-when-he's-good-for-you' theory.

According to the first of these – invariably known as 'voluntarism' in the industrial relations literature – the primary function of government and the various state agencies is to provide a framework of ground rules within which employers, employees and their respective organisations can conduct their affairs in peace and harmony untroubled by the stultifying mechanistic interference of lawyers and judges. It has much to recommend it for, provided there is protection of individual rights and legal limitations on what employers and trade unions may and may not do to each other in the course of their sometimes stormy relationship, it is flexible, efficient at managing change and, at the very least, gives those involved the impression that they have some direct control over their working lives. But a critical component of this approach is that governments remain above the conflict, acting as an independent arbitrator or referee who maintains the balance of power between the interests of labour and capital and adjusts the law accordingly. This is an appealing theory and one much beloved by successive generations of politicians for it permits them to indulge in their favourite pastime of having it both ways. When governments intervene they invariably justify the action in terms of realigning the power balance between the two sides – their reluctant intrusion is simply to make the world more equal once more. Alternatively, the same theory allows governments to wash their hands of all responsibility for industrial relations. 'Look', they say, 'no hands! It is not government policy to interfere in industrial disputes. That's a private matter between the employer and the trade unions.' Such postures can be struck without a trace of hypocrisy even – as was the case during the 1984–85 miners strike – when the government itself, in the final analysis, is the actual employer. Any theory which encourages politicians to deny responsibility – and which is supported by both employers and trade unions who have no desire to have their activities limited or scrutinised by the law – is bound to command much support for all are shielded. The wrath of the electorate, the demands of capital investors and the expectations of the membership can be deflected by blaming the other actors for *not* doing something.

But by far the greatest advantage of the Pontius Pilate theory to governments is that it begs the whole question of where the mystical balance of power actually lies: their concern, at least publicly, is simply to maintain a stable balance. The consequences of this can be easily illustrated.

The law regulating the employment relationship itself – that directly between the employer and employee – finds its origins in the contractual arrangements which emerged between medieval merchants and was later codified into the law of contract. Not so long ago the sale of labour was regulated by the Master and Servant Act and, although the language has since been sanitised, the balance of duties and obligations between employer and employee has not seen any dramatic change over the years. In legal terms, then as now, the employer and employee were regarded as free and equal partners to the contract of employment: they remain free to enter the contract, free to continue in it and free to withdraw from it. There are, of course, proper procedures to be followed and failure to respect them may result in the employee being held legally responsible for breaking the contract or the employer may be deemed to have dismissed someone unfairly. It is noteworthy that the penalties for the breaking of the contract are 'equal': the employer, at worst, may have to pay compensation – though this may be reduced if the employee is thought to have contributed in any way to the dismissal. In no case can the employer be legally compelled to take someone back; and the employees, at worst, will lose their present livelihood. Nonetheless, legally, the relationship remains voluntary and the two parties are treated as being of equal status. It is important to remember that this concept of legal equality has, naturally, been considered fair by those of Conservative persuasion while the Labour politicians, even in power, have never seriously questioned it.

In reality there is only an abstract technical sense in which the individual looking for work may be considered to be on equal terms with a prospective employer. In most cases, and especially during times of high unemployment, there exists a gross disparity in the power of the two actors. Even Adam Smith, the much-maligned fountainhead of laisser-faire economic thought, was moved to remark, 'In the long run the workman may be as necessary to his master as his master is to him; but the necessity is not so immediate.' And it was such immediate necessities that stimulated the then dangerous task of building trade unions which seek to superimpose *collective* rights over those abstract technical *individual* rights which continue to be enshrined at the heart of the contract of employment. In other words, trade unionists – through collective bargaining and such devices as the closed shop – seek, as they see it, to redress what is regarded as an unacceptable imbalance of power which permits employers to employ whom they like, specify how much will be paid for the labour and determine how that labour will be deployed.

In summary, the legal and *social* priority accorded to individual over collective rights is of vital importance in any attempt to grasp the historical significance of the Pontius Pilate approach to statutory regulation. In particular it helps us to understand three features of industrial relations.

Firstly, it highlights the deeper rationale which lies behind trade union antipathy towards the law. Trade unions, as we have seen, are engaged in a constant struggle to establish collective rights but their efforts have always been frustrated by the central principle which, for all but very short periods of time, has always characterised the law relating to employment: the principle that, first and foremost, the law must ensure the primacy of individual over collective rights. And, no matter how idiosyncratic the case – whether it be the right of Grunwick's Mr Ward to employ whomever he chooses and sack those who go on strike for the right to have trade union representation, or the right of Helen Jones, a member of the Plymouth Brethren, to refuse to join a closed shop on religious grounds – individual rights have invariably triumphed. In a social democracy such as Britain this will *always* remain a troublesome dilemma for trade unions for, despite their ideological convictions about the supremacy of collective rights, many, if not the majority, of trade unionists would prefer to see the continuation of the uneasy co-existence of individual and collective rights rather than the suppression of one or the other.

Secondly, it helps us to understand why the law itself – in that it expresses a priority for individual over collective values and subjects such disputes to the finest legal minds – can be a significant source of industrial conflict. Let us retain a religious flavour and return to the case of Helen Jones, a television technician whose employer has happily negotiated a closed-shop agreement with the technicians' union. This can be an emotive topic and one which is deeply misunderstood for the closed shop is invariably presented as nothing more than a union device to prevent employees from exercising their individual rights. Such a view is both simple-minded and very incomplete. For our purposes it provides the best and most dramatic evidence of the irreconcilable clash between individual and collective rights.

Helen is one of a hundred technicians, and the other ninety-nine have exercised their individual rights in choosing to endorse the collective values which lie behind the closed shop. In effect, having voted by an overwhelming majority to adopt such a principle they insist that Helen abide by the majority viewpoint. And this is when the trouble starts for, legally, those ninety-nine choices are not sufficient to override the alternative choice made by Helen Jones. Unlike many institutions – such as elections, Parliament itself, trade unions and local government – the democratic principle of rule by majority decision does not apply to closed-shop arrangements for each and every dissenting employee has an absolute individual right to refuse to join a trade union. It is one of the few situations in which the individual right of one person cannot be vetoed or out-voted by any number of other individuals making a different choice. This is not to suggest that it should necessarily be otherwise, but to illustrate the point that it is logically impossible to maximise *both* individual and collective rights at the same time. If Helen is forced to join the union her individual right has been violated – but if she has her way then the other ninety-nine *feel* that their individual rights have been denied.

The present legal position – which guarantees the right to belong to a trade union and also the right not to belong to a trade union – is the very quintessence of the Pontius Pilate principle for, in effect, the law appears to support two utterly counterposed positions. However, in a brilliant piece of legal doublethink, both those rights are construed as individual rights – there is no collective right to establish a closed shop. What this means is that when the ninety-nine technicians exercise their right to join a trade union, in legal terms, they do so as individuals and the moral view they express – that all who benefit from trade union activities should contribute towards the collective organisation by paying membership dues – becomes legally irrelevant. The fact that they are legally permitted to negotiate a closed shop doesn't help either: Helen can still stand her stubborn ground for her individual right is inviolate. In such circumstances it should be no surprise that most trade unionists regard the rights enjoyed by what they call 'free riders' as a denial of the democratic process. But, as we have seen, to override Helen's choice can also be regarded as a denial of her democractic right. In this unavoidable dilemma the law gives preference to Helen.[10] This conflict of individual and collective rights – for that is how it is perceived – is the major reason why the closed shop is such a controversial issue and why, on occasion, it can produce bitter disputes, for any attack on the closed shop threatens a fundamental principle of trade unionism: that the most effective way of ensuring the protection of individual rights is through collective organisation. However, philo-sophically, the law gives greater priority to individual freedom than it does to collective rights.

Thirdly, and finally, it helps us to understand that the initial power advantage enjoyed by nearly all employers over their potential employees derives not merely from their additional economic resources, not merely from the traditional mana-gerial prerogatives based on the rights of private property, but is also endorsed by legal statutes through the social and philosophical presumptions of the contract of employment. Since successive governments, in their role as the impartial referee ensuring fair play, have never seriously sought to make anything other than marginal adjustments to this pre-existing imbalance between employer and employee, it must be concluded that, as a society, we believe it right and proper that employers ought to enjoy such a power advan-tage. It is as if we believe in trade unions but don't want them to act in defence of their members.

This leads us conveniently to the second quasi-theory of statutory regulation which was characterised as 'Big Brother-is-bad-for-you-even-when-he's-good-for-you'. It may be cumbersome, but it does seem to capture the ambivalence in public attitudes towards any extension of statutory control to almost all aspects of social life. Even with the most convincing evidence and argument in favour of public control or public enterprise we continue to be sceptical or disparaging of their appropriateness. We all recognise public services must be provided, but we invariably detest paying rates and taxes; the efficiency of nationalised industry is regarded as a joke despite some quite phenomenal economic success stories; and, for most people, exercising our rights to claim social security benefits is little short of being reduced to the workhouse, despite the fact we pay for such benefits and that, on many occasions, there are simply not enough jobs to go round. Similar attitudes prevail with the statutory regulation of industrial relations when governments legislate improve-ments in the rights of trade unions or employees.

In the 1970s, for example, which saw a proliferation of such statutory rights, many trade unions remained suspicious of these advances, feeling that since the gains had not been achieved by their own direct efforts they could just as easily be lost with a change of administration. Such caution, of course, has since proved justified. Similarly, in 1977 when a government-sponsored Committee of Inquiry recommended changes in the law to facilitate trade union involvement in company decision-making and thus establish a system of industrial democracy, several large trade unions argued against such proposals. They did not want a statutory basis to industrial democracy but preferred to rely upon collective bargaining to ensure the defence of their members' interests. Reliance upon the law is seen to generate not only complacency but also dependence on the law. Self-help and self-reliance remain the only sure way to guarantee success.

Such attitudes have long been prevalent among British trade unions which, having secured legal protection for their organisation and funds, have been content to rely upon collective bargaining. And such a perspective has nearly always been endorsed in intellectual and academic circles. Somewhat perversely, Sidney and Beatrice Webb,[11] who were the mother and father of academic industrial relations, regarded statutory regulation as the ultimate objective of trade unions. They were the last of the great Victorian utilitarians and, as such, regarded state bureaucracies as rational, impartial and generally benevolent institutions created to serve the people. However, in a brilliant and scathing critique of their views, Belloc[12] sounded the theme which still dominates the attitudes of those engaged in the regulation of the employment relationship. With the use of a graphic metaphor, 'the servile State', he elaborated the social dangers of relying upon governments and state agencies to guarantee our rights. In particular, he insisted that once we allow ouselves to become dependent on the State for our needs we are likely to become incapable of providing them for ourselves. Once unemployment pay is regulated by a state agency how long, he asked, before those in employment are similarly regulated? Instead of the State serving the people, he warned, the people could end up serving the State.

Such concerns also typify some of the trade unions' resistance to incomes policy and the legislation of the 1970s. In similar vein, the dominant academic analyses of the 1970s also echoed Belloc's position. His dire warnings about the servile State were replaced by similar alarms about Britain becoming a corporate State – a society in which government, in exchange for giving statutory rights to employees and their organisations and for giving financial aid and guarantees to employers, demands, in return, obeisance to governmental policy in the direction of labour and capital resources. Such policies, despite being drawn up in joint discussions with employers and employees, would, it was suggested, lead to the creation of an ever more powerful State which could increasingly intervene in all areas of social life. It raised the spectre of totalitarianism and underlined the belief that Big Brother-is-bad-for-you-even-when-he's-good-for-you.

CONCLUSIONS

This chapter has focused, at some length, on the three major methods of regulating the employment relationship. It should be clear these methods are not distinctive alternatives but, in virtually all situations, will be found in some combination. Any particular pattern of regulation will depend on a complex set of factors reflecting government policies, economic constraints and the relative power of the actors. In addition, certain issues tend to be associated with one of these three means of regulation. For example, the distribution of the profits accuring from the exchange of labour and capital is invariably decided through unilateral regulation; statutory regulation has always determined the basic character of the contract of employment and, these days, is regarded as the primay means of regulating health and safety rules. In contrast, there are no issues over which collective bargaining enjoys exclusive domain. This should come as no surprise since collective bargaining is the product of the historical organisation of employees into trade unions. This occurred in stages through craft to unskilled and then white-collar employees and, in consequence, the use of collective bargaining developed unevenly throughout industry and between different occupational groups. Although it has never enjoyed unqualified support from governments or employers, the scope of issues it can cover includes all but the most important aspects of the employment relationship. Decisions about new jobs, redundancies, what to do with capital investment are invariably – but not always – the preserve of unilaterial regulation by employers and governments; and, despite the changing fashions in managerial style and government policies, collective bargaining – because it reflects such a fundamental social process – is likely to remain a very important means of regulation.

One final point on the analytical significance of governments to the overall character of industrial relations. Throughout the last four chapters there has been a steady and deliberate increase in emphasis on the part played by governments and state agencies in determining what happens in and about the employment relationship. Government is now by far the major employer in society, being directly or indirectly responsible for a massive proportion – 30% – of the total working population. Governments are also the incumbent general managers of the whole economy and, given the immense significance of events in the international economy on our own economic fortunes, must take economic policy decisions which can dramatically change the character of the employment relationship. Of course, the nature and extent of legislation governing the employment relationship is the sole preserve of governments. Taken together, these three inter-related aspects of governmental activity mean that the influence of government on the daily relations between employers and employees is extensive to the point of becoming pervasive. Given such a context it is difficult to see what trade unions, far less individual employees, can do – even with the most cohesive mutual organisation – to produce significant change in their position. Even when government publicly proclaims its deep aversion to any form of Big Brotherism, it is doubtful whether that government can, in fact, reduce the impact or significance of policy decisions; for no modern government can escape international economic forces. Big Brother may be bad for all of us, but there is nothing we can do to avoid him.

6

Red Moles and Blue Meanies

From their very beginnings trade unions have been publicly regarded as unnatural social growths contaminating the body politic. Originally they were described as 'an unseemly abomination operating in restraint of trade' and, as six farm labourers from the village of Tolpuddle discovered in 1834, individuals could be transported to the penal colony of Australia for 'swearing the illegal oath'; that is, promising to keep their membership secret.

Although times have changed – trade unionists now happily emigrate to Australia if given the opportunity – public attitudes to unionism have not been radically transformed. In the past 25 years each and every symptom of our economic malaise – low productivity, reluctance to accept new technology, strikes, balance of payments deficits, poor competitiveness, low morale, unemployment, or whatever – seems to be the result of something trade unions have done or prevented others from doing. For successive political leaders trade unions have become the bogeyman at the centre of our various socio-economic diseases and every aspiring journalist knows that 'shop steward' is an anagram for 'wrecker'. As recently as 1980, Sir Raymond Pennock, at that time President of the CBI, pointing to what he saw as the causes of our apparently malign industrial relations, observed: 'the British, alone among world industrial powers, are essentially confrontalist in their attitudes'.[1] But for trade unions, it seems, industrial relations would be perfectly harmonious.

Indeed, there are some companies, especially among the

larger multi-nationals, who have sought to avoid all possibility of contamination by refusing to admit they have any industrial relations. They, like ChemTar International, have dispensed with the traditional distinction between staff and weekly-paid, or 'payroll' employees, abolished clocking-on, employed consultants to tap the emotional needs of their workers and replaced every reference to industrial relations with the phrase 'employee relations' or, in latter years, 'human resource management'. While such deodorised terminology cannot provide permanent protection against the underlying potential conflicts, it does, perhaps, make them smell a little sweeter and can transform them into highly specialised technical problems. What was once a go-slow on the shop floor for an increase in the bonus – which was discussed by the personnel manager and the shop steward over pastie and chips in the works canteen – has now become a 3-day seminar at a country hotel to consider the 'motivation-gap among production staff resulting from poor job-hygiene factor-satisfaction'. In the management of discontent all roads are explored and all techniques, so long as they function to pre-empt the development of shop-floor frustration and thus prevent 'negative' attitudes or overt industrial conflict are, from the employer's point of view, a good investment.

THE PARADOX OF PUBLIC ATTITUDES

Any examination of public attitudes to trade unions reveals a consistent ambiguity, if not a contradiction, in the postures which are adopted. When pressed, people (and this includes politicians from across the ideological spectrum) will approve, albeit grudgingly, of trade unions. We believe in fair wages, that everyone should enjoy healthy and safe working conditions and that employees should be protected from excessive exploitation. But, in general, we disapprove of attempts by trade unions and their members to ensure such conditions prevail. Hospital ancillary workers – publicly acknowledged as being among the lowest-paid employees – strike to increase their wages and are immediately subjected to a barrage of moral blackmail for apparently threatening the lives of patients. In some instances this may have been correct, but why was there no equivalent public outrage because these workers were driven to such behaviour?

The manifest degree of public doublethink has been highlighted in recent years with the emergence of the 'Solidarity' movement in Poland which, outside the Soviet Union and Eastern Europe, was met with almost worldwide acclaim as a positive attempt at social change in a communist society. Once Lech Walesa and his acolytes had established 'free' trade unionism this would provide a basis for democratising such societies. It seemed as if the one thing approved by all social democratic societies was free trade unions. Yet, at the same time as the leader columns of national newspapers were extolling the virtues of the 'free' trade unions in Poland, they were also endorsing the proposed restrictions on 'free' trade unions in Britain resulting from the 1980 and 1982 Employment Acts which were deliberately designed to narrow the range of legal trade union activity and thereby reduce their power and apparent significance. Such a stance was illogical but not quite as irrational as it might seem: in supporting Solidarity the leader writers and politicians were saying that, in Poland, the introduction of 'free' trade unions would *increase* the degree of individual liberty, while their simultaneous advocacy of the proposed restrictions on British trade unions reflected the belief that, in Britain, trade unions had become so powerful they had effected too great a *decrease* in individual liberties and, in particular, the liberties of the employer.

Trade unions, in the process of attempting to establish standard terms and conditions of employment for whole categories of labour, inevitably interfere with the individual freedoms of both the employer and, by default, the employee. Just as trade union members will sometimes take action to ensure that the employer abides by the rules of any agreement reached between them so too, for all practical purposes, the individual employees covered by such agreements forgo the right to reach their own separate pay agreement with the employer. Philosophically, this may be a matter for regret but, in practice, as suggested in the previous chapter, any individual employee is likely to be at a distinct power disadvantage in relation to the employer. Thus the apparent sacrifice of such individual rights on the altar of trade unionism is, in most instances, likely to be the exchange of a worthless right for a tangible measure of economic protection in the labour market.

Nevertheless, as the carefully worded opinion polls consistently demonstrate, and as has been reaffirmed by the election of anti-trade union governments in recent years, the majority of the great British people seem to remain unconvinced of the logic of trade union organisation. Like snakes and sharks, trade unions are not to be trusted. In effect, it seems as if we endorse them in principle, but reject them in practice. We believe – or have been persuaded to believe – that if only trade unionism were not so powerful, if only individual employees were not forced to join closed shops, if only shop stewards were not genetically endowed with a militant tendency, if only trade union officials were prevented from pulling the wool over the eyes of the membership, and if only our economy were not so desperately damaged by strikes then our society would return to its natural healthy state. Or, even better, some would have us believe, we would become more like the Japanese for whom work is thought to be as exciting as winning the Pools.

But how serious is the disease? And to what extent are the symptoms real? The primary obstacle to answering such questions is that these images of trade unionism have become so deeply entrenched in our taken-for-granted knowledge that any attempt to discredit them is itself a source of instant suspicion! Thus it is necessary to proceed with caution. The general underlying theme which links all the images – the idea that trade unions and their officers enjoy too much power – will be deferred until chapter 8. However, in order to anticipate that discussion, two of the more persistent problem areas will be examined in some detail. The role of shop stewards is considered below and strikes are discussed in the next chapter.

SHOP STEWARDS

Our caricature shop stewards inhabit a subterranean world populated by well-organised industrial hobgoblins mercilessly plotting the downfall of the white knight, British industry, and his loyal servants, the employees. Disputes, poor productivity, the loss of export orders, the intimidation of non-striking workers, low investment, poor morale and virtually every other possible symptom of poor economic and managerial performance are put down to the malevolent action of shop stewards and 'union militants' whose sole objective, in this model, is presumed to be political subversion and the destruction of our industrial infrastructure. This nightmare was briefly made to come true in August 1983 when British Leyland sacked thirteen employees at Cowley, having discovered they had falsified their job-application forms. Between them, those sacked had not disclosed their full educational achievements – some were said to have been to university – and had manufactured fake references by using dummy addresses for previous employers. After 8 months in employment, five of the thirteen were said to have become shop stewards; and, most damning of all, all were alleged to be members of an obscure Trotskyite political faction. As a story, it was the dream come true for the newspapers.

Dubbed the 'amazing red mole plot to seize BL' (*Daily Mirror*), the nation's investigative journalists went on overtime. Six of the dismissed were women and much attention focussed on 'Red Steph' who admitted to the deception. She instantly became the 'punk girl behind the BL moles, the loudmouth leftie who couldn't resist bragging about how she conned the bosses' (*Sun*). The same newspaper informed us she wore a yellow blouse and green trousers with red turnups – clearly evidence of something nefarious; and the newshounds were undeterred by the fact that none of the 'Marxist masters of the BL moles' (*Sun*) were to be found at the 'nerve-centre of their amazing undercover operation, a shabby terraced house in a quiet suburb' (*Sun*). The eagle-eyed *Daily Mail* reporter espied 'books on Russia' through the window, and *Telegraph* correspondent James O'Brien was the only one to point out that the door of the house was painted 'pink and white'. Several unearthed the tell-tale destruction of secret documents; O'Brien again: 'Neighbours said there had been a huge clear-out of documents. At one time there were 30 black polythene bags full of files and rubbish.'

There is, fortunately, some analytical value in this hysterical tale from the quiet August of 1983. What remained unemphasised in the telling of the story were four facts: all thirteen suspect political activists had been sacked; their inept little plot had been shopped to management by a 'moderate' unionist; their trade union, the TGWU, only provided a routine defence when they appealed against the dismissals; and the Cowley workforce – which only a month or so previously had been involved in a bitter dispute over 'washing-up' time – took no action at all in defence of the thirteen. In other words, whatever the character and extent of infiltration, it received little or no support from the other shop stewards, the union or the 5,000 other employees. While many of those who stand for election as stewards are often politically active in one way or another, the vast majority of trade union members do not regard the workplace as an appropriate location for political activism. No matter what the tone of the political appeal – be it Trotskyite, Labour or Conservative – if the steward does not effectively represent workplace issues, such as pay, bonus payments, the allocation of overtime, discipline and personal grievances and problems, they are unlikely to retain the confidence of the employees. Since all stewards are subject to re-election, what little power they have can only be sustained provided their electorate continue to give the necessary support. Those 30 mysterious black plastic bags might have contained no more than the unsold copies of some Trokskyite newspaper.

One factor in the appeal of the 'Red Steph' model is that it fuels the industrial fantasies of both the so-called 'hard' Left – for whom stewards are the sleeper agents at the leading edge of the inevitable revolution – and of the so-called 'hard' Right which, having never met a live shop steward, places its trust in the *Daily Telegraph*. But the idea that stewards are red moles driven by revolutionary zeal or foreign agents is a million miles from the reality of their daily routines. If we have to employ a metaphor from the animal world, then all the available evidence we have suggests they are best regarded as pet moggies. On occasion they eat the foreman's goldfish and, even more rarely, like tom-cats, have to be doctored for causing too much noise at night. However, in the vast majority of cases they are ground down by the daily drudge of workers' grievances, most become lazy, are retired early and take to growing roses. They are very good at catching mice and this is all workers and management expect of them. Apart from the fundamentalist appeal to deeply held ideological convictions, the source of these misconceptions – both Left and Right – resides in a complete failure to grasp the structural context in which shop stewards operate and that the only occasions on which these factory pussy-cats come to public attention is when there *is* an industrial dispute. Once elected, stewards become the immediate focus of a series of competing and, at times, incompatible demands: they are imprisoned in a role in which they are asked to be all things to all people (see figure 6.1). Indeed, it could be said that it is a very slippery role at the 'hard' centre of daily industrial relations.

THE STEWARD AS EMPLOYEE

This can be illustrated by briefly returning to our real-life victim, Sam Hardhead, who exemplifies the typical shop steward. As an employee he valued his job: it was well-paid, secure and provided good working conditions; he got on well with his colleagues and, while he had had occasion to discuss grievances with his supervisor and Peter Warmly, the Personnel Manager, relations had always been congenial. As an employee, the company expected him to perform the job for which he was paid to the best of his ability – a demand recognised by Sam who had only rarely left his place of work to conduct union business without first informing his supervisor. He is paid by the employer to be a lagger – the

Figure 6.1   Complex role of shop steward

fact that he had been elected as a steward is recognised by the employer who permits him to leave his job when necessary since this facilitates the quick and peaceful resolution of grievances and potential disputes. He is aware that if he tries to 'take liberties' with management by abusing their tolerance of the time he spends on union business during working hours they are likely to withdraw this concession: for no deduction is made from his wages for time spent on union business but this has never been formally agreed to by the company.

As an employee the steward can sometimes experience difficulty in maintaining a good working relationship with the immediate boss or supervisor. This is partly because, at least informally, the steward's authority can undermine that of the supervisor. Foremen frequently complain that stewards do not ask permission to leave their jobs and, with anything other than a minor issue, stewards are prone to by-pass the immediate supervisor and take the problem to the personnel or industrial relations staff or the production manager. Any of these actions is likely to create insecurity and resentment, for it may appear that the supervisors are not doing their jobs properly. Where procedures exist to prevent such by-passing, there will nonetheless be occasions when even the most amenable of stewards – because the foreman is not available or because the issue cannot be resolved without the involvement of more senior management personnel – will tread on some toes.

In other situations, the actual job the steward does may be the cause of strain. For example, a few years ago there was a very emotive strike at the Great Ormond Street Hospital for Children. Porters, cleaners and catering staff went on strike following the sacking of their shop steward, a certain Conway Xavier, whose job was Deputy Head Porter. He had taken part in a 2-day strike by porters in support of staff at a nearby hospital and was accused of neglecting his duty, taking unauthorised leave and of disloyalty to management. 'I am a shop steward', said Xavier, 'and I do only what my members tell me to do.'[2] Leaving aside the merits of the case, the analytical point is that had Xavier not been employed in what management regarded as a position of some responsibility, his duties as a shop steward would not have led to his dismissal. He had to choose between two incompatible loyalties.

No such complications occur where – as in the case in many large unionised concerns – management agrees to having full-time shop stewards. These are taken off normal duties, usually paid the average earnings of their original occupation and often provided with their own office, telephone and, sometimes, secretarial assistance. Such investment in the management of discontent is as much a reflection of the need for such full-time shop stewards as it is a reflection of the extent to which stewards can bargain for such facilities. Where they exist, management rely very heavily upon them to sort out problems and, if possible, pre-empt industrial disputes. Full-time stewards do not, of course, guarantee permanent industrial harmony. The most well-known, for reasons we will come to, are those in the various car-manufacturing companies.

More generally, there are two simple but easily forgotten factors which go a long way in helping to understand the problematic role of shop stewards. First, anyone who becomes a steward can only do so because he or she is already an employee and, as such, has obligations toward the employer. Second, the precise nature of the occupation and its associated working conditions place constraints on the steward. A NALGO steward working in local government can pick up the internal phone and talk to all the members; in contrast, a bricklayers' steward on a large construction site may only be able to inform his constituents of a serious grievance by calling an unofficial lunch-time mass meeting. Shop steward organisation also reflects these features of the work itself. For example, where there is continuous production with three shifts, there is likely to be a steward for each shift to ensure that everyone is properly represented as communication between shifts is often difficult.

In maintaining harmony much depends on the way in which the employee balances the obligations to the employer with the duties of being a steward. On occasion, as with Conway Xavier, this can produce an impossible dilemma. Indeed, in most situations where stewards are disciplined or dismissed for flouting management authority it is likely to be the result of the zealous pursuit of stewardly duties rather than red mole-type subversive intentions. There is no way such conflicts can be avoided, for they reflect differing assessments of how far the steward is entitled to neglect his or her obligations as an employee in favour of those to the members.

Even where there are long-standing good working relationships problems can occur. Sam Hardhead, his supervisor and Peter Warmly had come to an understanding as to what was reasonable and, up until the laggers' dispute, there had rarely been any serious disagreement between them. Yet, on the day he and the other five laggers left the job to put their case, Mr Warmly donned his stiffest shirt and informed them they had left their work without permission, were thus in breach of their contracts of employment and, if they did not return immediately, they would be suspended pending a disciplinary hearing. This is merely one of the consequences of being an employee.

THE STEWARD AS ELECTED REPRESENTATIVE

Just as Peter Warmly was representing managerial interests, so too Sam Hardhead was expected to represent the interests of the laggers. In the circumstances, they felt they had little choice but to call an unofficial strike. No-one could say they were looking for an excuse to take such action – least of all brave Sam who, like all the others, not only lost his wages but was instantly elevated to immediate notoriety as an industrial hooligan and was still expected to negotiate a winning solution. Like the policeman – or blue meanie – the stewards' lot is sometimes not a happy one.

They are unpaid, have little training for their duties and frequently spend long hours on union business. These are some of the reasons why, in many instances, they do not face a great deal of opposition from alternative candidates at election time. Technically, all stewards are elected, but about 75% are returned unopposed and, once in office, may remain there until someone else can be persuaded to take over. This does not mean they are unrepresentative or retain their post through undemocratic means, for they have to be formally re-elected every 1 or 2 years. A long unchallenged term of office may reflect not only the absence of serious employment issues but also the skilled work of the steward in pre-empting such difficulties. The greater their experience in the post, the less likely it is the members will wish to replace them. And the one overriding lesson stewards learn from experience is that if they fail to reflect the wishes of the membership then they are instantly criticised and may be forced to resign. It is for this reason that most stewards regard their primary function as representing the interests of their electorate.

The duties and responsibilities this involves vary considerably from one situation to the next. In the engineering industry (which includes car-manufacture) their role is probably more extensive than elsewhere. This is partly for historical reasons – it was there the shop steward role first became important – and partly results from the character of collective bargaining in that industry. As noted earlier, the national engineering agreement only specifies minimum terms and conditions of employment. This permits the stewards much greater discretion and means the workforce feels more directly involved in wage-determination. Where piecework pay systems operate it is even more important to be well organised. In other words, it is because plant bargaining is more significant that *everyone* – managers, stewards and employees – is more directly involved. Not surprisingly, therefore, stewards in engineering tend to be more actively involved not merely in pay issues but all issues – overtime rotas, discipline, grievances, dismissals and production itself. In contrast, where the national agreement is a detailed specification of terms and conditions – such as in large areas of the public sector – shop stewards' visibility and activity across the whole range of potential issues tend to be lower.

Despite what is said in public, stewards are not only supported by their members but also tend to be seen in far more positive terms by management than we have been led to expect. In one large-scale national survey, 93% of the senior managers interviewed thought stewards were reasonable to deal with and 79% agreed that stewards helped to resolve problems. Nor do stewards blindly represent only one side of the issue – in the same survey, 36% of those managers thought stewards took a 'fifty–fifty' attitude on points of worker–management conflict. This is a reflection of the mediating element in the shop steward's role for, in representing employee interests, they have to make judgements about what can reasonably be asked of management. Even the employees recognised this for in the same survey 54% of the workers also thought stewards took a 'fifty–fifty' attitude.[3] Analytically, this highlights a very important constraint operating on stewards, for, to remain an effective representative, they not only have to persuade management to make concessions but must also persuade the membership to accept less than they demanded. This balancing act can become very difficult if the steward represents different job-categories composed, perhaps, of both male and female employees whose particular interests may come into conflict.

Such dilemmas are more likely to occur where the trade union organises across the whole range of occupations. In local government, for example, NALGO members are found throughout the administrative hierarchy. An employee's supervisor might also be the shop steward and this could create problems should the employee have a grievance against the supervisor. A rather bizarre case, which highlights this problem, occurred a few years ago in one of our august universities. A lecturer was accused of falsifying his educational qualifications – an offence meriting dismissal. The chairman – or senior shop steward of the local branch of the Association of University Teachers – the organisation which put his case – was also his Head of Department and foremost amongst his accusers. Needless to say, it was a dispute which took a very long time to resolve.

THE STEWARD AS UNION REPRESENTATIVE

Shop stewards, apart from the demands made upon them as employees and apart from the demands made upon them by their members, are also, of course, representatives of particular trade unions which, in turn, also expect certain things. At a minimum, unions expect stewards to recruit new members, collect union dues,[4] keep members informed of union affairs, abide by union policy, and, where necessary, represent and negotiate on behalf of members.

But the union is an external organisation with its own interests and, historically, shop stewards have not enjoyed a particularly honoured place inside the formal trade union organisational structure. There has been a more or less permanent tension between shop stewards and full-time trade union officials which stems, once again, from the structural context in which shop stewards operate. They have their own constituencies and their own very localised workplace problems and interests; issues which may be of concern to national officials may not only be viewed with studied disinterest by the members but may also come into conflict with membership interests. In such situations the stewards have to choose and – since they are answerable to the membership – will invariably side with the membership. One simple example is the overtime issue. Most trade unions have national policy documents which commit the union to aiming for the reduction of overtime working. It would, however, be a foolish shop steward who insisted the members refuse all overtime work in line with such policies, for overtime earnings are often regarded as a significant part of the wage-payment.

Historically, the most dramatic example of this tension came during World War I, which produced what is actually referred to as the 'Shop Stewards Movement'. At the request of government, the national officials of the engineers' union (the AUEW) agreed to what was called 'dilution'. In effect, this meant that employers would be allowed to use technically unqualified men to do the work of skilled craftsmen. This was bitterly resented by many skilled engineers and a source of continuous industrial conflict throughout the war. In order to prevent it, workers formed their own closely coordinated local negotiating committees – composed largely of shop stewards – to fight the issue.

Other evidence which reflects this tension comes from the involvement of stewards in the union itself and their contacts with full-time officers. The ordinary union *members'* involvement in trade union branch activity is notoriously low – the most recent survey[5] suggests, on average, there is about 7% attendance – and, as expected, shop stewards are likely to comprise the bulk of those who do go. But stewards themselves only attend about half the meetings in any one year. The same survey established that, on average, senior stewards met with their full-time union officers about 2.5 times per year and meetings involving senior stewards, full-time officers and management representatives occurred, on average, only once a year. This last statistic emphasises the extent to which management prefer to negotiate with their own stewards rather than involve a full-time officer who is unfamiliar with the problem, does not really know the employees and whose views may only complicate the issue. Indeed, one important report suggested that management may even encourage the separation of the steward from the union organisation, for management 'have built up the authority of senior stewards as part of a deliberate policy of retaining the control of industrial relations matters generally within the organisation'.[6]

THE STEWARD AS WORKPLACE COORDINATOR

This structural tension between shop stewards and their unions is sometimes reinforced and increased by the existence of shop steward committees, composed of stewards from all the various trade unions at the workplace. Informal contacts between different unions in an organisation – with the purpose of exchanging information and enlisting sympathy support when required – are commonplace. In the larger organisations – and especially where pay is directly negotiated at plant or company level – these contacts are likely to generate what is, in effect, an almost autonomous multi-union organisation. Such organisation springs naturally from the bargaining structure: if there is a joint negotiating committee which processes all the major issues then it is logical for stewards to establish a united front in order to prevent each category of employee being picked off one at a time.

Such committees sometimes take on a life of their own, focused entirely on the plant or company and outside the control of the full-time trade union officers. They are responsible only to the collective membership of the organisation and develop policies and strategies which may have little relationship to those of the trade unions as such. In rare instances they may even establish international linkages, as has from time to time occurred when stewards from various Ford Motor Company plants across Europe have met to try – unsuccessfully – to create a wider bargaining base.

THE BLUE MEANIE MODEL

This brief account of the complex role and structural location of the shop steward leads to two important conclusions. Firstly, in the day-to-day regulation of the employment relationship, in the event of a disagreement or dispute of any variety, the shop steward is likely to be a key figure in the management of discontent. Given the strains and tensions inherent in the often competing interests they are expected to defend they might, with charity, even be regarded as the unsung heroes of British industry. Sam Hardhead should not be regarded as untypical except in the sense that his dealings were with a progressive employer which was, and still is, intent on minimising industrial conflict through a professional approach to the management of discontent. Elsewhere, in smaller less secure concerns, he would not have enjoyed such cooperation from management.

Secondly, shop stewards are essentially peace-makers, actors who seek to resolve rather than create differences: they catch the mice that constantly invade the larder of industrial harmony. On those occasions when a dispute arises, the employees expect them to do their best to resolve the issue quickly and favourably. In turn, when management make concessions, they expect the steward to persuade the employees to accept any such proposals. All the survey evidence available confirms not only that the vast majority of managers are happy to deal with shop stewards but also that the rank-and-file members tend to be more 'militant' than their stewards. This is not to suggest that shop stewards never act independently of the membership or that they are all docile Social Democrats – for they are elected in order to represent employees and this involves, in some circumstances, taking an uncompromising stance on particular issues. It would not be reasonable to expect employees and their representatives to accept peace at *any* price.

Of course, every once in a while, a shop steward will do something which appears very damaging to the image of trade unionism. But to take such incidents as being symptomatic of shop stewards in general would be the same as treating skin-head Paki-bashing as a normal feature of behaviour among all young people. Few of those directly engaged in industrial relations – managers, stewards, employees and academics – would disagree with the conclusions of the 1968 Royal Commission which was set up precisely because unofficial strikes had become defined as a major socio-economic problem. It reported that shop stewards were 'more of a lubricant than an irritant' in the system of industrial relations. 'Trouble', it said, 'is often thrust upon them. In circumstances of this kind they may be striving to bring some order into a chaotic situation, and management may rely heavily on their efforts to do so.' Further, 'they are rarely agitators pushing workers towards unconstitutional action . . . but . . . commonly they are supporters of order exercising a restraining influence on their members in conditions which promote disorder.'

It is this less vivid but more securely grounded empirical account which gives rise to the 'blue meanie' model of shop steward behaviour. What this states is that the stewards, by entering into arrangements with management, making agreements, processing grievances and generally plastering over all the cracks and strains of the employment relationship, have, in effect, become a police force operating on behalf of the employer. Having institutionalised industrial conflict shop stewards (and trade unions) have not only established a truce between the endlessly warring factions of capital and labour but, in their attempts to enforce order through joint agreements, actively perpetuate the monstrous exploitation of the workers under capitalism. Shop stewards are little short of cuddly toys for management.

Stewards have been duped by the promise of managerial blandishments – the good steward, once spotted, is often promoted to foreman or better – and are further shackled by the constant stream of bourgeois ideology. This operates as an anaesthetic to all effective initiative and masks the coercive reality of capitalist work relations. If only they could escape its clutches, raise the political consciousness of the workers and fight the good fight, we might all be led to the promised land. This is a tall order; and one which is severely hampered by the persistent refusal of most employees to ever see beyond the next hire-purchase repayment and the next wage-packet. They too, of course, have been seduced by the materialistic mystifications of capitalist society.

As one might expect in a nominally free society such as Britain, there are a minority of shop stewards who operate with this frame of reference. Their impact on industrial relations is very difficult to assess but, if the experience of the BL 'red moles' is anything to go by, then it is extremely limited. The greatest obstacle to progress is not the mole-hunters of Fleet Street or the Economic League's blacklist, but the fundamental caution and suspicion of employees who, despite the occasional historical hiccough, have persistently refused to take any interest in revolting.

As the account of the complex role of the shop steward indicates, both the red mole and blue meanie models are grotesque parodies of the everyday realities faced by shop stewards. Their appeal lies in the grain of truth that each contains and in their simplistic self-fulfilling character. The Right-wing political scientist observes that strikes are advocated by Left-wing propagandists and such activists are also seen on picket lines supporting shop stewards. Therefore shop stewards are red moles.[7] The Left-wing sociologist observes that shop stewards do sign agreements and do get promoted. Therefore they are blue meanies.[8] Both conclusions are simplistic and naive in that they completely ignore the context of social action: in order to survive, the steward must represent the daily demands of the membership *and* come to working arrangements with management. It is never a question of doing one or the other for the two are interdependent. In practice, this means that there will be occasions when the employees demand industrial action and also occasions when they agree to management's offer, irrespective of the advice given by their stewards.

THE MYTH OF THE WRECKER

If, as is being suggested, shop stewards operate as mediators

166

between the unrealistic expectations of both members and management, then why is their conventional public image such a gross distortion? A full answer is complex but two critical factors are the context in which shop stewards are brought to public attention and, secondly, what happens when news is packaged for sale.

Normal everyday life happenings do not make 'news': it is the exceptional and the extraordinary which captures the front pages. So far as the public is concerned, unless they have a particular interest, if all that is ever presented by way of information about industrial relations are the exceptions rather than the rule then it is entirely possible that the exceptions *become* the rule: the image becomes everyday reality. Since the shop steward occupies such a critical role in maintaining the continuity of the employment relationship on the shop floor, the only time we see him is when that relationship has broken down and, quite legitimately, becomes a focus of public concern. On virtually every occasion that a dispute reaches the 'Nine o'clock News' there is a shop steward shuffling his feet outside the factory gates or a union official tediously elaborating the convoluted reasons why it was management which 'failed to abide by the agreed procedure' and thus forced the employees to go on strike. Not only does no-one understand what he is talking about but, even among those who are listening, there are even fewer who regard it as an appropriate justification for such drastic action. Given this 100% correlation between industrial disputes and the appearance of a union representative defending whatever action has been taken, it is no surprise that we also assume he is the cause of the dispute: without him it would not have occurred.

In this respect, the shop steward enjoys a high profile: the press photographers and TV cameras are never there when a worker is sacked or when management change working arrangements without prior notification, or when it is actually decided to close a factory or make 300 employees redundant. But they are always there when the shop steward is addressing a mass meeting, and when pickets are standing around a brazier drinking tea from vacuum flasks in breaks between intimidating workers and fighting the police. In terms of the social visibility of industrial relations, it always *looks* as if the shop steward or trade union is the individual or institution which has actively started the dispute. It is they who call the strike – not the manager; it is the workers who have stopped working – not the management. What management has done or is not doing remains invisible: they are seemingly inert, on the receiving end. In such circumstances it is easy to forget that conflict is the product of a joint relationship, not something one actor engages in independently of the other; and thus to forget employees on strike are *reacting* to something management have or have not done. It is remarkably easy to forget that, on all the other 364 days of the year, the steward is acting positively to prevent such disputes by signing new agreements on working conditions, consulting with supervisors on overtime, negotiating bonus rates and piece-work prices with rate-fixers or representing workers before disciplinary panels. Such activity is rarely, if ever, reported – because it is normal.

This unwarranted wrecker image is further enhanced by the constraints which are imposed upon the presentation of news. There are three major sources of distortion: political colouring, competition for sales and the inherent limitations of the media themselves.

All major newspapers have a political frame of reference which colours the tone of reporting and determines the way in which news is presented. Such political bias is not, of course, the preserve of the capitalist press but a source of distortion common, in varying degrees, to all newspapers from *The Times* and the *Morning Star* to the Soviet Government's *Pravda*. Among the national British newspapers, all but one or two would be regarded as Conservative in tone. There used to be a distinctively pro-Labour newspaper – the *Daily Herald* – but this folded in 1964 and, despite increasing concern among Labour politicians and trade union leaders, attempts to remedy what they regard as a very significant political imbalance in newspaper reportage of their views and actions have been unsuccessful.[9] It is also alleged that television news reporting – despite the statutory requirement to present a balanced coverage of differing viewpoints – is sometimes far less balanced than is desirable. Detailed research by the Glasgow Media Group[10] concluded that the way in which industrial relations issues are presented is invariably more favourable to the interests of the employer.

The political bent on news coverage – most obvious in newspapers – is, of course, unavoidable and inevitable. Indeed an 'objective' account of any dispute is impossible since all perceptions of the social world are located within particular frames of reference. Distortions occur when one frame of reference comes to dominate all discussion of the issues, creating a rather one-sided and thus very incomplete view of social reality.

As a source of analytical distortion, political bias is not insuperable and is, perhaps, less important than the distortive consequences of circulation battles between the press barons. Newspapers, like cornflakes, are products which are pack-aged and sold and, in this process, it is not surprising that, particularly among the mass-circulation newspapers, the packaging can become more important than the content. Just as a new blue ingredient sells more of a particular brand of detergent, so too a new red variety of industrial militant may sell more of a particular newspaper product. Functionally, if it makes little difference whether it's 'red moles' or 'blue meanies' being given the shock-horror massage on the front page or Bingo on page five – so long as it sells more newspapers, it works. The actual news events become a mere vehicle for the most dramatic angle which, in some cases literally, can be created. A vivid example of this occurred during the waterworkers' strike of 1983 when one newspaper headlined the story of a woman who was divorcing her husband – a waterworker on strike. Whatever complex personal tragedy lay behind this news item was not clear, but the message was: here, at last, was a true patriot, someone who – like the nation as a whole no doubt – felt so deeply about the traitorous behaviour of her husband, a waterworker on strike, that she could no longer stomach living with him. This practice of packaging 'news' in such a way that it increases the marketability of the product is a distinctive and potentially dangerous source of distortion. It is unfortunate that, at times of high unemployment – which intensifies the degree of competition between the mass-circulation papers – newspaper editors seem to be under greater pressure to resort to such practices to increase circulation.

However, by far the most enduring source of distortion comes from the inherent constraints of the media itself. If news reporters have only two minutes screen time or five column inches in which to tell their stories, the likelihood of oversimplification is extremely high. In the case of the laggers' dispute, for example, when Sam Hardhead was interviewed by the reporter from the *Clearwater Mail*, he gave a full explanation of the relationship between the company pay scheme and the national agreement pay scales for thermal insulation engineers. Peter Warmly, as ever eager to please, also detailed this issue as well as explaining the consequential effect on the company job-evaluated scheme should the laggers claim be recognised. The reporter sat, nodding intelligently, and wrote down everything the two men said. Having written it up it came to 5,000 words and, back at the office, the editor decreed there was only space for 500 words, so it was gutted to give only the salient points. The net result was the story headed: 'Six militants threaten 1,400 jobs' – the sub-editor thought it was a catchy headline.

So, the next time you see a shop steward or union official on the television news insisting that their 'injustices' must be remedied or their 'aspirations' met, take pity and remember this was the only part of what was said which the video editor could fit into a 2-minute slot; the part where the dispute had been explained had to be cut 'for technical reasons'. And nothing, least of all accuracy in reporting the complexities of an industrial dispute, can be allowed to interfere with the technical demands of the medium.

None of this is to suggest that journalists are part of some grand malign conspiracy on the part of those who control capital: they are, like the shop steward, trapped within the constraints of their work situations. Indeed, one journalist, a Labour Affairs correspondent, recently penned the following: 'Sweet reason dominates most of British manufacturing industry. Disputes are unpopular among stewards and workers, just as much as they are in the boardroom.' In support he cited some research findings of the Department of Employment which concluded that, in 1976, 98% of all plants in the manufacturing industry are strike-free in any one year. Sadly, this quote is not from the *Daily Mail* or even the *Observer*, but from page 203 of a very detailed analysis of trade unionism.[11] That which is normal does not make news.

Shop stewards are, of course, not alone in suffering the defects of media news reporting although few groups of people in society can have enjoyed such consistently negative treatment. This, combined with what amounts to little short of public ignorance about the role of shop stewards and the context in which they operate, is the primary source of the grotesque image which is passed off as the conventional shop steward. Red moles are found in industrial relations about as frequently as honest politicians in Parliament; and, once discovered, both are usually sacked.

Although estimates vary, it is reckoned that there are about 290,000 shop stewards distributed throughout British industry. On average, though it varies from year to year, some 5,000 (i.e. 1.75%) of them may be involved in an industrial dispute which includes strike action. It is the other 285,000 who have a normal year. The image of shop stewards as peaceable but watchful pussy-cats is even more vividly illustrated by one of the conclusions in a massively detailed study of strikes which suggests that at least 99% of the bargains struck between employers and employees are achieved without resort to strike action.[12]

7

The Striking Paradox

If there is one feature of industrial relations which is even more misunderstood than the humble shop steward, it is the strike. Like the steward, the presentation of strikes suffers from the same distortive media limitations, and it is easy to conclude that we are a nation of strike-happy robots when every day there is another dispute to be given the shock-horror-crisis make-up. In addition, a much less obvious factor which interferes with coming to a more dispassionate understanding of what causes strikes, how costly they are and how to resolve them is the behaviour and attitudes of those directly involved in the issue. This point requires particular emphasis. Earlier, it was pointed out that strikes can only be understood as part of collective bargaining, a process through which conflicting interests are accommodated. As noted above, in 99% of cases this does not involve strike action though it may involve other forms of pressure and threats – such as an overtime ban or management saying they will close down the factory rather than concede a particular wage increase. Each side is testing, probing and pushing the other in order to force them to lower their demand or increase their offer. Going on strike or imposing a lock-out[1] is the most extreme and most socially visible tactic available and, for employees, invariably the last resort.

The critical point to remember is the strike is part of an *ongoing* process: bargaining has not stopped when a strike is in progress; the verbal cut-and-thrust has merely been temporarily interrupted while all those involved show off their muscles to each other and, of course, to the public. What was a private, secretive process of negotiation is, all at once, thrust into the floodlights and transformed into a public contest of rhetoric, propaganda and bluster. Thus, when any of the principal protagonists talk to the media they are, of course, also talking to each other and to their own supporters. It is in the interest of the employer to present a picture of dire consequences if the employees do not return to work, and employers always stress the catastrophic economic consequences, emphasise the number of redundancies there will have to be and bemoan the definitive loss of export orders. This is done in order to persuade those on strike to weaken in their resolve and, if possible, to mobilise public opinion against them.

Logically, it is in the interests of the employer to overstate the possible consequences. The strike leaders are similarly engaged on creating an image of total unanimity of purpose and solidarity among those on strike, of the fundamental justice of their case and of the utter intransigence of the employer. This is done in order to ensure the continued resolve of those on strike and, if possible, to mobilise public opinion in favour of their position.

THE LOGIC OF STRIKES

All this public posturing is often accompanied by a range of 'dirty tricks' tactically designed to undermine the position of the other side. Employers take out full-page adverts in newspapers putting their case to the public, send letters to the homes of individual strikers, enlist the public voice of politicians as available, and may even – as the employers in the London Docks did in September 1984 – finance a ballot of the employees on strike in order to embarrass the union and, if possible, break and strike. This latter tactic is brilliant because the employer can't lose: if the ballot produces a majority vote in favour of a return to work – no matter how unrepresentative that group might be – they can accuse the union of being undemocratic bully-boys; and if the vote is in favour of staying on strike they can shrug their shoulders in despair and point out that the strikers are cutting off their nose to spite their faces.

On balance, the strikers have a narrower and more fragile range of 'dirty tricks'. They can – as occurred during the national miners strike of 1984–85 and also in the national dock strike of August 1984 – play strictly by the union rules in order to declare a national strike. Such action may be legal and legitimate according to the rules but leaves the leadership wide open to attacks on their integrity and accusations of having manipulated the strike. They can try to increase the solidarity of the strike or spread its economic impact by picketing, which has always been a double-edged tactic for, to be effective, it depends not only upon total solidarity among the group on strike but also on sympathy from other occupational groups. Neither of these is easy to achieve and, where they are absent, peaceful picketing easily drifts into intimidation or violent confrontation with the police. Potentially, the most effective 'dirty trick' is to persuade other occupational groups to take some form of sympathy action. If the miners in 1984–85 had managed to persuade electricity power station workers or dockers to come out in support, this would probably have produced a quick and favourable settlement.

It is not only the double-edged nature of the 'dirty tricks' available to strikers which gives them their fragility. Not only are there severe legal limitations on picketing and sympathy strikes but everything they do is much easier to see. This means the behaviour appears as a crude exercise of brute force which is joyfully reported by an essentially unsympathetic press. In contrast, the 'dirty tricks' available to governments and employers are far less open to public scrutiny. If an employer claims the strike is costing £2 million a day in lost production how do we know it is true? No-one but the employer has access to the relevant data. If a government claims there is no more money available to pay higher wages how do we know this is correct? Or if a nationalised industry deliberately makes an offer which, secretly, it knows will produce a strike, the only way we find out about it is if someone leaks it to the press.

Depending on our sympathies – or frame of reference – we may approve or disapprove of each and all of these various 'dirty tricks'. However, in coming to a better understanding of what goes on in industrial relations, the critical point to recognise is that the use of such devices is a normal and predictable feature of strike situations. Given the vested interests of the major actors – governments, employers and unions – it is natural to use whatever means are available and appropriate to strengthen their position or damage the case of opponents. Such behaviour, to be effective, also involves putting out public misinformation, for the actors continue to bargain even if they are not actually talking directly to each other. Paradoxically, it is often as the strike is coming to its end that the actors become most strident in their assertions about not compromising. The union agrees to talks but insists 'under no circumstances will we retreat from our fundamental demands'; the employer declares 'there is no question of raising our last offer'. They talk, come out smiling and, having agreed 'to hold further talks about introducing positive improvements in the efficient allocation of resources' – which can mean anything – both announce that the strike has been settled on their terms. As was noted earlier, precise details are often quite deliberately fudged. The union side says 'The deal is worth 7.8% addition to earnings', while the employers insist 'the agreement will add 6.7% to basic rates'. It matters not which is accurate; for the strike is over and each party has retained its dignity. Analytically, such deliberate obfuscation merely adds yet another layer of distortion to the image of strikes presented in public. 'Why?' says everyone, 'couldn't they agree to that 6 weeks ago?'

A final reason why strike behaviour remains a continued source of public perplexity resides in the very nature of the strike as a social act. It is a dramatic and perhaps brutal rupture of the employment relationship. Employees stop doing their work, goods are not produced or services cease to be provided. No cars are manufactured or all the commuters from the south-east suburbia are stranded at Waterloo station. Those on strike suffer an instant loss of income and the employer appears to lose whatever profits would have accrued from the lost production. Taking strike action, self-evidently, automatically involves immediate economic losses. Thus strikes – unless they are in Poland – are always a bad sign, a symptom of industrial disease caused by trade unions; yet another nail in our economic coffin.

It is not easy to step back and attempt to understand strikes in a more systematic and critical fashion. Instant gut reactions have a powerful appeal and the real strength of this strike image lies in the one indisputable truism that the image contains: on strike, employees have ceased to work. The rest of the image depends on a series of assumptions which, on examination, turn out to be less than satisfactory. The most important of those dubious assumptions are (1) strike action is a major cause of economic losses; (2) because trade unions or shop stewards instigate strike action they are also the cause of that action; (3) employers derive no benefits from strike action; (4) there are never any good reasons for strike action; and (5) there is a clear-cut distinction between 'political' and 'industrial' strike action.[2]

STRIKES AND ECONOMIC LOSSES

Despite the certainty with which the news media report the cost of strike action in terms of lost production, lost sales and the additional burden they impose on our balance of payments, the one thing that all those who study strikes agree upon is that it is extremely difficult to assess such economic losses with any degree of confidence. As ever, everything depends on the context in which we seek to understand the issues and the kind of measures used to assess economic costs.

For example, despite all the images of doom and destruction, if the economic losses are measured by the absolute amount of working time lost due to strikes then – however perverse this may seem – strikes are almost irrelevant to our economic well-being. As the figures in table 7.1 demonstrate, between 1946 and 1973 the absolute amount of working time lost was 0.07%. What this means – if the losses are spread evenly throughout the working population – is that every employee loses 20.16 seconds in an 8-hour day through strikes. Even this is an exaggeration for it assumes that all employees are fully productive throughout the 8-hour day. Snatching 5 minutes for a chat or a cigarette, returning late from a tea or lunch break or sneaking off home 10 minutes early – and many of us do all of these things – are all, in comparison, quite horrendous sources of lost working time. But, because no one measures them – and it would, to say the least, be a difficult task – we never think about their cumulative effects.

Table 7.1   Strike activity

Years	Workers involved as a percentage of all employees	Working days lost as a percentage of potential working time	Working days lost as a percentage of time lost through unemployment
1946–52	1.3	0.03	1.3
1953–59	2.6	0.06	3.6
1960–68	5.3	0.05	2.6
1969–73	6.5	0.20	5.9
Overall: 1946–73	4.0	0.07	3.8

Source: Durcan, J.W., McCarthy, W.E.J. and Redman, G.P. (1983), *Strikes in Post-War Britain*, London: Allen & Unwin, p. 175.

Even where there are some reasonably reliable data available for comparative purposes there is no real attempt to put the losses due to strikes in perspective. For example, as table 7.1 shows, the working time lost through strikes between 1946 and 1973 amounted to only 3.8% of that which was lost through unemployment – and it was not a period in which unemployment was particularly high. The amount of productive working time lost through unemployment – like strikes – can have many possible causes but it constitutes a far more significant source of economic loss than do strikes. So too do the losses from industrial accidents and certified sickness. Hyman gives figures for 1970 – a year in which the losses from strikes reached a new post-war record of about 10 million working days. This, however was only 50% of the losses due to industrial accidents (20 million days), 5% of the losses due to unemployment (200 million days) and 3.3% of the losses due to certified sickness (300 million days). At that time the losses due to sickness did not include absences through sickness which lasted less than 3 days and, thus, did not require a medical certificate. As Hyman remarks, 'an effective anti-influenza vaccine – or stricter control over unsafe working conditions – would be likely to save far more working time than the most draconian of anti-strike laws.'[3] In addition, with unemployment now seemingly settled at around 3 million, the comparative losses due to strikes are extremely small. In 1983, for example, unemployment averaged 3,104,700 which, assuming there are 48 5-day working weeks in the year, produces a net loss of 745,128,000 working days through unemployment. In contrast, strikes accounted for 3,513,000 lost working days which amounts to only 0.47% of that due to unemployment.[4]

Nonetheless, no matter how dramatic the statistics, for many people they remain abstract, unconvincing and, perhaps, even irrelevant. It might be suggested that strike losses are avoidable while no-one deliberately has an industrial accident or induces their own sickness; that unemployment is a natural economic hazard in a market economy and, some say, is increased by strike action. In short, the bare statistics grossly undervalue the economic losses and provide a measure of strike costs which is equally as misleading as the one provided by the news media.

It is, of course, important to be aware of the limitations of global statistical analyses and, as with all statistics, interpretation of their meaning is more important than the actual figures. Those detailed above are subject to all sorts of qualifications and their purpose is merely to indicate general tendencies. Thus, even if the suggested comparisons with other sources of lost production are thought to be invalid and even if the figures themselves are 100%, 200% or even 300%

inaccurate, it would still be extremely difficult to avoid the conclusion that the economic impact of strikes has been grossly overrated. But there are more tangible reasons than mere statistics to justify this conclusion.

Firstly, the distribution of strikes between different occupations and different industries is not even. Since 1946, in general terms, about 65% of all strikes, 75% of all the workers involved and 80% of all the days lost have come from six industrial sectors: coal mining, dock work, shipbuilding, vehicle manufacture, engineering and iron and steel production. Yet, between them, they account for only about 20% of the total employees. There are particular reasons why each of these sectors has been characterised by relatively high degrees of overt industrial conflict and although very difficult to draw secure generalisations, with the exception of engineering, all these sectors are – in various ways and for a variety of complex reasons – in a process of economic decline. For example, since 1955 the number of coal miners has been reduced from 700,000 to below 170,000; output has dropped by 50% and now provides less than 30% of our basic energy supplies; in 1955 it supplied 90% of these needs.[5] Work in the docks – although it remains critical economically – is no longer labour-intensive: in 1950 there were approximately 75,000 registered dock workers, by 1984 this had fallen to 13,500.

Secondly, the vast majority of strikes are small localised affairs of short duration. Almost 60% of strikes involve less than 100 employees, 71% last no more than 3 days and in only 17% of strikes are more than 500 working days lost.[6] The actual economic losses incurred are impossible to calculate with any degree of accuracy, for much depends on the nature of the product, the market for the goods or services, and the consequential knock-on effects. A strike in the newspaper industry or public transport involves an immediate and irrecoverable loss of revenue, but with the majority of products – especially if the disruption is no more than 2 or 3 days – the lost production can be made up afterwards through overtime so that actual economic losses are minimised.

Thirdly, there may be occasions when the production which is lost through the strike could not have been sold because there was no-one to buy it. This is particularly relevant to those products which have a cyclical pattern to their sales – such as motor cars.

Fourthly, even with major strikes, the stocks in hand may be sufficient to maintain adequate supplies to the market even though the workforce is on strike. The 13-week steel strike of 1980 did not cause any serious loss of sales because stocks were so high and even after a year of the 1984–85 coal dispute there were no power cuts. Like boy scouts, the NCB and the government had come well prepared. Coal stocks were high and more oil than usual was used to generate electricity.

None of this should be taken to suggest that strikes do not involve economic losses, for clearly this is not true, but such features do mean that the economic losses due to strikes are far less than we have conventionally been led to believe.

One further objection to this conclusion is that the real economic losses due to strikes – however small they might be in simple money terms – are intangible. That is, the uncertainty and unpredictability of strikes leads customers – and especially customers in those countries to which we export goods – to lose confidence in their British suppliers and take their custom elsewhere. This is not an argument which can be easily dismissed, for the kind of evidence required to refute it is impossible to collect. Strikes will, from time to time, undoubtedly interrupt supplies and – where an overseas customer requires a completely uninterrupted supply – may lead to orders going to foreign competitors. However, in the international league table for strikes, Britain invariably comes below Italy, Canada, the United States, Australia, France and sometimes even Japan. While it is not easy to assess the extent to which the strikes of these countries affect the purchasing behaviour of importers, the fact that such countries often lose proportionately more working days through strikes than we do is not something British consumers think about when buying imported goods. It might just be that our politicians and our news media are more concerned about the effect of strikes on exports than are those who buy our goods. Once again, this is not to minimise such consequences, but to put them in a broader perspective.

The widespread belief that those who call a strike are also the cause of strikes has become an almost unquestioned truism. It is understandable but deeply misleading, for it completely neglects the fact that strikes occur in the context of an employment relationship and, as such, can only be understood as a product of that relationship. This does not mean trade unions and shop stewards do not call for strike action, but they do so in response to something which the employer has or has not done. Technically, this could be taken to mean that virtually all strikes are caused by employers since they are formally in control of the terms and conditions of employment: it is they who decide whether changes to the existing practices will be made. However, this is to walk down exactly the same blind alley as those who insist all strikes are caused by trade unions or shop stewards.

Initially, it seems useful to briefly reiterate some of the analytical points made earlier. The key actors – employers, employees and governments – have their own particular interests, and their own frames of reference in which they come to decisions about what action they will take. They calculate the consequences of such decisions and, on occasion, are aware that one of the possible consequences will be conflict of some kind. This may be resolved through bargaining or it may produce overt conflict in the form of a strike. Any one of our actors can miscalculate and face unwanted but, perhaps, unavoidable strike. During pay negotiations an employer, in making the 'final' offer, could underestimate the determination of the employees to insist upon more. But the 'final' offer has been publicly declared and it would be unwise to revise it too quickly because this might lead the employees to hold out for an even greater increase. Trade union officials can argue themselves into similar corners either by raising the expectations of employees to an unrealistic level or by misjudging the real position of the employer. But not all circumstances involve miscalculations or errors of judgement.

Some strikes occur over what are called 'perishable' issues. This refers to those situations where, if the employees do not take immediate action, they will lose the issue by default. For example, if an employee or a shop steward is sacked and escorted off the premises, sometimes the only way to secure their reinstatement is to take immediate strike action. This only occurs when the employees regard the dismissal as victimisation or grossly unwarranted. To take such cases to an industrial tribunal is by no means a guaranteed route to reinstatement. Even it the case is won, employers sometimes refuse to reconsider such decisions – which may have been made in the heat of the moment. Employees may respond in a similar frame of mind and down tools until the decision is reversed.

Similar action is often thought necessary when – as has been known to occur in car-assembly plants – management increase the speed at which the assembly line is moving without prior consultation. Such action may be in contravention of an existing agreement on line speeds and, once discovered, is likely to produce an instant protest strike in order to reverse the decision. Such covert changes in the production process not only produce an outraged reaction but also do little to breed confidence and trust in the employer–employee relationship. Many of the instant strikes over piecework prices are also of this perishable and almost bloodless variety.

Establishing clear-cut proof of management or the employer deliberately provoking a strike is by no means easy. No employer would admit to such seemingly irresponsible behaviour and, in terms of public opinion, it is clearly not in the employers' interest to be seen as the obvious cause of a strike. Despite this, there is, occasionally, very powerful circumstantial evidence to suggest that, even if employers do not actively instigate a strike, they sometimes do very little to discourage strike action. In a now famous analysis of strikes in the motor-car industry[7] in the 1950s and 1960s it was demonstrated that, for the employers, strikes function as a means of suspending production at times when there were adequate stocks to supply the market demand. Analysis of the strike pattern showed that the greatest loss of working days tended to occur when the demand for new cars was low – precisely when any 'lost' production could not have been sold. The researchers suggested, that at such times, management did not pursue solutions with any great degree of energy until existing stocks had been depleted. Such episodes, to anticipate the next section, may have distinct advantages for management. They make financial savings on wages, raw material costs and overheads; they avoid all the problems associated with short-time working – which is administratively complex; and they retain their workforce through not having to declare redundancies, which, apart from its financial costs, means that former employees who have been trained, once stocks are depleted or the market picks up, may not return to the plant because they have found more secure employment elsewhere. Hence, not all the allegations that management have provoked a strike should be dismissed as red mole rhetoric – for there are clearly situations in which a strike may be of advantage to managerial objectives.[8]

By far the clearest evidence of management starting strikes comes from the rare occasions on which somebody grasses. This occurred, for example, in 1980 following the 13-week national strike in the steel industry. The strike was called by the steel unions after abortive wage negotiations in which the BSC (British Steel Corporation) decision-makers – headed by Mr Ian McGregor who subsequently presided over the national coal strike of 1984–85 – made a final offer which even the traditionally non-militant steel workers could not accept. After 13 weeks the employees returned to work on terms which were hardly victorious. Not long afterwards, *The Times* – on information provided by a managerial employee who, not without irony, came to be known as the 'steel mole' – revealed that BSC management must have known that their initial final offer would almost certainly cause a strike. At that time – for reasons we shall come to – the strike suited managerial purposes.[9]

Governments too, given their extensive and sometimes intensive involvement in industrial relations, may also be regarded as the causal agents in some strikes. Decisions to pass new laws which will have the effect of restricting trade unionism are often accompanied by demonstration strikes – in 1971 there were two 1-day national strikes against the proposed Industrial Relations Act. Leaving aside the question of whether or not workers ought to strike for such 'political' purposes, the analytical point is that had the Government not announced its intention to pass the Act against the collective wishes and advice of the TUC and virtually all the trade unions, these strikes would not have been called.

Similarly, governmental decisions about their direct involvement in the regulation of industrial relations may be a cause of industrial stoppages. In their detailed statistical voyage in search of an explanation for the increase in strikes in Britain after 1950, one of the conclusions reached by Durcan, McCarthy and Redman (see table 7.1 source-note) is that some of the increase was due to deliberate governmental decisions to reduce the availability of independent conciliation and arbitration. This is not to say there was a deliberate provocation of strikes but – in the pursuit of wage-restraint – governments decided to restrict the use of arbitration since this was seen as one of the mechanisms through which wages were increased. In effect, government were prepared to exchange more strikes for lower wage increases. Similarly, the same study also established clear links between government attempts to directly regulate wages and the level of strike activity. They conclude: 'all the evidence indicates that on balance incomes policy has both provoked particular strikes and done a great deal to raise the general level of strike activity'.[10]

On other occasions the inadequacy of union representation may be the most important cause of a strike. This was the case in the 1970 strike at Pilkington's Glass Works in St Helens referred to in the story of the laggers. On the surface, the cause of this strike – which lasted 7 weeks and spread to most of the company's plants elsewhere – was a small number of miscalculated wage packets. Within hours, however, the dispute escalated into a substantial wage claim and within days became a strike against the union itself for failing to provide effective representation.[11] At the time the strike was celebrated by some on the political Left as a great act of working-class self-liberation, an explosion of working-class consciousness; and there was much dark and irrelevant talk of political subversives. It undoubtedly reflected a range of long-suppressed and deeply felt frustrations about the employer and the union but, once the grievances had been aired and, to some extent, remedied, work life once again settled to its peaceful, hard-working routines. Virtually nothing has stirred at Pilkington's since that time.

The purpose of the foregoing examples has not been to allocate blame to any specific individuals or any particular organisations. Indeed, all attempts to specify such responsibilities are likely to be no more than expressions of our own preferred political frame of reference. The point which this chapter seeks to secure is that any analysis of strikes in these terms will produce nothing but crude stereotypes; a social world peopled by red moles, blue meanies, wicked capitalists and a manipulative, all-pervasive State. Sadly, such caricatures are not unknown in the industrial relations literature and, like the media images, do little to enhance our understanding of the employment relationship. The first step in this process is to stop looking for someone to blame and start by examining the social, political and economic contexts in which strikes are generated.

WHO BENEFITS FROM STRIKES?

Once it is recognised that all of the actors involved in the regulation of industrial relations can take decisions that may result in strike action, the belief that employers or governments never derive any benefits from strikes becomes highly suspect. The idea that employers or governments may have good – and defensible – reasons for provoking strikes is not one that fits easily into the conventional imagery. Indeed, the question of who profits from strikes is not one that is often asked at all.

It has already been shown that, under certain circumstances, car manufacturers can secure a range of positive benefits by not preventing strike action; and the possible rationale behind the British Steel Corporation (BSC) decision to allow the 1980 strike to proceed lies in the political and economic context of the steel industry at that time. Government policy with regard to nationalised industries was to take whatever action was required to make them 'more economic'; a phrase which, for the steel industry, meant a drastic reduction in the amount of steel produced and in the number of employees. Hence, Mr MacGregor was appointed Chairman of BSC with instructions to reduce the very heavy losses. At that time there was a worldwide excess of steel production capacity and also pressure from the EEC to make significant reductions in our steel production. Even before the strike a heavy closure and redundancy programme was under way and, at the time of the strike, it was estimated that BSC was losing about £1 million a day.

In these circumstances the strike had considerable potential advantages for management objectives. It saved money on wages; it saved money on new materials; it stopped the production of steel which, with the exception of specialised steels, could not have been sold anyway; it reduced steel stocks – which cost money to store and tied up valuable capital resources; it provided a political justification for further redundancies, for the strikers could be accused of having thrown their jobs away; and it weakened the resolve of the unions to resist redundancies after the strike was over. It could be said that, in the circumstances, it was good management to allow the strike to go ahead – it undoubtedly helped reduce financial losses being incurred by overproduction and thus reduced the amount of public funds required to finance those losses. The steel industry became more economic – the initial government objective. There were, of course, other costs external to the industry but it seems likely, once the initial policy decision had been made, the BSC board and the government concluded the longer-term benefits were greater than the short-term costs.

Somewhat perversely, perhaps, there are even occasions

when the employer might actually make a profit out of a strike. In 1971 there was a national strike by postal workers in pursuit of a wage claim. Unfortunately, they took action when both the letter and parcel services were losing money and wage costs constituted a high proportion of total costs. At that time the Post Office was also responsible for running the telephone system. One analysis[12] suggested the disruption to the letter-post had only a marginal effect because consumers – and especially business consumers – simply switched to telephones. This large increase in the use of the profitable side of the Post Office business – some of which was sustained after the strike – actually produced a greater profit than would have been the case had there been no strike. Needless to say, since there were no real economic pressures on the employer, the union was almost bankrupted by the strike which, in so far as such judgements can be made, was unsuccessful.

What these examples suggest, when analysing a particular strike, is the necessity of trying to perform a 'cost–benefit' analysis for all the various actors. Since all are involved as part of the cause so too all are subject to various costs and derive various benefits. These examples also highlight a much more troublesome issue: to what extent do *employees* benefit from strike action? As with all the other questions posed, this is far more complex than it might seem.

The most troublesome element of this issue comes from the widespread conviction that strikes are a means through which employees pursue economic goals. It is a view which is encouraged on all sides. Our media image is dominated by the economic damage which results from the disruption of productive activity; academic analyses focus on the statistical surface of strike behaviour – everything which stops is counted – and on the real and imagined impact of strikes on output levels, wage costs and a wide range of other economic indicators. Even trade unions themselves stress their role in defending and improving the terms and conditions of employment of their members, a claim invariably taken to mean increasing economic returns. This carefully nurtured public image highlights their function as economic interest group organisations; and, at least during the good times, the prevailing conventions admit that, although undesirable, strikes in pursuit of economic objectives are legitimate while the use of strikes for political ends are almost always condemned as unjustifiable. In most cases those leading a strike regard the accusation of 'political motivation' as a damaging smear and vigorously defend themselves against such slanders. In short, so long as strikes are about money and economic rewards the behaviour of employees remains understandable; but as soon as it appears to go beyond this – by protesting against government policy or striking against a proposed new law, there are cries of 'Foul, that's political' from all sides. It is not merely a mistaken view of strikes but also an extraordinarily blinkered account of the social phenomenon of strike behaviour. In particular it grossly distorts the motivation of those who strike and misrepresents the presumed benefits of strike action.

Firstly, if we examine the range of nature of the *issues* which are said to be the cause of strikes it is difficult to sustain the view that strikes are solely or even primarily economically motived. An economically motivated strike is one where those on strike expect to extract some financial gain or economic benefit from taking strike action. The Department of Employment collects data on the principal causes of strikes and their most recent account is reproduced in table 7.2. This shows that, in 1983, some 40.5% of strikes were classified as wage strikes and such disputes accounted for 58.1% of the working time lost. Similarly, in the study cited earlier,[13] it was found that, between 1946 and 1973, 49% of strikes were about wage issues and these accounted for 65% of the time lost. But, as the researchers point out, the way in which these data are collected and classified means, at best, they provide no more than 'a rough guide to the main *precipitating* factors which were quoted at the time' of the strike, and 'it is dangerous to assume that what appears is capable of being used as part of a *causal* explanation'.[14] In other words, although there are many strikes which are classified as being about money – and thus reinforce the idea that strikes are economically motivated – in reality a complex range of grievances and motivations may have become crystallized

Table 7.2 Causes of Disputes, 1983

| | Official cause | | | | | | | |
	Pay	Hours of work	Redundancy	Union issues	Working conditions and supervision	Manning and work allocation	Dismissal and discipline	Totals
Number of disputes	548	49	136	70	134	288	127	1,352
As percentage of total	40.5	3.6	10.1	5.2	9.9	21.3	9.4	100
Total workers involved	290,100	20,300	93,700	9,900	27,000	63,000	38,600	542,600
As percentage of total	53.5	3.7	17.3	1.8	5.0	11.6	7.1	100
Total working days lost	2,311,000	104,000	658,000	78,000	172,000	321,000	336,000	3,980,000
As percentage of total	58.1	2.6	16.5	2.0	4.3	8.1	8.4	100

Source: Department of Employment Gazette, vol. 82, no. 7, July 1984, p. 309.

into a wage dispute. In this way the demand for more money becomes, for official purposes, the principal cause of the strike.

Thus, for example, both the laggers' dispute and the strike at Pilkington's – where the demands for more money became the *symbol* through which the employees concerned could process their complex grievances – might well have appeared in the official statistics as wage disputes. Similarly, many of the strikes over piecework prices relate not to *absolute* increases in the money paid for particular jobs, but to the *relative* returns of one job compared to another. That is, such disputes are about establishing comparable or fair prices for different jobs – but they would be classified simply as wage disputes.

Nor, in this context, should we forget the constraints on our beleaguered official collectors of statistics trapped on the sixth floor of a government building in London. They are expected to squeeze each and every strike brought to their attention into nine albeit rather vague categories, of which, if the laggers' dispute is any guide, the person doing the work might perm any one from five. It is no surprise so many end up as wage disputes and such a large proportion come to rest in the 'miscellaneous' category. No matter who owns them, bureaucratic mincing machines have a tendency to produce gross over-simplifications.

The purpose of all this scepticism is to emphasise that, in trying the grasp the complex pattern of expectations that go into what employees regard as strike-benefits, the greatest danger lies in treating the strike as a one-dimensional form of behaviour. As has been emphasised throughout, the employment relationship involves both social and economic exchange. It is therefore reasonable to assume, in any dispute over the terms under which work is provided, social values, norms, ideas about fairness and justice and, on occasion, even the personal idiosyncrasies of a Margaret Thatcher or an Arthur Scargill, will be equally, if not more, significant than the simplistic maxims of economic man.

Support for this view comes from many many sources. In the account of the managers of discontent it was noted that, at least since the work of the human relations thinkers in the 1930s, severe doubts have existed concerning the effectiveness of simple economic incentives. Economic rewards are merely one among a bewildering variety of possible expectations from employment – the need for security, social status, a sense of responsibility or a preference for autonomy in the work itself, can all operate not merely to condition economic motivation but, in many circumstances, to replace it. Similarly, they can all be regarded as the expected benefits of strike action. Studies of how local labour markets work in allocating labour between competing employers demonstrate that most employees remain stubbornly attached to their present employers despite the existence of well-advertised higher-paying comparable jobs in the locality. Lower-paid employees, even where they are relatively well-organised – as in the National Health Service – remain very reluctant to strike simply for higher wages. A national strike by nurses, who enjoy widespread public sympathy, could bring extreme hardship and suffering and, if they were determined to force the issue, no government could resist their demands for long. But nurses have never taken such drastic action and show little sign of ever doing so. It is not that their economic needs or motivation are any less pressing than, for example, those of car workers, but the social expectations they bring to their work and the work-culture they inhabit make strike-behaviour metaphorically, if not literally, unthinkable.

In contrast, our car workers, who enjoy the somewhat doubtful reputation of being highly instrumental in their expectations of work and occupy a work-culture in which strike action, according to some, is almost second nature, are assumed to be the archetypal example of real, live 'economic man'. Indeed, it could be said that the car-manufacturing industry, with its highly repetitive monotonous production technology and cyclical demand for labour, created economically motivated workers – for money is the only work-reward clearly available.

Logically, if strikes are designed to produce real gains then it would follow that the more strikes the greater the real gains, and it would be reasonable to expect that if any one occupational group has managed to benefit economically from strike action it would be the car workers. Once again, however, there is evidence to confound the image. In the most recent study of earnings in the car industry, it was concluded: 'There is no evidence to support the view that the higher level of strike activity in motor vehicles raised the relative wages of that industry.'[15] Even when the researchers tried to relate the number of strikes and the number of working days lost to the actual changes in earnings throughout the period (1949–73) they could find no consistent relationships. So, despite their overt economic motivation to maximise monetary returns, even car workers, with their higher strike rates, have been unable to translate such desires into real gains. At best, strikes keep them where they are relative to other groups. In other words we are faced with the curious conclusion that economically motivated strike action may produce no real economic benefits.

One final indication why we should not regard strike action as being primarily directed toward simple economic objectives comes from the official statistics. Despite the weaknesses noted above, the Department of Employment figures suggest that 59.5% of strikes are from causes other than single wage issues while the Durcan *et al.* analyses of the years between 1946 and 1973 – which is based on the DE annual figures – produced a comparable figure of 51%. There can be little doubt almost half the strikes that occur involve something other than wages. It might be objected that the majority of other issues reflect economic concerns and such issues might function as substitutes for increased earnings. If correct, then the economic motivation model remains untroubled. But the opposite assumption – that demands for extra economic returns of all kinds are merely the symbolic medium through which the complex mix of employee demands for autonomy, fairness, status and recognition are processed – seems equally valid.

One final piece of this jigsaw must be added before trying to reach a conclusion. This concerns the cost of strikes to those who take strike action. In the vast majority the income losses to strikers are negligible and, in most cases, can be made up after the strike. But for any strike lasting longer than a week the income losses reach levels which take a much longer period to recoup. Logically, in terms of a model of economic motivation, those on strike should increase their demands the longer the strike goes on – for their immediate losses become greater the longer they stay on strike. For example, if a group of employees who earn £100 per week go on strike for a 5% increase and stay on strike for a week, at which point the employer concedes, it will still take 20 weeks for them to recoup the loss of the £100. If they stay out for 2 weeks it will take a further 40 weeks to make good their strike costs.[16] Once a strike goes beyond 2 weeks all sorts of other costs begin to arise – mortgage, rent, hire purchase repayments, gas and electricity bills still have to be met and, even if repayments are delayed, become an increasingly menacing source of anxiety and pressure. At some point all these outstanding debts have to be repaid – in effect, those on strike are mortgaging their future income as well as losing their present income.

Seen in this light, the real costs of the 1984–85 miners' strike to individual miners and their families become almost incalculable. Throughout the coalfields, building societies agreed to suspend repayments and most banks were – initially at least, quite happy to allow overdrafts. Such practices are not unusual during strikes for they produce unanticipated additional interest earnings. Nor are there many risks involved, for 85% of all strikes last less than 7 days and only 4.4% last longer than 18 days.[17] However, after 6 or 7 months it becomes a source of growing concern, particularly for the banks. Building societies are secured against defaulting by their first claim on the family home, but banks, even if they initiate bankruptcy proceedings, may lose their money. Thus, if you owe the bank £500 it is your problem, but if they allow an overdraft to rise to £5000 it is their problem. The severe hardship that accompanies all long strikes and the relatively massive debts that begin to accumulate can, of course, generate very strong and bitter feelings which, on occasion, erupt as violence on picket lines. Such behaviour becomes understandable if not justified when – as happened during the 1984–85 miners' strike – the drivers of lorries going through picket lines taunt those on strike by waving wage packets at the pickets. It also helps to explain why those on strike display such ferocious animosity to those who remain at work.

Two important conclusions follow from this. Firstly, not only are the vast majority of employees generally reluctant to strike at all, but when they do they are extremely reluctant to remain on strike for more than 6 days. Any stoppage lasting longer rapidly becomes a very expensive enterprise and, somewhat paradoxically, we could conclude that it is the economic needs of employees which *stops* them from taking strike action. Quite simply, they cannot afford it and, in economic terms, it is a very poor investment. Secondly, those who stay on strike for any longer than 6 days are – in terms of any model of simple economic behaviour – crazy, for the additional cost of staying out rapidly outweighs any additional benefits that might possibly accrue from even a favourable settlement. This means almost any strike over a wage issue which last longer than about a week cannot be explained by reference to economic motivation alone.

These two conclusions also indicate why we should not be surprised that strikes involve such a small proportion of the working population, why they are largely confined to a small number of industries and why the economic losses are so trivial, despite the intangible costs. Some 85% of stoppages involve only very marginal costs to both employees and employers, and it is not unreasonable to conclude that money becomes the flashpoint at which all kinds of other issues and causes – such as inadequate methods of managing discontent, poor working conditions, insecurity, unrewarding work, arbitrary management, notions of fairness about relative rewards or even habit – become focused.

Of course, this does not mean that money is not a major source of conflict in the employment relationship. For most employees and union members it has always been the primary focus of collective bargaining activities and, as noted earlier, some 99% of bargaining is concluded without resort to strike action. What it does mean is that when strikes are said to be about a wage issue there will invariably be a set of underlying and related issues which are non-economic in character.

This brings us to one final irony in the complex arguments about the economic costs, losses and benefits of strikes. The one outstanding conclusion which has emerged is that, for employees, strikes really are economic madness. In the 15% of strikes which last longer than 6 days it is almost certain that those on strike will incur real financial losses. In contrast, as illustrated above, there are circumstances in which employers can make real economic savings and it may, on occasion, be in their economic interest to have a strike. This should not be taken as a suggestion that employers and their managers conspire over whisky and cigars to deliberately provoke a strike but that, for some employers, labour is merely an economic resource. As such, it is employed only at such times as it is profitable to do so. Thus, in making economic decisions about how much labour costs can be increased, where production can best be contracted, or whether or not to close down a particular plant because the product can be bought in cheaper from abroad, managers may dismiss the probability of strike action in response to their decisions as being of no consequence. Such action may even produce financial savings or make the implementation of the decision easier than it would otherwise have been.

WHY STRIKES ARE GOOD FOR US

The uniformly negative public image of strikes has led us to believe that, in our society, there is never any good reason for a strike, they are always avoidable if common sense prevails, and they, and their organisers, the trade unions, are symptoms of social disease. While no-one would disagree that all those involved in the regulation and control of the employment relationship should constantly seek to improve the quality of working relations and, where possible, resolve conflicts of interests without resort to strike action, it would be dangerously misleading to conclude the ideal situation is one where there are no strikes at all. Just as strikes may have intangible economic costs so too they may have intangible benefits, some economic in character.

Apart from the occasional windfall savings that employers reap from some strikes, there are sometimes other beneficial consequences for the process of socio-economic exchange. For example, at one time, the recognised national procedure in the engineering industry was extremely time-consuming. One analysis found it sometimes took 3 months for even the most trivial of grievances to be processed and, even then, there was no guarantee the issue would be resolved. This meant that those employees who behaved 'responsibly', and took their problem through the procedure often found it not only took a very long time – during which their problem remained and, particularly if it was an urgent issue, caused further resentment and frustration – but by the end of the process, the national representatives of the trade unions and the employers' association might say the problem was too localised to deal with and send it back to be resolved at local level. This often exacerbated the problem, for the employees – having been stone-walled for 3 months – became more determined not to compromise than they had been at the outset. Not surprisingly, engineering workers often concluded the procedure was merely being used by management as a delaying tactic and, increasingly throughout the 1960s, groups of workers would strike rather than go through procedure.[18] Such strikes, in effect, forced management to take immediate steps to resolve the problem, prevented issues from becoming more important than they really were, and stopped the build-up of frustration and feelings of neglect which can have a negative effect on productivity and morale. Some managers – who could not afford publicly to be seen to break procedure – welcomed such short stoppages because it meant problems were resolved quickly and efficiently. Management were happy because everyone went back to work with greater enthusiasm and the employees were happy because, even if the issue had not been resolved fully in their favour, they had vented their feelings and relieved the tension.

Similarly, with many of the instant strikes associated with

piecework, a stoppage forces the two sides to reach a quick agreement. If a disputed piecework rate has to go through a time-consuming procedure it means, while the issue is being processed, the employees have to work at the rate specified by the rate-fixer or that work on the specific job is suspended pending the outcome. Neither of these solutions is likely to be beneficial to either side, and a short sharp strike rapidly focuses the minds of the shop steward and the rate-fixer. Once again, such methods may be more effective and more efficient than not allowing the strike to take place or insisting that all such disputes must, in every case, go through procedure.

It is not easy to appreciate the real benefits which accrue from the 'tension-release' function of strike behaviour – partly because of the difficulties we have in believing strikes have any positive outcomes and partly because, unlike adding up the number of strikes that occur or counting the number of working days lost, we are unable to measure it with any precision. There is, however, powerful circumstantial evidence.

For example, it is now well established that strike action is merely one way or one form through which employees express their dissatisfaction, contempt, or outrage at what is happening to them in their employment relationship. Like the imposition of a ban on overtime, a work-to-rule or a policy of non-cooperation, such action has to be organised and orchestrated to have any effect. Alternatively, in the absence of a trade union or some other form of social cohesion and solidarity, employees have to take individual action. One way is simply not to go to work – this is referred to as absenteeism. Another solution is to withdraw from work completely, leave the job and search for alternative, more congenial, employment – this is referred to as turnover. All the evidence suggests high rates of absenteeism and turnover are associated with high levels of dissatisfaction with work. This may be caused by any one or several of the following: the nature of the work itself, the level of rewards, the behaviour of management, the absence of any cohesive work-groups, or ineffective means of resolving disputes. All of these features can be found in combination with poor morale, higher than expected rates of accident and low productivity.

It has also been clearly demonstrated that absenteeism, turnover and lower productivity can operate as *alternatives* to strikes. In the early 1960s, for example, one motor-car manufacturer sacked a number of shop stewards who had been defined as trouble-makers. This did appear to produce a reduction in the number of strikes but was accompanied by an increase in the levels of absenteeism, and accidents and the turnover rate trebled.[19] Later, in 1973, a report by the National Economic Development Office[20] pointed out that while the British motor-car industry was characterised by relatively high rates of strike action it showed markedly lower rates of turnover – 5% – than those found elsewhere: Japan had 20%, Italy had 14% and the Swedish motor industry had rates of about 75%. (This meant that in any one year the equivalent of three-quarters of the labour force left to find work elsewhere.)

What these examples suggest is that removing the symptoms of industrial conflict – by dismissing shop stewards – does nothing to diminish the underlying causes and that high rates of strike action are not necessarily a bad sign. The organisational and economic costs of high rates of absenteeism – which can be very disruptive to production schedules unless management employ a sufficient number of 'spare' employees to cover for absentees – and turnover – which may increase selection and training expenditure – may be greater than the losses incurred from strike action. The collective worker organisation necessary for strike action is also often the source of increased worker solidarity and better morale: the employees feel they do have some control over their working lives and can, if necessary, take some action to remedy their grievances. In this respect strikes may lead to greater social integration of the workforce as well as defusing potentially explosive situations.

This occurred most dramatically in the Pilkington's strike of 1970 when individuals on strike expressed feelings of great relief and even a sense of freedom at having taken strike action.[21] Similarly, at one time, car workers developed a habit of having what they called 'downers': very short strikes lasting maybe only an hour or so, often in the afternoons. One car worker explained that these were to break up the monotony and boredom of the work – were more frequent on hot sunny afternoons than during winter – and that they were good for making the assembly-line workers feel better and work better.[22] There is even some famous evidence[23] which suggests that if the frustrations of work do not find a clear outlet, it may result in an outbreak of psychosomatic disorders amongst employees as well as seemingly inexplicable losses in productivity. All these examples reinforce the suggestion that, despite the various kinds of costs associated with strikes, these may be far less damaging than those resulting from other manifestations of industrial conflict.

However, even if the possible socio-economic benefits of strike action are discounted, it is difficult not to appreciate the potentially dangerous political consequences of suppressing strike activity altogether. In an extreme case, such as Chile, it is accomplished through straightforward military repression. Elsewhere, as in some East European societies, it is achieved through a combination of autocratic organisational structures and careful policing. But the maintenance of such controls makes great demands on financial and manpower resources and is still no sure guarantee of social and economic stability or growth. Although employees in such societies do adapt and find ways of accommodating to such relatively high levels of social coercion, there are periodic accumulations of social tension and pressure and those in power cannot afford to relax the controls. This makes the social order unstable and, as occurred in Poland in 1980, can, in a severe economic crisis, lead to demands for radical social change. Similarly, following the final days of General Franco's authoritarian rule in Spain, there was an explosion of trade union organisation and an epidemic of strikes. Nor does suppression exempt the employment relationship from other manifestations of the underlying industrial conflicts. Managers in the Soviet Union have to cope with very high rates of alcoholism which, apart from absenteeism, does little to improve the quality of production. In Poland, morale and productivity were very low prior to the creation of Solidarity in 1980 and, after the imposition of martial law in 1981, in some factories it became extremely difficult to get any work at all completed on schedule. Such symptoms, reinforced by non-cooperation and widespread acts of sabotage, reflect the consequences of society-wide suppression of autonomous trade unions.

Such examples may seem far removed and unthinkable in a British context but, nevertheless, they remain as sombre warnings to the potential consequences of banning strikes or making trade unions illegal organisations. In practice, it seems necessary to do both for there have been two recent periods in British history when strikes have been outlawed. This was during the two world wars and the reason why these are not particularly well-remembered events in the history of British industrial relations is because the legal prohibitions made little difference to the number of strikes – indeed, in 1944 there were over 2,000 recorded stoppages for the first time. Elsewhere, in Australia, there is a compulsory arbitration law which effectively outlaws strikes, but there, on average, there are more strikes per year than in Britain. The reason for this is quite simple for, in the absence of military repression or a police state apparatus, it is impracticable to enforce such prohibitions. If strikes had been illegal in Britain in 1984 and the government had tried to enforce such a law against the miners just what could have been done? There are not enough jails to hold that number of people and, even if there were, who would mine the coal if 70% of miners were in jail? More significantly, perhaps, what would be the general consequences of such repressive legislation for the quality and character of the management of discontent?

Autonomous trade unions are a well-established feature of all social democracies and, despite historical variations in their fortunes, they should be regarded as a necessary part of any civilised society. In order to function effectively as the representative voice of employees it is also essential they be allowed to call on strike action. Economically, socially and politically the elimination of strikes by law or force would entail serious and, some would say, totally unacceptable costs for it would fundamentally undermine the social fabric of social democracy. Seen in this light, the existence of trade unions and the toleration of strike action operate to institutionalise or regulate socio-economic conflict in such a way that it increases rather than undermines the stability of the existing social order. In so far as either merit serious consideration, it is the 'blue meanie' rather than the 'red mole' model which most approximates the reality of trade union behaviour and impact on industrial relations. Strikes, on the whole, are better than no strikes.

INDUSTRIAL DISPUTES AND POLITICAL STRIKES

Academics splitting hairs and trade unionists taking strike action which endangers their jobs are not alone in adopting seemingly irrational postures. Similarly, journalists and politicians, through a process of constant repetition, have deluded themselves there exists a clear-cut distinction between industrial and political strikes. And, what is more, they have persistently tried to persuade the rest of us that, while 'society' reluctantly permits industrial disputes, political strikes remain an unjustifiable form of action. This distinction is wheeled out when governments or employers wish to increase the degree of public outrage over a particular dispute and, as a propaganda tactic, has much to commend it.

Some strikes are overtly political in the sense that they are called directly in response to some government action or intended government action. In 1969, for example, there was a 1-day strike in protest against a Labour government's proposals to change the law relating to industrial relations; four similar 1-day strikes were organised by the TUC against the 1971 Industrial Relations Act; and again in 1979 and 1981 the TUC mobilised 1-day strikes to highlight their objections against forthcoming anti-trade union legislation. Events such as these have clear political effects and, since they are not specifically directed against the various employers of those on strike, might best be regarded as political demonstrations since their object is to express the disapproval of at least one group of citizens at what government intends to do. Nevertheless, such acts also have economic or industrial objectives in the sense that they concern the way in which the employment relationship will be regulated.

Another kind of political strike are those which are called against the government as an employer. For example, in 1970 there was a 2-day stoppage of Post Office workers in protest at the dismissal of their boss, the Post Office Chairman; and, in 1980, Health Service trade unions organised 1-day national strikes against proposed cuts in expenditure on the National Health Service. Strike action to protect the boss may seem somewhat curious, but if it has the effect of preventing policy changes which would have a detrimental impact on the job interests of employees then it makes sense. The Post Office workers' political strike had a clear economic objective. Similarly, strike action against a reduction in government expenditure may, if successful, preserve jobs but it would be naive to claim such action is directed solely to 'industrial' ends. Indeed, in practice, since government occupies a central role as employer, legislator and economic general manager, almost any strike in the public sector is unavoidably political since action is taken in defiance of the elected representatives of the people. It is impossible for such strikes *not* to have a more or less obvious political dimension.

Ultimately, the distinction is specious because it ignores the context of strike action. For example, there was another miners' strike in 1984. It involved 40,000 miners who stopped work in support of their 18% pay claim. The strike lasted several days during which there was considerable police violence against pickets – some of whom died in the pitched battles that took place. But the miners eventually accepted an offer of 14% which was considered to be an historic victory. This industrial dispute took place in South Africa; those involved were black gold miners staging their first legal strike. At the time of their action they were being paid only 20% of the wages received by white miners doing exactly the same jobs. Although the strike was ostensibly 'economic' in objective it is, of course, impossible to ignore the immeasurably more significant political implications and consequences for the policy of apartheid in South Africa. The success of black gold miners could fuel the economic and political aspirations of all other black South Africans.

It would, seemingly, be dangerous to draw any close parallel between the fortunes of black South African gold miners and British coal miners. But, analytically, the example does highlight one vital common feature which illustrates the critical weakness in the conventional distinction between political and industrial or economic strikes. Economic issues – whether it be the relative wages paid to black workers and white workers or the number of jobs that will continue to exist in the coal-mining industry – are always intimately and extricably bound up with political issues. In reality, 'economic' issues are never exclusively economic in character and it is not necessary for those on strike to have a clear-cut political objective for a strike to have a political dimension or political consequences. This is most obvious where strikes directly involve government in one or more of its several roles in regulating employment. The national coal strike of 1974 had the ultimate effect of bringing down the government of Mr Heath even though the strike was 'simply' about wages. Similarly, the 1984–85 miners' strike – ostensibly fought over the issue of pit closures – had clear and, perhaps, quite fundamental political causes and consequences for all those involved. More importantly, there is the broader question of how we think about the employment relationship and what we think those who regulate it are actually doing.

Earlier, it was stressed that work does not simply involve economic exchange but has social and political dimensions and much emphasis has been placed on the various ways in which the rules which regulate employment are made and unmade. Collective bargaining, for example, creates a complex of rules in order to ensure a reasonable accommodation of the mutually conflicting interests. Normally, despite the pressures which are exerted, both sides agree to abide by such rules even though they do not have the 'force of law' behind them. These rules are often very stable and endure because employers, employees and trade unions believe that such rules ought to be respected. They are often seen as a sort of

informal 'legislative framework' which reflects prevailing
conceptions of fairness and justice at work. Seen in this way,
collective bargaining is a social mechanism which functions to
establish countless systems of 'industrial justice' throughout
the various employment relationships in which it is found.
Employers and employees are mutually involved in creating
and maintaining a moral order in work relations.

It is not the only source of such rules: some are imposed
unilaterally by employers or trade unions; some come from
employment legislation and still others are derived from
custom and practice. Not surprisingly, some rules enjoy
greater support than others but, taken collectively, the rules,
whatever their origin, reflect how those responsible for
making them think the employment relationship ought to be
regulated. Hence the rules constitute the 'informal laws' of
the *status quo* whether this be in the factory, the office or the
mines. When an employer, a trade union or a government
breaks the existing rules or refuses to abide by them any
longer and insists on negotiating their revision they are, in
effect, challenging the *status quo*. Any such challenge, at
whatever level in the industrial or social hierarchy, is *by
definition* political in character since it represents an attempt to
modify or, in more extreme cases, even change the prevailing
social order.

In the vast majority of situations where the *status quo* is
challenged the issue is resolved through the normal process of
bargaining. In some cases these processes are defective or
break down, but in others the issue is so important to those
involved that the matter cannot be resolved until each actor
has tested the determination of the other. In these situations,
and they are not unusual, a strike indicates that one side or the
other regards the readjustment being demanded as unacceptable in principle and requiring determined, even fierce,
resistance. The 'full force' of the laws – both informal and
statutory – may come into opertion. Strike costs, dismissals,
redundancies, picketing and legal actions may be the result.
When this occurs the actual economic costs may become
irrelevant to both sides – as was the case in the 1984–85
mining dispute – for the issue concerns the *principles* upon

which the employment relationship is based and not merely the terms of the exchange. One or more of the participants is saying 'what you propose is so unjust that we are prepared to accept real economic losses in order to remedy the situation'. Thus, when trade union officials or shop stewards appear on the television screen and explain their action in terms of this or that particular 'injustice' they are invariably 'telling the truth' as they or their members see it.

Even when the dispute concerns an apparently straightforward wage issue, the fact that employees take such a drastic step is, in itself, usually a strong indication it is not the only, nor even the most important, aspect of the conflict. On careful examination there will invariably be some additional issue of principle. It might relate to the fairness of a management decision or the belief the employer has reneged on a previous commitment or some other perceived gross inequity in the particular situation which is deemed to merit such a determined response. This is why, no matter what the specific issue in dispute, *all strikes are political* since they reflect attempts to modify, change or, in some cases, maintain the *status quo*. Although, at first, this may seem to be a perverse conclusion, it should not be regarded as controversial for it is the only way to make sense of those situations where the strike costs far outweigh any economic gains that might be made.

One final problem remains. If all strikes are political, why is it most employees who take strike action do not see them in this way? There is no simple answer to this question. Ironically, part of the answer lies in the very success those deluded journalists and politicians have had in sustaining the spurious distinction between economic and political disputes.[24] Political action has come to be regarded in very narrow terms being restricted to behaviour of an explicitly party-political kind or action designed to insidiously subvert the social order and overthrow the government. There are a minority of such political activists among trade unionists who harbour such wild fantasies. However, the vast majority of those who challenge the *status quo* in vigorous defence of their 'rights' or to remedy some manifest 'injustice' entertain no such objectives, and, for the most part, remain oblivious to the genuine political dimension of their attempt to create or restore the moral order of their employment relationships. In this respect, conflict in employment has become de-politicised and it is only with events such as the 1984–85 mining dispute that we are forcibly reminded of the inherently political character of industrial disputes.

This is also reflected in the widespread public belief that trade unions are far too deeply involved in politics. Opinion polls have consistently confirmed, even among trade union-ists, a commonly held belief that trade unions should confine their attention and activity to 'industrial' matters. However, in practice, it is impossible for trade unions to pursue economic or employment issues *without* being actively involved in politics. This apparent paradox provides a second element of the answer to the question of why strikers do not seen themselves as engaged in political acts.

Even the briefest historical sketch of trade unionism instantly demonstrates why political involvement is, and remains, inescapable. Their legal right to exist and pursue their everyday activities was not finally secured until the TUC had been actively involved in creating the Labour Party in 1900. Subsequently, their cooperation was sought by governments during wartime to more easily facilitate produc-tion and, since 1945, successive governments have endeavoured to involve the unions to a greater or lesser degree until the late 1970s. Since then, with the election of Mrs Thatcher's Conservative administration, there has been a dramatic and, for the unions, a seemingly traumatic refusal to countenance any form of collaborative or consultative policy formation. Nevertheless, during periods when unions have enjoyed political influence, they used it to shape socio-economic policies in ways thought to be beneficial not only to their membership but also to the wider society. Not surprisingly, given their close ties with the Labour Party, such efforts have invariably been shaped by some form of socialist philosophy.

However, the central analytical point is that unions did not become involved in politics because governments courted their cooperation nor because trade union leaders exploited their role as representatives of an economic interest group in order to pursue their own private political ambitions. In order to effectively pursue the economic interests of their members it has been essential to be actively involved in politics. Trade unions can only influence the laws regulating the employment relationship by directly seeking to introduce or change legislation. The rules governing the contract of employment, the role of trade unions, the employment of children, equal pay, discrimination at work – and many others – are not created through the forces of economic exchange. Similarly, especially in the 1960s and 1970s, the unions from time to time supported various kinds of incomes policy in order to maintain overall levels of employment and thus create a more secure and planned economic environment for their membership. Such goals – which they regarded as being to the general benefit of all employees – cannot be pursued through conventional economic exchange processes nor even through collective bargaining. Some kind of centralised governmental regulation is necessary and this requires an active involvement in formal politics.

This more or less direct political role has invariably created tensions and strains within individual trade unions and the last example demonstrates why this is so. Trade union officials – in agreeing to accept the restrictions on collective bargaining which invariably accompany incomes policies – do so in order to further the general interest of labour and regard such policies as operating to the general advantage of their membership in so far as they help to contain inflation and, perhaps, reduce the threat of redundancies. But specific categories of labour or certain occupational groups – particularly if they enjoy a favourable position in the labour market – may see such policies as operating against their particular interests. In other words, the structural location of the leadership in relation to their members means they interpret the economic interests of the membership in a different light to the members. The latter, whose primary concern is likely to be their own particular wages and conditions of employment, may reject the political activities of their leaders on the grounds that it does not further their specific interests. Thus it is that even ordinary trade union members come to agree trade unions should not be involved in politics. Such a view, as suggested above, is, analytically, wishful thinking and the result of operating with an extremely narrow and incomplete frame of reference.[25]

CONCLUSION

In recent years the idea trade unions are a major cause of our present economic difficulties has gained much credence. Trade unions are seen as being economically obstructive and destructive and, in general, as having too much power. Shop stewards appear as termites undermining industrial harmony, and calling economically devastating strikes. It has been shown that, whatever may or may not be the social, political and economic consequences of trade unionism, it is by no means as cancerous as the conventional images suggest. In particular, two issues – the role of shop stewards and the impact of strikes – have been elaborated in order to demonstrate that, with a more considered frame of reference, there is evidence to suggest that both stewards and strikes fulfil positive social functions.

Finally, this is not to suggest such issues should not be a subject of deep and continuing public concern nor that trade unions, like governments and employers, can be exempted from at least some responsibility for our present economic ailments. However, what it does suggest is that unions have become the scapegoat of successive governments since the late 1960s. The political obsession with 'settling the union problem' has, perhaps, resulted in a failure to see the activities of unions in a realistic context and an associated failure to address the more significant variables influencing our economic decline.

8

Power and the Employment Relationship

In any attempt to arrive at a more disciplined account of industrial relations, it is necessary to set up a basic *analytical framework*. This is a device through which we describe, analyse and, if brave, try to explain some part of the social world. In the language used so far, an analytical framework is the social scientists' 'way of seeing'. It helps us to do three things. Firstly, it acts as a check-list telling us what information to collect and what kinds of questions to ask. Secondly, it permits us to see beneath the surface of the action by forcing us to examine material which is not immediately visible. Thirdly, it directs our attention to the all-important 'how?' and 'why?' questions.

Throughout previous chapters there have been a number of recurring themes which, when linked together, comprise the elements of such an analytical framework. In the account of the laggers' tale the different interests which characterise the employment relationship were related to the different frames of reference held by the actors. Then, in chapter 3, the organisations created by employers and employees to pursue these interests more vigorously and, they hope, more effectively, were examined. Our central focus – on the administration and control of the employment relationship – was then elaborated with descriptions of the important managers of employment and the methods they use to regulate industrial relations. Throughout there has been a constant emphasis on the idea that industrial relations is about social relationships. The initial focus on the employment relationship between two people was superseded by a more emphatic concern with the complex *structure* of interlinked relationships – between trade unions, employers' organisations, governments, financiers and even oil sheiks – which impinge upon and constrain the behaviour of individual employees and employers.

At this point the all-important questions for the reader are 'how does all this fit together?' and 'why should we approach it from this direction?'. In order to provide some answers it is necessary to dig a little deeper into some examples and to come clean about the concept of 'power' which lies at the centre of the frame of reference which informs this book.

THE WAY WE ARE

When an immediate boss issues instructions to supervisors, why do they do as they are told, and how does the boss ensure they obey? If employees are informed they are to be made redundant or that they will be docked 15 minutes pay if they are 6 minutes late for work how are such decisions enforced? If a shop steward is sacked for holding a lunch-time meeting with employees, how come the steward can sometimes be reinstated after a threat of industrial action by those employees? Such questions may seem a trifle naive because, at one level we all 'know' how such acts are secured. Indeed, we know the answer so well we rarely bother to reflect upon it – everyone 'knows' they have to do what the boss tells them, that's what bosses are for; we all 'know' that, when business is tight or orders are down, employees are made redundant – that's the way of the world; and management reinstate the steward in order to avoid a strike. But 'knowing' in this context refers to our intuitive grasp of social realities, to that which we 'take for granted'. The object of a social scientifically informed approach is to penetrate these surface realities and go beyond such taken-for-granted notions in order to observe the inner workings or internal dynamics of the social world. What *really* makes it work? How is it all held together?

For this a more detailed account of these examples is necessary. What do all these situations have in common? They are all events which commonly occur in the employment relationship and all imply the use of *social sanctions* by one actor on the other. The refusal of supervisors to obey the boss is likely to invoke disciplinary action, and, should they persist in their waywardness, could get them dismissed. One implied obligation of the contract of employment is that the employee has to come to work on time and failure to meet this obligation could also result in dismissal. These days, occasional over-sleeping is tolerated, but if you're not there to work, you don't get paid. The employers' right to determine what to do with the capital employed is matched by a parallel right to declare redundancies – in many situations these rights are put to use as a sanction on employees: 'If wages go up, I'll have to close down the factory.' And if the employer does not agree to allow the shop stewards to return to their nefarious activities, sanctions – in the form of a work-to-rule, a ban on overtime or a strike – may be imposed by the work group.

Like bargaining, the use or potential use of social sanctions is also a pervasive feature of social life. Pre-school children may have their sweets taken away if they do not behave; at school the stick rather than the carrot ensures discipline; in some religions a visit to hell operates as a quite singular sanction on sinful behaviour; and in politics MPs have to abide by the party line if they wish to advance their careers. In fact, it should be clear bargaining and sanctions go hand-in-hand – the one is not feasible without the other. In order to bargain you have to have something the other actor wants – it could be wages, jobs, work, cooperation or simply peace – and it is the withholding of the desired object which constitutes one possible sanction. If you have nothing to bargain with, the other side can simply impose whatever terms they choose.

The process of collective bargaining frequently produces the use or threat of sanctions. In the attempt to persuade the other side to develop more 'realistic' aspirations, both parties may engage in bluff and counter-bluff. 'If there is not a substantial improvement in the offer I'll be powerless to prevent a strike' is countered by 'Any more than 2% on the gross wage bill and we'll be forced to close the plant.' On sober reflection – which can take much time in collective bargaining – each side plays the waiting game while making careful calculations about the capacity and willingness of the other to carry out their threat; and the use of threats requires fine judgement, for an idle boast may be interpreted as a sign of weakness, or worse, desperation and produce the opposite of its intended effect by strengthening the resolve of the other party. Thus, to be effective, sanctions must not only produce negative consequences but also be enforceable.

Nearly all of the sanctions available to employees and their organisations depend upon circumstances. Among these the most dramatic is the temporary withdrawal of labour: the strike. As we have seen, these are by no means as effective as the headlines suggest and not easy to enforce. Other sanctions, such as a proposed overtime ban when an employee has, seemingly, been unfairly dismissed, also depend upon circumstances. In the month before Christmas, for example, there are likely to be difficulties in making the ban effective because many employees will be concerned to earn as much as possible to finance the festivities. So, unless the employee is held in very high esteem by the work group it would be wise to forgo any action that might precipitate an instant dismissal until January. In contrast, some of the sanctions available to employers – and especially those relating to work discipline, such as faithfully carrying out the employer's instructions or arriving at work on time – have a basis in law and are enforced as a matter of routine.

One of the most significant characteristics of sanctions – which reveals much about the public reaction to events in industrial relations – is the way some are regarded as being legitimate or justified, whereas others are deemed to be unjustified and thus non-legitimate. For example, management are generally thought to have the *authority* or the right to direct supervisors, dock the wages of latecomers or make employees redundant. In contrast, even where management have clearly over-reacted, we tend to think of workers using *power* to force the employer to reinstate a shop steward.

Despite the justification for the threatened action – it was the only means through which the work group could protect their representative – its legitimacy is suspect, for all we see is one actor coercing another. And that, somehow, is not cricket.

This conventional distinction between managerial authority and worker power is no mere linguistic convention. It reflects the dominant values of our society in which there is a widespread taken-for-granted assumption that, in general, the rights of management and employers enjoy a more deeply-rooted legitimacy than those of employees. Further, it also reflects the fact, despite 200 years of existence and a long struggle to achieve *legal* legitimacy, that trade unions have yet to secure a permanent measure of *social* legitimacy for their activities. The analytical problems this creates can be considerable – especially for the newcomer to industrial relations – for it is sometimes extremely difficult to prevent such taken-for-granted assumptions (our initial frame of reference) from having an unwarranted influence on how we interpret events.

Paradoxically, in operation, power and authority can have virtually the same effect. In the examples above, no matter how we choose to dress it up, the employees may have no option but to accept redundancy just as, in some situations, management may feel they have little choice but to reinstate the steward. The effect is only virtually the same because, in these particular examples, there remain important differences. The employer has a legal right to declare redundancies while the shop steward – even if an Industrial Tribunal declared he had been unfairly dismissed – would not necessarily be re-employed. His entitlement is to compensation, not to get his job back. This latter 'right' can only be secured if the employees mobilize their collective voice on his behalf and successfully compel the employer to change the decision. Nonetheless, in both cases one actor is imposing – or attempting to impose– an unacceptable choice on the other. Analytically, the fact a sanction is legal does not make it any less coercive to those on the receiving end.

Management, in performing their functions, have to respond to the interests of shareholders or the employer, and have to react to such contextual factors as may impinge upon the organisation. This may result in employees being moved from one job to another, having their social life disrupted by working shifts or being made redundant. Such decisions are not necessarily arbitrary or without justification, but, in many cases, are implemented against the wishes of the employee and, where they exist, trade unions often oppose them. That the employer is legally empowered to enforce such decisions does not mean they are experienced as legitimate. It is for this reason that, in practice, there is no clear-cut distinction between power and authority and, conceptually, authority is often defined as *legitimate power*.

In any attempt to analyse industrial relations in a disinterested fashion it is therefore vitally important to be aware of the initial inbuilt disadvantages of employees. They have no 'right to a job' and almost any sanction threatened by their trade unions tends to be greeted with public disdain and regarded as non-legitimate. In contrast, employers', drawing on law and the long-established goodwill of property rights, enjoy an almost unquestioned right to exercise their legitimate power. This may seem a partisan view and anything but a disinterested conclusion. However, two points can be made in its defence. Firstly, even if there was much greater social support for employee rights and sanctions or the power advantage of employers were greatly reduced, this would not necessarily reduce the incidence or ferocity of industrial conflicts. No matter what the balance of advantages, the potential for such conflict is a permanent feature of the employment relationship. Secondly, it is *not* being suggested we ought to change the existing power balance in society. The objective of the analytical framework is to provide a more disciplined basis for *understanding* industrial relations behaviour and, in this respect, the conclusion reflects 'the way we are', no more and no less.

POWER AND POWER RELATIONS

All the various employees, managers and employers encountered so far are individuals who, in various ways, are both

214

acting and being acted upon in their employment relationships. Although often displaying different frames of reference, they are all seeking to persuade, cajole and control the other actors around them in such a way as to optimise their own particular interests. In order to improve their chances they may join interest group organisations, such as trade unions, or contribute to particular political parties which promise to change the law in their favour. They may become engaged in collective bargaining and, on occasion, feel impelled to impose sanctions on the other. The underlying common thread which knits all these forms of behaviour together is the acquisition, mobilisation and use of power. The actors, their organisations and the structures they inhabit can be seen as a series of interlocking power relationships. Power relations can be mediated in a variety of ways, the most important of which in industrial relations are unilateral, joint and statutory regulation. It is through the use of an analytical framework such as this that all the elements, levels and complex array of contextual variables discussed in previous chapters can be related to each other in a reasonably coherent fashion and one which, used insightfully, should take us beyond the surface ripples which dominate the headlines of industrial relations.

In everyday usage the term power conjures up ugly connotations of force and restraint – images which those who exercise power naturally seek to avoid. Thus, in social democracies, with our institutions of free speech, free association and universal suffrage, there is a tendency to equate power with coercion and non-legitimacy and, as such, its use is treated as a temporary aberration rather than a *normal* phenomenon. In order to justify the daily use of power and explain away its effects we have invented a stream of euphemisms to distance our actions from any unsavory judgement. Pride of place goes to 'upholding the rule of law' – a notion used to describe the seemingly unchallengeable right of governments to exercise power which, by definition, is legitimate. Of more obvious relevance to industrial relations is the way major changes in the employment relationship are sometimes explained. When a company is taken over by another company this sometimes results in large numbers of redundancies – a process often described as 'rationalising the resources' or 'streamlining the organisation to improve efficiency'. Even better is the practice of explaining away such an exercise of power as the 'inevitable consequences of economic necessity', a phrase which attributes responsibility to a set of unknown, other-worldly mystical forces, completely outside the control of those involved. Significantly, when new jobs are created, those same anonymous forces rapidly take on human form; and much credit is claimed by bold politicians increasing public expenditure or by a Board of Directors – perhaps with a government grant in their back pocket – placing their investment and faith in a reliable British workforce. Their benevolent re-emergence is a timely reminder that behind every event in industrial relations lies a process of human decision-making in the context of a complex set of power relations.

Although we are publicly reluctant to recognise the use of power and prefer to believe it is only employed as a last resort it is, like bargaining, a pervasive feature of social life and, indeed, can be observed in *all* social relationships. This does not mean everything is reducible to the simplistic question 'who's got the most power?' or that the use of power is necessarily coercive in character – as was indicated above, one *form* of power, authority, is legitimate. The easist way to avoid analytical confusion is to see the distribution of power – as reflected in the hierarchial character of society – as both the scaffolding which holds social relations together and the motive force of social change – for those who have power can use it to shape the social world around them. Viewed in this light, power is neither good, bad, nor indifferent: it is simply a functional prerequisite for society to exist in the first place. Social relations are thus naturally power relations. As such, they may be more or less equal, more or less coercive. In practice, power may be used well or badly, to the betterment of individual, collective or even public interest and – as the participants to political debate consistently demonstrate – there is endless argument about how the use of power should be controlled and about the purposes for which it should be employed.

There are four fundamental and related assumptions which, taken together, help us to avoid most of the common misconceptions and ideological quagmires which have characterised the discussion of power.

1. Power is forever

The first of these assumptions has already been touched on: the idea that power is neither good, bad nor indifferent. This means power is seen as a 'technical' feature of all social relationships. In some accounts of power it is portrayed simply as a kind of malevolent force in the hands of a few who use it to oppress and suppress the rest of us; and, come the revolution or whatever, we will be able to get rid of power by creating new democratic forms of social organisation. This is not the view taken here: power is something which is always with us no matter how we arrange or re-arrange society. Indeed, in order to achieve a successful re-arrangement a great deal of power needs to be mobilised – and, once mobilised, power is not in the habit of draining away like water through sand. Power, like love, is forever.

2. Power only exists in social relationships

Despite the existence of decision-makers who exercise power, power is not something which can be 'possessed' by individuals in their own right. Individuals may own or control considerable power resources but power itself only comes when those resources are put to use in the context of a relationship with others. For example, a person with a million pounds to invest is, *potentially*, a very influential social actor: put to use such funds could be used to exercise considerable control over the lives of others. Used to manufacture chemicals it could create many jobs for, amongst others, laggers. Take it out of chemicals and buy property to rent and all those jobs could disappear. However, if this person and the million pounds are on a desert island with no hope of escape, the power resource – the million pounds – is worthless except for lighting fires. But if, before the first match is struck, our forlorn person is teleported to the Stock Exchange, she is instantly transformed into a potentially very influential social actor. In short, outside the context of a social or, in our case, socio-economic relationship, power resources are useless. Power is not a property of individuals but of social relationships.

This conclusion has profound implications for the way we conventionally think about those who exercise power. For example, one of the more contentious issues is the question of trade union power. We are frequently told that 'trade unions are too powerful' – a belief much supported by opinion polls. But what does it mean? As it stands, the statement is little different from saying 'marooned millionaires are too power-ful'. Since it tells us nothing about the resources of trade unions, nor does it specify in which relationships they are deemed to exercise 'too much power', it is not a very informative statement. We can only make sense of it by translating it into what it really means: trade unions have *more* power than we think they *ought* to in relation to the other actors. It expresses a vague generalised preference for a different distribution of power between the actors; and, since trade unions are considered in isolation from the other actors, the statement has as much bearing on the reality of the situation as the claim of a football fan who says, 'Chelsea are the best team in the league', irrespective of Chelsea's position in that league. To believe something does not make it true.

3. *The nature of power relations*

Power relations always involve mutual dependence and mutual antagonism. In the context of the employment relationship, employers are dependent on employees to perform work tasks to make a profit or, as with public employees, to provide a service. In parallel, employees are dependent on employers to pay wages or salaries so they can live the good life. In simple terms, they come together because each wants something the other possesses: in this respect they are mutually dependent. Work or labour is exchanged for money or goods.

However – and this is of fundamental importance – mutual dependence should never be confused with *equal* dependence. Employer and employee may need each other, but their respective needs may not be of equal magnitude. Much of this differential dependence can be explained in terms of the initial resources which the two actors, employer and employee, bring to the relationship. For example, in a company town where there is only one major employer there may appear to be an equivalent degree of need between the two: the employer can go nowhere else for his labour and the employees can go nowhere else for work. This ought to make for harmonious and congenial interdependent relations. Often it does but, in practice, it is usually on terms which can be paternalistically dictated by the employer. The reasons for this lie in who has the right to take important decisions – like whether to increase or decrease investment, to expand output, or to employ more people – and differences in the flexibility and transformability of the respective resources controlled by the actors. The employer's capital can be put to many uses other than providing employment in a particular town: it can be realised and put into another town, put into property, or even transferred to another country where labour is cheaper. Labour, in contrast, is a much more cumbersome resource. It is inflexible, being capable of only a small range of tasks; gets sick and old, and is relatively immobile geographically for it resides in communities. Nor, for the most part, can labour take important decisions – it can only *react* to the decisions of employers. Such initial differences help to account for the almost universal imbalance of power between employer and employee and, despite their mutual needs, generally means employees are far more dependent on the employer than the employer is on them. There are exceptions but these are rare.

The fiction that mutual dependence should be taken to mean equal dependence, as we saw earlier, is something which finds reflection in the philosophical underpinnings of the contract of employment. Employer and employee are treated as equal partners. But this apparent flaw is not merely to make life easier for our finest legal minds; it also reflects and reinforces the dominant values of our society: the way we are.

Further support for this fiction can be found in the abstract minds of some abstract economists, who use the label 'labour market' to locate the place where the economic forces regulating the demand and supply of labour work themselves through: those who seek employment are deemed to freely enter a labour market where they compete with others of similar disposition for the available jobs. But the labour market is not composed solely of the hopeful unemployed; there are also various prospective employers in that market-place competing with each other for the services of those available for employment. Of these, some will have skills or qualifications which are in great demand and, where such jobs exceed the workers available to fill them, the price paid will be bidded up by the competing employers. In the reverse situation, where there are more job-seekers than jobs available, it is the prospective employees who compete and the price paid by the employer will be the lowest amount employees are prepared to accept. Thus the free forces of competition produce a balance between the supply of and the demand for labour.

This marvellously simple set of propositions can be used to produce elegant, compelling theories and pretty diagrams of demand and supply curves. It is, of course, only an abstract model of how prospective employers are matched up with aspiring employees: nevertheless, it remains at the root of most modern economic thought. Few modern economists would claim it accurately reflects how the process operates in practice and, in order to preserve its integrity, have added a whole series of qualifications – referred to as 'imperfections' – to accommodate the waywardness of the real world in the face of such a pleasing economic logic. Imperfections cover such problems as the initial inequality of power between the employer and employee, the fact that some employers enjoy a monopoly position in the labour market while others get together – sometimes openly, sometimes in secret – to fix the maximum price they will pay for particular kinds of labour. Other sources of imperfection include trade unions which attempt to interfere with 'pure' market forces and governments, whose influence, as we have seen, is so great they can cause gross distortion of 'pure' market forces. Indeed, as this last example suggests, the list of imperfections is now so long, and their impact so extensive, the only place where the model appears to work is on the pages of economics textbooks.

There are two reasons why this seemingly irrelevent and naive model of how employers and employees come to satisfy their mutual needs is of particular importance to the way we conventionally understand industrial relations. The first lies in the image of a world without power which is projected on to the employment relationship. Employers and employees freely allow themselves to be herded into a sort of economic melting pot, the labour market, where all compete against all: employers bid against each other for labour resources and employees bid against each other for jobs; and the outcomes are subject only to the arbitrary and autonomic operation of market forces – those hidden hands which, provided we do not interfere with their delicate functioning – massage the price of all commodities to their natural level. None can gain unfair advantage because everyone is subject to the same set of autonomic forces which, because of the open competition, cannot be controlled by any one employer or employee. The price paid for labour is determined not by any human decision-making but by 'the market'. There are, of course, inequalities of reward, but these reflect our value as an economic commodity, not any initial difference in power resources. Thus it is that 'the market' – which abhors any concentration of economic power – decides what we shall be paid.

This brings us to the second feature of the model which is significant for our purposes. Since it is the market and its mystical non-human forces which produce the hierarchy of employment rewards, there is a sense in which those differentials and inequalities are seen as the product of a

221

natural economic ordering: we get what we deserve. The model provides a rationale which says those who husband their economic resources wisely in the pursuit of self-interest will find their just rewards in the great plastic bag of life. Market forces smile benignly on those who make the most of their opportunities, but if you haven't got a job it's your own fault; if your profits disappear to a competitor's product it's your own fault. In this way – since what we have and what we are is a natural reflection of how well we have optimised our economic opportunities – the model provides a set of political arguments to justify the existing distribution of rewards, income and wealth. And woe betide anyone or any institution which seeks to disrupt the free flow of economic forces: we have a Monopolies Commission to ensure large companies do not unfairly dominate any particular market and there is very careful scrutiny and regulation of the activities of trade unions which, by organising the employees, function to prevent market forces from reducing wages.

Such measures are but symbolic gestures designed to preserve the myth of 'free' market forces. The model itself is pure fiction but can still be persuasively used to explain away the existing economic order. How is this possible? The vital clue lies in all those imperfections, for the model works not in spite of them but *because* of them. The model describes an idealised economic utopia; the imperfections describe the real world of people, those economic sinners who consistently refuse to have faith in the beneficence of pure market forces. 'Look here', says the abstract mind, 'we have devised a beautiful way of creating economic balance. Now, all you've got to do is behave in an economically rational self-interested fashion, everyone will get their just deserts, and I won't have to waste my time thinking up new imperfections to prove my model would work if only the world were perfect.' Curiously perhaps, everyone is sympathetic. Employers say, 'Yes, of course, we'd like to help, but our problem is trade unionism: they have monopoly control in the labour market and this stops us reducing wages to their true market value.' Even some unions – and especially those which represent the higher-paid occupational groups – will give qualified support for 'free' market forces. During periods of incomes policy, for example, they will point out that all sorts of 'anomalies' have been created, occupational groups are having their differentials reduced and the governmental ceiling on wage increases only serves to prevent their members from receiving fully deserved productivity payments. 'The sooner we get back to "free" collective bargaining – which is the best way to reflect market forces – the better.' Governments, of course, display different levels of ideological commitment to 'free' market forces. But, however vociferous they may be in public, they all, in private, have to say to our poor economist, 'Now see here, old chap, we understand your problems but try to see our position. We have social responsibilities as well: if we don't build roads, sewers, hospitals, schools and keep standing armed forces and police at the ready, who will? We can privatise bits of it, but we haven't had private armies since medieval times and society wouldn't stand for a private police force.'

All this is but lip-service to the dominant social values which inform our culture and, in the daily business of regulating the employment relationship, both sides operate in the labour market according to their intuitive understandings of how it really works. Labour markets are not power vacuums where 'free' market forces regulate price, but socio-economic arenas where each actor – in bargaining about the terms of the transation – will employ whatever power resources they can muster in order to increase the dependence of the other and thus achieve a more favourable price. Logically, it is in the self-interest of each employer to buy labour as cheaply as possible and, in parallel, it is in the self-interest of employees to sell their services at as high a price as they can.

This conflict of interests is not something which only exists during the process of establishing the terms and conditions of the exchange but, like the relationship itself, is a continuing and permanent feature. This is why it is referred to as an endemic structural characteristic. It is always there because it is in the *nature* of the employment relationship – and this feature accounts for the mutual antagonism alongside the mutual dependence. Ideologically, this antagonism is reflected in 'them–us' attitudes and, behaviourally, in various forms of industrial conflict; it is regulated and controlled by the various managers of discontent who employ various means, tactics and strategies in order to reduce the overt expression of such conflicts to a minimum.

Mutual antagonism, despite what it seems to imply, does not mean the employer and employee are in constant readiness for war or continually engaged in guerilla raids on each other's territory. Such a description may sometimes be appropriate, but is unlikely to be sustained. There are occasional phases of bitter conflict – usually centred on some fundamental issue or reflecting particularly aggressive tactics – but, for the most part, there exists a negotiated truce. Conflict resolution has become institutionalised with annual collective bargaining characterised by a great deal of loud talking. In Japan – currently heralded as the mecca of industrial harmony – there is a 'strike season' in spring when the major negotiations are in process: there are strikes, well-organised military-style demonstrations and ritual encounters with the forces of law and order. Then everyone, having made their point, goes happily back to work until next season.

In many other situations – such as at IBM – the mutual antagonism almost never becomes overt because management work extremely hard at staying on top of it. Such behaviour provides an indication of why there is no permanent state of open conflict: at any one point in time the likelihood of overt antagonism depends on the extent to which there is satisfaction with the terms of the mutual dependence. Management at IBM are constantly monitoring the situation to ensure the level of employee satisfaction never falls to the point where overt conflict is preferable to the benefits of the existing accommodation. The key analytical point in all this is that the employment relationship is not one of harmonious coexistence nor one of irreconcilable conflict: it is one in which mutual dependence coexists with mutual antagonism. The tension between these two creates constraints and limitations on the way in which *both* sides exercise their power.

4. *Conflict is normal*

Nonetheless, the analytical consequence of this permanent tension between the needs and demands of the actors is that periodic conflict is a predictable and normal feature of the employment relationship. The potential for disagreement over the existing terms of the exchange is always present because, in reality, the social world is never static. For example, once a particular business begins to make profits, the workers may feel the terms initially agreed are no longer a 'fair' rate of exchange – they have worked hard to expand the business and feel entitled to share in the profits. The employer and management may agree – in which case there is no problem – or they may not. Should this occur then the employees, if they wish to pursue the claim, must seek to change their view by putting pressure on them. They may, ultimately, go on strike and the employer – if he is George Ward of Grunwicks – may respond by sacking them all and employing new staff who are prepared to accept the existing terms. The sacked workers might respond by recognising the need for collective organisation and form a trade union – to which they must recruit the workers who replaced them. And so it goes on until we reach the complexities of 20th-century industrial relations. It did not, of course, actually happen like this – historical social reality is infinitely more colourful than any analytical conceptual framework – but it does reflect the developmental logic which generated trade unionism.

More concrete evidence of this tension and its accompanying conflict was revealed in the laggers' tale. In that example the soft-hearted Peter Warmly is employed to carry out the work of administering the employment of others such as Sam Hardhead, the lagger. One of his work tasks is to ensure the continued effectiveness of the system of financial rewards and this requires, from time to time, that he will talk to, bargain and negotiate with employees and their representatives when any disputes occur concerning how the system operates. In this process of managing discontent he is both assisted and hampered by the actions of his fellow managers of discontent, the two District Officers, Golightly and Ratchett. All three have to 'balance' a variety of competing and conflicting demands. Golightly, for example, signed the original agreement which allocated laggers a lower pay rate than the skilled engineering fitters and, at a later date in a separate context, signed another agreement defining thermal insulation engineers as equal to the fitters. In resolving one problem yet new – and more difficult – ones are sometimes created.

Union officials are constantly in the process of making, breaking and revising the terms and conditions under which their members will be employed. But other actors, such as Peter Warmly, depend upon the Golightlys and Ratchetts of this world to deliver 'peace in our time' with as little organisational disruption as possible. This is not always a simple task for their 'indirect' employer – the membership whose interests they are paid to represent – calls on them from time to time to improve the terms of the 'peace treaty'. And if the only circumstances in which the employer is prepared to agree to such revisions is when the employees, as a collectivity, threaten to or take offensive action, then intermittent overt struggles are inevitable. As emphasised earlier, this does not mean there is a permanent open war being fought between employers and employees – for manifestly this is not the case – but that personnel managers and union officials cannot avoid being both the creators of social order in the employment relationship – in that they sign agreements – and also the apparent cause of social disorder – in that they actively support the abandonment of such agreements. Analytically, they are not the 'cause' of consensus *or* conflict: their role is to reflect, interpret and convey the positions of the other social actors. They are the middlemen of conflict resolution.

In summary, these four assumptions about the nature of power and power relations –

(1) that power is neither good, bad nor indifferent but is found in all social relationships;
(2) that power is not 'possessed' by individuals but is a property of their relationships;
(3) that power relations necessarily involve both mutual

dependence and mutual antagonism; and
(4) that power relations are naturally prone to periodic conflict, if only in institutionalised forms –

are, as has been briefly demonstrated, essential for a disciplined and realistic analysis of the socio-economic world of work and employment relations. Their distinctive advantage in coming to the study of industrial relations for the first time is that they cannot be seen as being either pro-management/ employer interests or pro-union/employee interests: they refer only to features which appear to characterise *all* socio-economic exchange relationships irrespective of the political or economic system. They would be equally valid and useful for analysing industrial relations in London, Los Angeles or Leningrad.

THE SOURCES OF POWER

There is one further element of the analytical framework which requires elaboration. Having identified the major figures who occupy positions from which they can exercise power; having detailed the most common methods they use to regulate their interactions; and having outlined four key assumptions which can be made about power and the nature of power relations; it is also necessary to summarise what is meant by power resources and how these fit into the analysis of an industrial relations situation.

Power and dependence are intimately related, for having power resources permits a greater degree of freedom in choosing between alternative courses of action. In any given relationship the distribution of resources is critical to the distribution of dependence. More directly, some people are less on the receiving end because they enjoy access to greater power resources than others. Mohammed has virtually no resources except the £1.50 a week his father pays him and, even if he chose to invest all of this in Krugerrands, it would be a while before he became independent of his employer. Alternatively, he might be able to produce a dramatic increase in his resources by putting the £1.50 on the Football Pools and – having won a few first dividends – he could invest the spoils, retire early and spend the rest of his life doing anything within the compass of his monthly investment income. Such power resources permit an enormous degree of freedom. Money may not bring happiness, but it buys the social space for us to try.

Not all power resources are as flexible or as transformable as hard cash. Rachel, despite her educational resources, has been unable to find an employer who wishes to purchase her skills and, for the moment, has little choice but to remain under the greasy thumb of her menopausal manager. So long as she remains unable to find an alternative source of income she must to continue to endure the questionable benefits of her present post or face unemployment.

As both these examples demonstrate, the value and effectiveness of power resources depends entirely upon specific circumstances and any attempt to make generalised statements about power and power resources has to be approached with caution. Just as there are considerable differences in the power resources available to trade unions so too with their officials. For example, an official of the TGWU (Transport and General Workers' Union) employed to represent and negotiate on behalf of TGWU members employed in the hotel and catering industry on the south coast is likely to feel, like an ambassador to Haiti, he has been sent to penal servitude. The typical labour force in hotel and catering is low-paid, very poorly organised (i.e. only a relatively low percentage are members of a trade union), and characterised by high staff turnover (i.e. people do not stay long in any one job). In addition, the demand for labour is seasonal so that permanent employment is the preserve of a select few. In such circumstances the union official can do very little to pressure an employer to change or improve the terms and conditions of employment. Since the employees will not act together against the employers there are no 'persuasive' sanctions available to the official.

However, should the same official be moved to the Midlands and given responsibility for the TGWU members in the car-delivery industry it would be akin to our ambassador being transferred to Washington. The car-delivery business is responsible for transporting newly manufactured vehicles to car showrooms. It is the critical step in the process of making profit in car manufacturing. If no cars are delivered for sale it not only means the manufacturer cannot recoup his costs (and collect the profit) but it can also mean the production process will have to be halted once the available transit parking space for newly manufactured vehicles is used up. (The price of land around car-plants enjoys a very high value and companies try to minimise such parking costs.) Hence any disruption in the car-delivery process is likely to be an expensive affair and some manufacturers have been prepared to concede considerable rewards to car-delivery firms rather than face an interruption to their business. In consequence, from time to time, the employees – such as the drivers of car transporters – have exercised powerful leverage in their dealing with employers, and any trade union official who represents them can, within limits, enjoy great influence. Not only is it possible, relatively speaking, to negotiate very good working conditions and high wages, but, if the official secures control over the number of people to be employed in individual firms, it is also possible to determine which of the individual TGWU members will get such highly paid and highly prized jobs. For a trade union official to enjoy such power is rare but not unknown.

The power resources which employees in the car-delivery industry draw on come not from their financial resources, nor from their skills or value in the labour market – for anyone who can drive could do their work. They can exercise considerable influence because they are well organised and because the delivery cost is, in many cases, paid by the purchaser of the car; their employers and the manufacturers are therefore not too concerned about their price. However, it is very important to remember there are significant limits to such power. Car-delivery firms exist in the context of several power relationships and should the customers complain too much about delivery charges or, worse, start to buy another brand of car, the manufacturers could take drastic action. They could buy-out the car-delivery firms and control the delivery system themselves or reorganise the whole process and use rail instead. It is uncommon for employees to enjoy such industrial leverage, but the example does illustrate the significance of workers who occupy a *strategic position* in the overall production process.

But having potential muscle does not necessarily mean it will be used because, to enjoy the benefits of power, the employees or the employer have got to be willing to take the necessary action. Some employee organisations – such as the nurses' Royal College of Nursing, the RCN, and the Association of Professional Teachers, the APT, which is composed of a minority of school-teachers, have publicly declared they will not take strike action. In so doing they not only bring a quiet smile to the face of their employers but also express their rejection of certain power resources. This, in turn, reflects their social values concerning how they think nurses and teachers ought to behave.

Other types of employee are able to rely almost exclusively upon specialised skills or talents which give them a high market value. Computer programmers, financial analysts, creative advertising people, and others may not see themselves as being in need of a trade union. Indeed, it may be regarded as a disadvantage, for success in such jobs depends upon being better than others engaged in similar jobs: the task itself depends upon competitive individualism rather than collective cooperation. This is particularly evident in professional sport where the individual's capacity or skill in direct competition with others is the major criterion of 'successful employment'. In such instances, despite a relatively short working life, the possession of particular skills can ensure very high financial rewards for a small number of individuals. Similarly, in the industrial relations of the entertainment industry small numbers of individual actors, singers and other specialised performers can command very high fees. Meanwhile, the vast majority of 'the profession' scratch out a meagre living and regard periodic unemployment as an occupational hazard. There are so many aspiring talents whose sense of realism has been blinded by the beckoning bright lights that Equity (the actors' union) and the Musicians' Union try to enforce a strict pre-entry closed shop[1] in order to minimise unemployment in their industry. It is one of the closed shops which budding employees are sometimes desperate to join. In effect, the closed shop – as a power resource – operates as a disincentive to all but the most determined of would-be stars and prevents employers from paying even lower wages.

A TYPOLOGY OF RESOURCES

Even with these few brief examples, it should be clear the power resources available to particular categories of employees vary enormously, and, in any specific situation, the total configuration of power resources available is likely to be composed of various elements reflecting the actors' access to and control over political, economic and social power. In the process of identifying the resources available to laggers or car-delivery drivers, it is vital to bear in mind such resources are extremely difficult to measure in any absolute sense. This is partly because they vary over time and partly because the *effectiveness* of any resources can only be assessed in relation to the resources held by the other actors.

Political Power Resources

Access to and control over political power may be regarded as the most desirable type of resource for it ensures influence over policy decisions which can radically transform the total context in favour of one or other set of interests. Not only this, but the capacity to utilize such resources – if it flows from a governmental decision – enjoys an almost unquestioned legitimacy.

The actor with the greatest access to and control over such resources is, of course, government itself. As described earlier, in performing the related roles of legislator, national economic manager and largest employer, governments invariably occupy centre stage and can, directly or indirectly, pull all the important strings which adjust the level of employment and determine the general character of industrial relations. Changes in the law, the level of public expenditure or budgetary adjustments can have a dramatic impact on the power resources of private employers and employees alike.

All governmental decisions are made in the context of a particular ideological frame of reference. When steering the ship of state they choose what they see as the most appropriate routes to political stability, economic well-being and social justice. Governments often encourage us to think that whatever 'practical' course of action they take has been 'forced' upon them – either by the gross navigational errors of the previous administration which took us down the wrong road or, as we saw above, by the mystical imperatives of 'economic necessity'. Alternatively they can opt for an appeal to the supreme all-purpose banality, the 'national interest'. It is all-purpose because it can be employed to justify anything and because, by definition, no matter what governments do it is in the national interest. It is banal because changes of government are invariably accompanied by a complete redefinition of what is in the national interest. Its supremacy lies in the fact that it explains nothing but justifies everything. Although it is not unknown, this is not to suggest governments tell lies: they merely provide us with the truth *as they see it*.

While it is clear governments, under the guise of 'redressing the balance' can exercise power in favour of employer or employee interests this, quite emphatically, does not mean they are being 'even-handed' or 'disinterested'; for they have their own interests which may or may not coincide with those of employers and employees. For example, under the administration of Mrs Thatcher we have seen both record levels of unemployment and record numbers of bankruptcies. In terms of her definition of what the 'national interest' demands, both the interests of labour and capital have had to take the same medicine and suffer accordingly. A judgement on which set of interests has endured most is, of course, a matter of political prejudice.

One of the more obvious redefinitions of how best to pursue the national interest coincided with the election of Mrs Thatcher in 1979. Under the outgoing Labour administration the Social Contract had been drawn up in collaboration with the TUC. In return for income restraint the government agreed to pursue a particular set of social and economic policies ostensibly designed to operate in favour of trade union and employee objectives. With the return of the Conservative government in 1979 this route to social and economic well-being was replaced by a radically different set of policies which, among other things, involved eliminating all the political power resources which the TUC had formerly had access to. And since then all attempts by the TUC to reopen a dialogue with government – which has long been a central feature of policy no matter which government is in power – have been rejected.

A good example of how successive governments, in exercising their power to implement policy decisions may – despite their undoubted good intentions – be regarded as the prime cause of some industrial disputes comes from the seemingly uncontentious issue of which energy policy is in the national interest. The deeply divisive miners' strike of 1984–85 was a product of how this policy has been developed. Britain, in having both oil and extensive coal reserves, is happily placed in being able to choose between the use of oil, coal and nuclear power. However, government decisions on the balance between the three have a crucial impact on the level of employment in the mining industry, since coal production is far more labour-intensive than oil or nuclear energy.

In 1955 there were some 700,000 miners and coal provided 90% of our energy needs. By 1984 the number of miners had dropped to about 170,000 and coal accounted for only 36% of total energy consumption. This process of change, as one observer put it, was 'an act neither of God nor of the market. Coal's demise has been executed from Whitehall and Westminster'.[2] Throughout the late 1950s and 1960s the run-down of coal was pursued against a background of relatively low world oil prices and a growing optimism about nuclear power. Some of the most dramatic reductions in the mine labour force were made by the Labour government of 1966–70. Then coal was catapulted back to central significance by the oil sheiks' four-fold increase in world oil prices during the early 1970s – a period which also saw two major national strikes by miners in 1972 and 1974, the second of which was accompanied by the fall of a Conservative government. This revival of the miners' power resources came from the renewed economic significance of coal and, once again contrary to media opinion, illustrates it is the vested interests of the Sheik Yamanis of this world rather than the purple rhetoric of trade union leaders which carries real significance for the outcomes of collective bargaining.

A temporary halt in the process of decline was achieved in 1974 with the jointly agreed Plan for Coal, a policy intended to increase investment, modernise and develop new pits. But the election of a new government in 1979 saw a significant shift in emphasis, for it was announced that ten nuclear power stations were to be built. This decision, combined with a failure to meet the output objectives of the 1974 Plan for Coal, convinced the leaders of the NUM their industry was facing an ever-declining future unless they took industrial action to prevent it. Strategically, in terms of the balance of power resources, a governmental decision to increase our reliance upon nuclear rather than coal-fired power stations has the effect of reducing dependence on coal and therefore makes it easier for the government – and subsequent governments – to resist the demands of coal miners. Indeed, there were some strong indications this was the specific intent of the government in 1984. The central point, however, once we dig through the surface allegations of political chicanery and get beyond the collective belligerance of the key actors, is that the real cause of the dispute lies in changes in energy policy. And these, while guided by the views of the NUM and the NCB, remain the responsibility of governments.

In meeting such responsibilities and in exercising their legitimate power, governments override the sectional interests of others and, on occasion, this also involves brushing aside legal rights. The best recent case of this was in 1983 when the government decided to prohibit trade unions from organising at GCHQ, the top-secret government communications centre. Employees who were already members were instructed to give up their membership and were offered a cash inducement to do so. The cash incentive was extremely important for, by accepting it, employees were effectively waiving their right under law to join a trade union. The case went through the courts and although one court declared the government action to be illegal because they failed to consult the unions and ignored the rules of natural justice, a higher court overturned this ruling by arguing that in matters of national interest – in this case, national security – the government was entitled to act as it saw fit. Leaving to one side the question of whether or not the potential threat of trade union action does constitute a serious threat to national security – which was the government's case – what the example illustrates is that there are circumstances in which the exercise of government powers seems to be limited only by what the government decides to do.

It should not be concluded it is only Conservative governments which use their political power against trade unions or employees. Labour governments, despite the fact some 80% of the finances of the Labour Party come from trade unions and, at any one time, 50% or more of Labour MPs are sponsored by individual trade unions, have an almost equally distinguished track record. In 1966, for example, the then Labour Prime Minister, Harold Wilson, not only declared the national strike of merchant seamen to be against the national interest but also alleged it was the product of a communist conspiracy. A few years later, in 1969, that same government put forward proposals for the reform of industrial relations which, had they become law, would have imposed severe legal sanctions on unofficial strikes.

Apart from direct government action, one of the more obvious sources of political influence stems from the relationships between individual MPs and extra-parliamentary interest groups. In order to prevent MPs from quietly promoting any particular cause in which they have a vested interest, they are required to declare all such external associations and interests. One recent study of this register[3] found that half of the back-bench Conservative MPs were company directors and one-third retained as 'consultants' to companies. Only a small number of the directorships are held in major companies – the vast majority being in small or family businesses – while 29 of the top 300 industrial companies have appointed MPs as consultants. Of Labour MPs only 14% hold directorships and 5% are retained as consultants, while 58% are sponsored by trade unions. (Trade union sponsorship means the union provides funds to the local constituency organisation; the MPs themselves receive no payment.)

Such figures reflect the natural interest constituencies of the two major parties and come as no real surprise. Just as the finances of the Labour Party come overwhelmingly from the unions so those of the Conservative Party come overwhelmingly from private enterprise concerns. Labour Research, a small trade union-funded organisation, publishes an annual survey of such contributions. In the most recent,[4] based on an examination of 3,000 sets of company accounts, they found companies had donated a total of over £2.7 million directly to the Conservative Party in 1983. This was an 80% increase over the previous year and the total sum will likely drop back again in 1984; 1983 was an election year. In 1983 a further £656,000 was donated by private companies to other organisations, many of them clearly identified with the Conservative cause.

These patterns of political association and influence reflect no more than the well-known political orientations of the two major parties and such information, while not always easily accessible, is public. However, in recent years there has been growing concern at the increasing presence of professional lobbyists and public relations people in and around the Houses of Parliament. In one report which examined the progress of proposed legislation to regulate the introduction of cable TV,[5] it was pointed out that during the committee stage at least half of the back-bench Conservative MPs who took part in the proceedings declared some direct or indirect financial interest: they were either directors of, or paid consultants to, companies which were or might become involved in cable TV. Their deliberations were assisted by lobbyists, with armfuls of briefing material, located outside the committee room. Another recent study has identified 20 MPs who are directors of, or declared advisors to, public relations firms and noted that 'almost all of these firms were created after the MP entered Parliament'.[6] Although such affiliations are public, if not widely publicised, there seems to be an increasingly ambiguous dividing line between private and public interests. Although, by its very nature, the impact of such activities is difficult to assess accurately, it would be naive to conclude it has no important effects, for why else would private companies employ lobbyists and public relations concerns and pay retainers to MPs?

Economic power resources

Economic power resources derive primarily from the possession or control of the classical 'factors of production': land, labour and capital. Ownership of land produces rent which can, if desired, be put to other purposes. Labour commands a market value in relation to both its skill or talent and also to the demand for different kinds of labour. Ownership of capital is accompanied by control over how that resource will be invested. In the analysis of industrial relations, the economic resources of labour and capital are usually seen as the most important of the three.

The economic power of a prospective employee, as noted above, is unlikely to be particularly significant in relation to prospective employers. Quite apart from the initial power disadvantage, individuals – unless they possess the market power of top entertainers or have other highly specialised skills – are in competition with others with similar economic resources for sale. Historically, the most obvious and important way individual employees have tried to increase their economic power resources has been to form trade unions. In doing so their fundamental objective was to reduce, if not eliminate, competition between individuals in the labour market while, at the same time, creating an organisation which could represent the collective economic resources of members to employers. As we saw in chapter 3, the tactics used in the deployment of this economic power resource have varied through time and on circumstances. Craft unions, for example, sought to control the supply of labour through limiting the number of apprenticeships, thus restricting the overall numbers who become available in that skill market. Professional associations – in 'qualifying' prospective members – perform a similar function. Unions of unskilled workers have pursued a different tactic: their objective is, if possible, to organise all potential employees in the much less discriminating market for the unskilled. Analytically, the function of unionism is to reduce the dependence of the employees and, thereby, increase their bargaining power.

Ideally, what trade union leaders dream of – if they dream at all – is a situation where the trade union, in effect, enjoys ownership rights over the available jobs. Hence, when there is a vacancy the employer comes to the union and asks it to find a suitable employee. In this way the union would enjoy the power to 'invest the labour' of the membership. This is comparable to the power of owners of capital to invest their resources but by no means equivalent, for capital remains a far more flexible and transformable resource than labour. In practice, however, this dream of what are usually called 'job property rights' has only rarely come true. Dock workers, after a century of being subject to all the evils attendant on casual employment, secured what is known as the 'Dock Labour Scheme'. Under the casual regime they only got paid when they were picked for the available work; and work was only available when ships docked to be unloaded. With the new scheme dockers became 'registered' – that is, 'licensed' to be employed as dockers – and allocated to a particular employer. Now, even when there is no work, they are paid a guaranteed minimum wage by the Dock Labour Board which is financed collectively by the employers. This scheme has provided an orderly means of running down the labour force at a time when due to, amongst other things, the containerisation of cargo, there has been a continued reduction in the demand for dock labour. The dockers' job property right lapses on retirement or if it has been bought out with a redundancy payment.

As a *negotiated* economic resource the Dock Labour Scheme – which does not cover all dockers – has functioned primarily as a means of securing continuous income during a period of falling demand for labour. The only other industry which has seen the establishment of important job property rights is the newspaper industry. Fleet Street print workers have been able to negotiate agreements that the wages of employees made redundant continue to be paid into a pool which is then shared between the remaining employees. As a tactic, it is a variation on the job property rights scheme – technically, the job remains even though no employee is actually in post. In this context it is important to remember that amongst manual employees – for all things are relative – print workers are among the most well-organised and cohesive occupational groups. This, combined with an historical lack of cohesion among the employers, has permitted them to extract relatively high returns from assiduous use of their economic resources.

Print workers are important for another reason. They are one of the very few manual occupational groups who have been able to employ their economic resources in a creative fashion, for in most instances trade union power is mobilized in defence of employee interests rather than to advance such interests. For example, most forms of industrial action involve employees losing something – wages in a strike, overtime earnings with an overtime ban, and bonus earnings with a go-slow or a work-to-rule. Similarly, the bitterest and longest disputes tend to be about defensive issues such as wage cuts, redundancies or job losses rather than wage increases.

In contrast, the economic resource of capital is immensely creative: those who control its use can construct or manufacture everything that is built and made. All wages and salaries are paid out of the profit or surplus generated by the deployment of capital resources. Since more jobs are invariably welcomed and opposition to new ventures or products is highly selective, those in control of investment finance have few restrictions placed upon their freedom of action. Hence they have considerable, if largely unnoticed, power and influence at all levels of economic activity. Their significance cannot be underestimated no matter how small their number. One unusually well-publicised group, the oil sheiks, play a very important role in the 'money markets' around the world, for decisions on where to bank the almost countless oil dollars have tended to push up interest rates – thus making entrepreneurial borrowing to finance employment that bit more difficult.

In the British economy the most far-reaching investment decisions are made by government ministers and the financial managers of insurance companies and pension funds (see chapter 4). Next in line among the most influential controllers of capital allocation are the multi-national companies, many with operations around the world. Such is their power, they can often play off governments against each other in order to get the best deal. Their own resources are frequently bolstered by government investment grants – as occurred in 1979 when the then Labour Government provided assistance to the Ford Motor Company to build a new plant in South Wales. With their international division of labour – Ford builds engines in Brazil, gearboxes in France, car bodies in Britain and has diversified production units in Belgium, Germany and Mexico – such companies have the capacity to actively disinvest in one country and expand in another, depending on circumstances. Such changes in policy – though not quickly implemented – may reflect labour market prices, the exchange rate of currencies or even the quality of productivity and industrial relations.

The threat of disinvestment – and Ford now have identical production units in Britain and West Germany – can be highly effective in bargaining with unions and Ford, on occasion, have resorted to such action. The more important point is that such a decision may have little to do with the character of industrial relations or productivity as such. In early 1984, for example, Ford announced the closure of their plant in Ireland and, almost simultaneously, that they were going to build a new plant in Mexico where labour is cheap, uncontaminated by a tradition of long-standing custom and practice and amenable to modern management. Ford truly operates in the world market while the labour it employs is trapped in the historical contexts of their own societies.

Decisions to build new car plants in South Wales or Northumberland – which may be taken in Detroit or Tokyo – are completely beyond the influence of aspiring employees. Similarly, a governmental decision to reduce the labour force in the steel industry by 30% in order to reduce economic losses remains – despite the lobbying of MPs or mass demonstrations – almost completely beyond the control of employees and their representatives. It is only recently that the significance of what might be called the 'geographical mobility' of employment has become clearly evident. The decision on that car plant may be contingent on the character and quality of locally available labour and the level of wages that will have to be paid; and it may be economically advantageous for the company to build the new plant in Spain rather than Britain. This international dimension of competition between labour markets is one of the key factors in the decline of British manufacturing. With the progressive deskilling of much work, economic logic will often dictate that investment be made in relatively cheap labour markets, such as India, Hong Kong or Taiwan.

In general, at the levels of economic investment which really matter, the flexibility of capital is invariably superior to the belligerence of labour. At the very least, withdrawn capital earns interest at the bank; withdrawn labour cannot even claim social security.[7]

Nor can employees draw much comfort from the economic resources available to unions. In contrast to those at the disposal of governments, financial institutions and companies, the economic assets of trade unions are pitiful by comparison. The total assets of TUC-affiliated trade unions in 1984 has been reckoned at £388 million and their recorded income in 1982 was £276.6 million, of which 90.5% came from membership dues. During the course of the year 78% of the income was spent on running the unions and a further 9.6% on benefits to members.[8]

It is not easy to put such figures into perspective. However, some rough comparisons can be made. Lonrho, the British multi-national company briefly discussed in chapter 4, has assets of £2 billion; while one of our most renowned family businesses, the J. S. Sainsbury supermarket chain, has assets of £760 million; and even the income of Britain's private schools, at £660 million, is well over twice the income of trade unions. On a somewhat grander scale the government, since 1979, has raised £7,440 million through privatisation, over half of this coming from the sale of British Telecom. (The cost of the BT share flotation in respect of advertising, administration and commissions paid to merchant banks and brokers has been estimated at over £75 million or 27% of trade union income in 1982.)[9]

Such comparisons may be regarded as inappropriate or even invidious. However, spread throughout the membership, trade union assets and income do not inspire any confidence in the unions' capacity to mobilise financial resources. If the value of the total economic assets were attributed equally, each union member owns a stake of £3.85, and unions spend 52p per week on each union member out of their income. This is hardly a secure basis on which to mobilise action against employer interests.

Social power resources

The employment relation has been portrayed as one of socio-economic exchange. It is not simply an exchange of labour for economic rewards, nor is it solely regulated by economic values but is also conditioned by social status, social values and social organisations: these play a critical role in cementing the relationship and facilitating or preventing change. Such factors may be regarded, analytically, as distinctive sources of social power. Generally, the term 'social power' is used to refer to all forms of power regardless of its source or base – thus 'social power' often incorporates those forms of influence deriving from access to and control over political and economic resources. In the present context, however, it has a more precise meaning in order to highlight those resources which are more specifically the product of social interaction.

Within the hierarchy of the occupational structure, professional employees, such as doctors, lawyers, accountants and dentists, can draw on their high social status to legitimise the large earnings they have become accustomed to command. This is particularly true of the medical and legal trades which, historically, have managed to persuade society – and we have been sufficiently impressed by their magical potions to go along with it – that their specialised skills are so valuable we ought to pay them accordingly. Their lofty position in the league table of earnings is accompanied by a similarly elevated position in the hierarchy of social status and prestige and this, in turn, is a reflection of the hierarchy of social power. But no more than a reflection for, clearly, not everyone gets what they might seem to deserve. Our wonderful nurses in all their various roles, for example, have never been granted a salary to match their social standing. In contrast, teachers are members of an occupational group which has lost much of the high esteem it enjoyed some 30 years ago. These examples illustrate the fragile character of such status for it depends upon public *perceptions* of value. Unless the higher-status groups also create a social organisation to propagate and defend that high status – an organisation such as the British Medical Association or the Law Society – such generous public esteem seems unlikely to be matched by public largesse.

But even high status and a powerful professional organisation are no guarantee of long-term security if the group concerned appear to be falling below their own immaculate standards or seem to be over-exploiting their monopoly of the work. In such cases an unquestioning public confidence may be replaced by aggressive public intervention. In recent years the legal profession – which has created the finest and most elegant set of restrictive practices known to man – has come under increasing pressure. Not only are solicitors likely to lose their monopoly over the house conveyancing trade – which accounts for about half of their income – but serious doubts have been cast on the effectiveness of the Law Society in adequately disciplining those who fail to maintain the proper standards of professional conduct. It is this second development which is the more serious for, if lawyers fail to control themselves, then someone else will. If that happens their autonomy will be threatened and their power to establish their own fees, to insist clients may only talk to a barrister through a solicitor (and pay for both), to double their fees for 'care and conduct' (doing their work properly) and, through the Law Society, to administer and dispense legal aid, will all become subject to much more careful public scrutiny and, doubtless, criticism.

Our belief in the rule of law and our demand that those who practise it be of spotless reputation rests, ultimately, in the realm of social values. Values, in the simplest of terms, reflect how we think society ought to be organised, how people ought to behave and the kind of laws we ought to have. They are *social* because they become established through social interaction; are transmitted and learned through various processes of socialisation – such as education, religion and propaganda; and are socially institutionalised in law. Indeed, it is in legislation that social values find their most enduring affirmation. Thus, for example, the laws regulating employment rights and trade unions can be seen as the embodiment of dominant social values.

This does not mean we all believe in the *same* values. In all societies there are competing values which reflect conflicting interest groups in society and the institutionalisation of some values can only be achieved by precluding or suppressing others. Maximising employee rights automatically requires a reduction in the rights of employers. Similarly, although we may try to fudge it, as we saw earlier, it is not really possible to maximise individual and collective rights at the same time. Some values are bound to become dominant.

In practice, interest groups are automatically characterised by differing preferences and will try to persuade others to adopt or support their particular values. This is why the ownership of newspapers – and thus the power to decide which political line the newspaper takes – is of particular importance, for newspapers can be used to promote certain social values. Those on the political Left in Britain – and this includes some trade union leaders – frequently launch bitter tirades against what they regard as prejudiced and biased reporting of employment relations. Indeed, paradoxically, such complaints have become so numerous that – like increases in unemployment figures – they are no longer 'news', and nobody really takes notice any more. It happens so frequently we accept it as normal.

It is through a similar process that the social values purveyed by newspapers become embedded in everyone's thinking and, even if not accepted, are very difficult to dislodge. If we are constantly being told 'trade unions are too powerful' then – as public opinion polls show – even trade union members express the same view. Similarly, if strikes are repeatedly described as causing job losses or seriously damaging the economy then these become the criteria through which we judge industrial action. It is in this way that control of the various media through which social values are trasmitted leads to the reinforcement of particular social values and orientations as opposed to others. In any dispute between employers and employees it follows that those interests which receive greatest support from the dominant social values are likely to enjoy greater public support. Such values play a critical role in shaping the public frame of reference and help us to appreciate why, no matter what causes a dispute, we invariably regard the employees as the aggressors.

Among the most deeply rooted and resilient social values are those which underpin our conceptions of fairness and justice in the distribution of the rewards of work. Excluding those who live off investments of various kinds, the occupational structure has, historically, displayed a remarkably consistent pattern of differential rewards. At the top are our lawyers, doctors, other professional employees and

managers; next come the white-collar occupations, technicians, middle and lower management; these are followed by
skilled and other manual workers. There are, of course,
overlaps between these occupational groupings and many
anomalies but, in general, this structure has remained
impervious to any substantial alteration.

White-collar, male employees have – since the 1880s –
almost continually received 20% more than their manual
colleagues. Female employees – who have traditionally been
paid less than males – were supposed to be paid equally from
1975. In 1970, when the Equal Pay Act was enacted, women's
earnings were about 63% of comparable male earnings. By
1975, when the new law became effective, the figure had risen
to about 72%. Since then it has only risen another two
percentage points. In low-paid jobs there are five times more
women than men. Not only do women experience very
considerable difficulties in entering managerial and professional jobs but, even at the bottom, are severely constrained in the choices available. A study in 1980 showed that
74% of all women employees are found in five occupations:
secretarial work, as maids or in similar service work, in
nursing, as canteen assistants or as sewing machinists.

Despite literally dozens of academic studies which have
consistently demonstrated the inequalities of opportunity and
reward at work,[10] and despite laws which prohibit various
forms of discrimination, the stubborn resistance of such
inequalities has never been an issue of major public concern.
Labour politicians have some well-polished rhetorical
routines which condemn it but, when in government, have
never got beyond token gestures when it comes to remedies.
The tabloid newspapers – except on those occasions when
Willie Hamilton is protesting about the wages paid to the
Royal Family – reserve their finest moral outrage for social
security scroungers. As for trade unions, they keep their
heads down and disclaim responsibility. The only time they
are genuinely stirred into excitement and action – as we saw
in the lagger's tale – is when the existing pattern of
differentials between their members and another group of
workers is threatened. And it would be naive to expect them

to act otherwise. While there is often fraternal support when their 'family' is threatened by outsiders such as employers or governments it is well known for brothers to squabble and compete in a pecking order. Members tend to regard success not merely in terms of getting more but getting more than the members of other unions – especially if the latter are considered to be less skilled or of lower status. Hence trade unions appear to work on the principle: 'what we have we hold'. A similar social value has, for the most part, informed various government incomes policies since the 1960s. Such policies have tried to ensure employees received more or less the same increases in pay.[11]

Evidence of how this pecking order has become socially ingrained comes from studies of how we compare ourselves. Manual workers contrast their earnings with what other manual workers receive; white-collar workers mark their progress against other white-collar employees. In effect, such groups do not see each other as making comparable contributions and only dream of putting themselves on a par with professional specialists: each tier in the hierarchy of inequality appears to be insulated from the others and the barriers between them – though in part a product of social ignorance – are constituted of unspoken taken-for-granted social evaluations. Such social values constitute power resources to the extent that they legitimise the existing hierarchy and justify action to ensure its continued existence.

The most obvious source of social power is social organisation itself. Employers' associations and employee organisations of all varieties are the most relevant for our present purpose. Although we are accustomed to think of unions as economic interest group organisations their economic resources are relatively insignificant and their access to political influence has tended to be intermittent and fragile. In addition, the sometimes competing demands of the leadership and the membership has created an existential ambivalence towards the pursuit of what are regarded as overt political ends. Like their partners in conflict, the employers, trade unions and their members will pragmatically use any power resources which are available in order to achieve what they regard as their legitimate ends. Nonetheless, in all cases, the *effective* deployment of those resources to produce a satisfactory outcome depends, ultimately, on the degree of solidarity expressed by the employees. Such cohesion can only be achieved provided the issue at stake is collectively regarded as sufficiently important for all, or nearly all, to support. Without such social collaboration, no matter what the potential effect of available resources, all may be in vain.

Even the most strategically placed group of employees who take action will be frustrated if others are prepared to do their work. This is why 'blacklegs' or 'scab labour' are regarded with such extreme hostility by trade unionists: their action is seen to undermine and negate the sacrifices of fellow workers. The legend seen on countless union banners, 'Unity is Strength', reflects the fundamental source of employee power. Labour history is littered with strikes which failed because the employer imported 'scab labour' or because some employees broke ranks and returned to work.

More recently, the brief period during which trade union leaders enjoyed an unparalleled access to political power resources – 1974–79 – was brought to an abrupt end by the breakdown of social solidarity which was required to sustain it. By the autumn of 1978 – when the then Prime Minister, James Callaghan, insisted wage increases be limited to 5% – it became increasingly clear that many employees, having experienced a real drop in income, simply would not accept such a low level of recompense. It was implemented despite the warnings of trade union leaders and only served to increase the rate at which they distanced themselves from the policy. The net result was the 'winter of discontent' which saw a succession of serious and bitter strikes – the most vividly remembered were those by dustmen and gravediggers and the most important, those of road haulage and petrol tanker drivers – which destroyed the last remnants of the Social Contract. It is no small irony that the social solidarity of workers in 1974, which had, following the miners' strike of that year, helped to produce the election defeat of Mr Heath's Conservative government, produced a similar effect when turned on Mr Callaghan's Labour administration. The bruising lesson for trade union leaders was that political influence, however attractive it may appear, is worthless without the continued support of the rank-and-file membership.

More recently, the fundamental importance of employee cohesion was highlighted even more vividly during the 1984–85 miners' dispute, a venture fatally undermined by the absence of solidarity among the miners themselves. Indeed, the whole episode could be fruitfully analysed in terms of the tactics employed by the NUM leadership to increase the degree of solidarity and the counter-tactics pursued by the NCB and the government in attempting to break the strike. The NUM Executive Committee persistently evaded calls for a national ballot – no doubt reflecting concern about the degree of active support for the strike – and concentrated its efforts in attempts to widen the industrial base of the dispute by securing the support of steel workers, dockers, transport workers and railmen. They met with mixed and often temporary support. Steel workers, chastened by the job losses of 1980 and fearful of further redundancies, had no choice but to accept reduced supplies of raw materials, but refused to take industrial action. Railmen 'blacked' the movement of raw materials by train, but their efforts were seriously undermined by road transport drivers who drove convoys of coal and iron ore to keep the steel mills operating. The dock workers – whose capacity to disrupt the relatively smooth-running economy was critical to the NUM – held a brief and abortive national strike in July and the disappointment at its end was only relieved by a similarly short-lived, partial and even more muddled national dock strike in August and September. There was constant argument about how many pits were still working – most of those in Nottinghamshire never actually stopped – and excessively excited public disagreement about the trickle of miners returning to work elsewhere.

At the same time the NCB and government ministers focused their tactics on inducing miners to return to work in combination with a predominantly personalised attack on Arthur Scargill. The former comprised a massive advertising campaign in the national press, individual letters to striking miners, scare-mongering threats to withdraw the existing offers and close even more pits than had originally been proposed. The objective of the latter tactic, character-assassination, was to pre-empt any potential public sympathy for the miners' case and try to isolate Arthur Scargill from the support of members.

This mix of tactics, combined with the collective intransigence of the principal actors, guaranteed a bitter dispute. For miners in particular, crossing picket lines is little short of a sacrilegious act, and this, combined with the very heavy and visible police presence necessary to ensure the right of all to work if they so choose, was what lay behind the sporadic but much-reported violence at the pits. In turn this reflected real differences of opinion for there was no unconditional support for the strike. Where there is solidarity, pickets are unnecessary except as a token presence. Potentially, where employees are resolved to fight the issue no matter what the cost, employee solidarity is the most effective of all power resources, for it is the product of social consensus.

In contrast, employers are not so reliant upon collective social organisation. This is particularly so for larger concerns – such as ICI or Ford – and for monopoly employers – such as nationalised industries. The labour force cannot be tempted to take their labour elsewhere for there is nowhere else to go. This lack of competition, combined with access to very considerable economic and, often, political power resources, means such employers have no need to organise collectively with others.

Elsewhere, employers' associations are key institutions in bargaining at national level though their significance as a source of collective power depends on the character of the particular industrial sector. In electrical contracting, for example, where the national agreement specifies actual rates of pay, such collective solidarity among the large number of small employers is significant for, with standard wage costs, it eliminates one element of competition between them and also pre-empts the employees – who are more or less unified under the umbrella of the EETPU – from bidding up the price of labour by attacking one firm at a time. In the engineering industry, where there is considerable variation in size of firm and range of products, the EEF (Engineering Employers' Federation), while it still provides a number of important centralised services, has only sustained its membership by allowing member firms to pay above the nationally bargained minimum rates of pay.

Earlier, the Fleet Street printers were picked out to illustrate how employees can effectively mobilise economic power resources. In part this was only possible because of a significant lack of effective social organisation among their employers. A combination of highly individualistic press barons and a succession of circulation wars has permitted the very well-organised printers to fruitfully exploit this employer competitiveness. Fleet Street employers are collectively organised through the Newspaper Publishers' Association but, despite a tacit understanding that if one of them is under pressure the others will help, it has not always been able to ensure such support. The temptation of owners to try to pick up the circulation of a competitor is sometimes too great to resist. Despite years of editorial pontification on how to improve industrial relations, as employers, the Fleet Street barons have an almost unrivalled record of managerial ineffectiveness with their own employment relations.

TO CONCLUDE

Understanding everyday industrial relations is no easy task; and if we are assailed with images of miners fighting with police or grave-diggers preventing the burial of the dead, it is extremely difficult to maintain a detached attitude. Nonetheless, if we wish to understand such episodes in a dispassionate fashion, it is essential to discipline our own frame of reference. In order to do this it is necessary to construct an analytical framework.

The framework developed in this chapter is centred on the concepts of power, power relations and power resources. This has advantages and weaknesses. The weaknesses are more apparent than real for they reside in our common-sense conception of power which is invariably associated with coercion, physical violence and civil repression. However, as the discussion has illustrated, these are merely the most socially visible modes of exercising power. They are storms on the surface of industrial relations which are symptomatic of – and sometimes mask – a great underlying structure of power relations which, in reality, *hold these relations together*. Once it is realised power is not merely a seemingly negative feature but is also the source of all creative social acts – such as manufacturing products, providing services and generating employment; and once we recognise all social relations are characterised by dependence, then the distinct advantages of using the framework can be built on to produce an insightful grasp of the deep structure of employment relationships.

There are three particular advantages which merit emphasis. Firstly, it specifically avoids asking questions like 'who is right?', 'who is wrong?', 'what should we – or the government – do about it?' By side-stepping this swamp of value-judgements we can instantly distance the analysis from our own frame of reference, and by doing so can postpone passing judgement until we have made some attempt to establish who is doing what to whom and why.

Secondly, the framework is extensive in scope. That is, it can be used to link a very wide range of industrial relations phenomena – interests, conflict, wage-payment systems, investment, national expenditure, public policies, the law and so on – in a meaningful and relatively coherent fashion. In this respect, like the advert, it refreshes the parts no other framework can reach.

Thirdly, provided we maintain our suspension of moral judgement on the behaviour of the actors, it is an approach which could be used within almost any frame of reference across the political spectrum. There will be fierce disputes as to which of the major actors – employer, employee or government – is right, and endless argument over how best to achieve more harmonious industrial relations but such issues are, quite deliberately, left outside of the analytical framework. Its purpose is to provide a more informed basis on which to pursue such quarrels.

Historically, conflict and cooperation, consensus and disagreement, stability and change are, observably, all part of
the natural behaviour both in society and between societies.
To conclude that any one of them is a symptom of social
disease which must be eliminated is to fundamentally
misunderstand that they are all essential ingredients for
freedom to prevail in social relations. Indeed, their interdependence is such that in eliminating one of them, we
destroy all of them. It can be done, but requires an act of
ferocious coercion. One of the more recent examples was the
elimination of Solidarity in Poland, but this was only
achieved through martial law at a social, economic and
political cost which is still being counted.

9

Industrial Relations, Social Science and Social Justice

Within the broad range of disciplines which comprise the social sciences – politics, philosophy, sociology, economics, social and economic history, psychology and law – the study of industrial relations has always enjoyed an ambiguous, peripheral, almost furtive academic existence. This is both curious and unwarranted. Curious because the focus of industrial relations on the nature of work and the regulation of employment reflects a quite fundamental dimension of social life found in all societies. And unwarranted because, as will be elaborated, it is one of the major substantive problem areas of social science which not only draws on all the core disciplines but also requires an integrative analytical framework. This is one of the reasons why it occupies an occasionally somewhat troublesome relationship to the seemingly more refined and prestigious core disciplines.

Another reason which helps to account for this uneasy academic status is the pervasive concern with questions of social justice. In the previous eight chapters this issue has never been faced head-on – although it has been impossible to avoid when seeking to understand the rationale for certain kinds of behaviour. However, it is an issue which no invitation to industrial relations can ignore since it is of vital significance to any account of employment relations and, for this reason, is the final problem to be considered. But let us turn, first, to the question of how the study of industrial relations relates to the more respectable social sciences.

THE CINDERELLA OF SOCIAL SCIENCE

Academic institutions have never been particularly enamoured of the study of industrial relations. In Britain there are only a handful of professors of industrial relations, few journals and less than half a dozen university departments of industrial relations. Where it is taught, it is usually found as a subordinate section in a management or business studies department or, in some cases, tucked away in a disreputable corner of a department of economics. Every 10 years or so some economist, sociologist or, more rarely, a political scientist, will claim industrial relations belongs to their particular discipline.

Curiously perhaps, those who have chosen to make their academic careers in industrial relations, often relatively starved of resources and subject to these occasional predatory attacks, have never really made any concerted attempt to stake out their own exclusive claim to any specific academic cabbage patch. Nor, perhaps even more curiously, has our lowly status ever really been a source of intellectual insecurity.

There are three major reasons why this is so. Firstly, for a set of complex historical reasons which need not trouble us, industrial relations emerged too late to make any authoritative claims on any particular problem areas. It was peopled by labour historians and frustrated or 'failed' labour economists – failed in the sense they could not solve the intellectual puzzle of how to account for the price of labour without leaving the framework of conventional economic thinking. Secondly, industrial relations developed as a multi- or inter-disciplinary field of study and those who ventured in did so from the warmth and security of their parent discipline – usually to examine a particular aspect or dimension of employment relations. Hence there are numerous books with titles like: the *Economics of Trade Unions*, the *Sociology of Industrial Conflict* or the *Politics of Industrial Relations* and, within the core disciplines, there are distinctive specialisms which focus on employment relationship: labour economics, industrial sociology, organisational sociology and occupational psychology being the most well known. One consequence of this academic division of labour is that there are no books which vigorously assert, 'this is the discipline of industrial relations and here are our founding mothers and fathers'. Indeed, leaving aside the futility of such an endeavour, it would, in any case, be regarded as an ostentatious and vulgar display of academic imperialism.

Thirdly, if only by default in the failure to declare our autonomy, industrial relations academics have actively connived in the maintenance of their own subordination. Many regard the field as an adjunct to economics or sociology and others see it as being nothing more than the study of how to create the best methods of managing discontent. The latter – who can be characterised as the social workers of industrial relations – are primarily concerned with practical issues such as how to develop and implement effective personnel policies or how to reform collective bargaining or trade unions in order to 'improve' industrial relations. Such work is obviously important but the highly pragmatic orientation it requires can lead to misleading and sometimes specious conclusions. For example, if you set out to reduce strike behaviour it is all too easy to assume the *elimination* of strikes would, necessarily, be in everybody's best interest. In the earlier dicussion of strikes it was shown such an assumption is simplistic to the point of being socially dangerous.

For all these reasons and more, industrial relations has been the Cinderella of social science. It has little in the way of its own distinctive theoretical clothing and, in the areas of both teaching and research, much energy has been devoted to clearing up the messes left by its ugly social scientific sisters. It is common, for example, for economists to analyse strikes in terms of their presumed economic causation and consequences; and political scientists have invariably treated trade unions as no more than pressure groups for specific employee interests. Indeed, the idea that there exists a workable, if not always entirely clear distinction between the economic and political activities of trade unions has persisted even in the writings of those academics who are primarily or exclusively working in the field of industrial relations.

   Paradoxically, such weaknesses – which result from the use of a frame of reference which is too narrow to accommodate all the salient factors – would not be resolved by trying to establish a distinctive 'discipline' of industrial relations. That would merely create yet another analytical enclave which would 'exclude' certain variables as belonging to the territory of another. In the study of industrial relations, as the examples in this book have consistently demonstrated, any such enterprise is likely to produce little but a distorted, one-dimensional image of what is taking place. The pursuit of academic purity may produce impressive algebraic equations, lead to rational and intellectually satisfying models of employee behaviour and even high academic status, but it may also require an unjustifiable degree of oversimplification. The employment relationship cannot be treated as primarily either economic or political or social or psychological in character without serious risk of actively misunderstanding the complexities, the apparent irrationalities and contradictions of the social behaviour typical of industrial relations. The trick, and one which is extremely difficult to perform, is to avoid the intrinsic limitations of a disciplinary framework while retaining a disciplined frame of reference.

THE NEED FOR INTEGRATION

In the discussion of shop stewards, one reason advanced to account for their distorted media image was because we never see or hear of stewards unless they are in belligerent mood or engaged in some *abnormal* activity. We are consistently presented with a very one-sided view of their activities. Similarly, we will only receive a distorted academic account of any aspect of industrial relations if our perspective is limited to any one of the core disciplines. Like journalists and newspaper proprietors, social scientists have to simplify the social world to make sense of it, but, in doing so, great care must be taken to avoid becoming fixated within the conceptual apparatus of any one approach. Indeed, at the risk of offending many colleagues, it could be said one of the reasons why our common-sense understanding of industrial relations is so bedevilled by the various misconceptions and myths briefly considered in previous chapters, is that such notions have been reinforced and fuelled by the pronouncements of some social scientists. This can easily be illustrated by a brief reconsideration of collective bargaining. What would be lost when collective bargaining is analysed from a singular disciplinary perspective?

An economist would focus on collective bargaining as an economic mechanism which regulates the price at which labour is to be sold. It is seen by many economists as a mechanism which 'interferes' with the free play of market forces – an alien element distorting the proper functioning of the labour market and pushing up the price of labour to a level it would not 'normally' reach. In the abstract world of the free-market mentality, this is correct. However, as a description of the real world of employment relations it is bizarre. Not only does it imply the real world ought to conform to the abstract models we have constructed to help us understand it, but it completely misses the point that collective bargaining is not exclusively or even primarily an economic process. The image has taken precedence over the complex reality.[1]

Collective bargaining also has political dimensions and the political scientist, in contrast, might relegate the economic effects of bargaining to the periphery of the analysis. It is likely to be analysed as a method through which the vested interests of labour, or particularly categories of labour, are institutionalised and expressed either to specific employers or to governments. As a political mechanism it permits employees to take part in determining the rules – or 'legislation' – which governs their employment relationships. In this context the economic spin-offs may be regarded as less important – or even irrelevent – when compared to the political significance of collective employee organisation. As suggested earlier, trade unions, irrespective of their economic activities, can be seen as vital institutions in the maintenance of social democracy and political stability. Collective bargaining is thus a means whereby grass-roots participation in the politics of organisational life is ensured. This view is endorsed by experience for many of the rules created through bargaining concern the allocation of work, the representational rights of employee organisations and the scope of managerial authority. Although currently unfashionable, one of the major issues of industrial relations concerns how to create a workable system of industrial democracy. Some think it has already been achieved through the existence of collective bargaining while others insist no true industrial democracy can be realised without an authoritative employee voice in the boardrooms of industry.

Once again, however, there are dangers of over-interpretation. Right-wing political scientists are prone to interpret any display of trade union political power or any proposed extension of their political functions as undermining parliamentary democracy. Such a view can only be sustained provided they ignore the economic achievements of collective bargaining and trade unions. The manifest failure of collective bargaining to produce a significant redistribution of income, and the abject failure of trades unions to prevent dramatic increases in the general level of unemployment, hardly suggest unions are possessed of too much political or economic power. Similarly, those on the left of the spectrum sometimes expect momentous political changes to result from the occasional breakdown of collective bargaining. Strike action may be endowed with almost magical properties: they are seen to reflect the casting off of bourgeois ideology, the first seminal stirrings of a total rejection of the capitalist system and the birth of a new consciousness. And there is no doubt some strikes do transform employee attitudes.

Nonetheless, both right and left tend to over-politicise the behaviour of employees and trade unions. The vast majority of trade unionists display no genuine inclination to overthrow the system. The primary concern of the average bus conductor, car worker, hospital cleaner or computer operator is unlikely to be the political subversion of liberal democracies, though they can become very agitated about their terms and conditions of employment and, in particular, in securing what they consider to be their 'rights'. Revolutionary class-consciousness is not a precondition for demands to sustain a customary standard of living or to maintain allegedly uneconomic coal mines. Such a conclusion comes from an over-zealous concern with the political dimension and can also lead to the image taking precedence over the complex reality.

It is our trained legal minds which possess the most myopic view of collective bargaining. A legal analysis would focus almost exclusively on the ways in which the terms of the contract of employment are modified through the rule-making activities of the bargainers. These, of course, may have considerable significance for individual employees and employers in the event of a breach of contract. This may, on occasion, produce some interesting technical niceties, but any legalistic analysis is invariably extemely limited. It ignores the context of social action; is oblivious to the process of bargaining and the rationale behind demands; and, ironically, is most unlikely to pass comment on the 'justice' of the claim.

However, the most bewildering account of collective bargaining is likely to come from social or organisational psychologists. They tend to regard the process as one designed to remedy the consequences of faulty or defective communication. Beware, for this is the third great lie of Western civilisation.

No textbook on how to improve industrial relations, or on the principles of good management, is complete without a chapter on how to communicate effectively. Clear instructions from supervisor to employee and the precise specification of a grievance or industrial relations issue are obviously prerequisites to harmonious employment relations. However, in advocating such good practice the writers of such texts are prone to regard the absence of such harmony as the result of poor or ineffective communications. Industrial conflict thus ceases to be a structural phenomenon which is endemic to the employment relationship and is presumed to be no more than a 'technical' failure in the machinery of managerial communication. While there are undoubtedly occasions when disputes could have been avoided with clearer communications, it would be deeply misleading to regard this as a major or significant cause of industrial conflict.[2]

To focus exclusively or even primarily on the way in which collective bargaining improves the transmission of communications is to ignore not only the structural context but also the fundamental underlying character of the bargaining relationship. The quality of communication depends on what the bargainers are seeking to achieve. Tactically, they may deliberately misinform each other and, at other points in the process, will make themselves understood as clearly as possible. Both sides may be only too well aware of what the other is proposing – and both may simply refuse to accept the crystal-clear communications passing between them. It is not that they misunderstand each other, but the conflict of interests which sometimes openly characterises the employment relationship has, temporarily, produced a genuine disagreement over what should be done.

The purpose of these criticisms is not to dismiss such analyses out of hand – for they may all tell us something about collective bargaining – but to highlight the dangers of a one-dimensional approach to any aspect of industrial relations. The administration and control of the employment relationship in industrial societies requires, at the very least, a multi-disciplinary frame of reference and, if possible, an integrative conceptual scheme. The central focus of the study of industrial relations – the employment relationship – is, as repeatedly demonstrated in previous chapters, legal, economic, social, political and psychological. In any particular analysis it may not be possible to hold all these dimensions in the air at the same time, but in emphasising one we should never forget the others, for there is a permanent interdependence between them. A change in the law regulating the contract of employment is *never* an autonomous 'legal event' but the consequence of a decision by those who exercise political power. And the correlation between a decrease in the political influence of trade unions and increasing unemployment is no historical accident: high levels of unemployment greatly reduce the political and economic clout of trade unions.

CONFLICT AND CONSENSUS IN EMPLOYMENT

One of the major themes which dominates many texts on industrial relations and the management of employment is the question of how to create and maintain harmonious relations between employer and employee. It is a theme which has been carefully avoided in this book – the aim of which is far less ambitious, being merely to provide some evidence and justification for a particular 'way of seeing' industrial relations. Nevertheless, it is a theme which is reflected and contained within the definition used throughout: the administration and control of the employment relationship in industrial societies. The use of the term 'administration' implies the idea of management and the existence of rules and regulations; and the inclusion of the term 'control' evokes the notions of power and authority relations which are always potentially conflictual. Indeed, the full definition indicates not only that employment relationships are ordered but that such order may well be problematic for all those involved.

In more general terms what this definition alludes to and, indeed, the unstated question to which this whole book has been addressed, is the theoretical issue of how social order is maintained in the employment relationship. This problem is not merely of academic interest to social scientists but also of central practical significance for all those who are engaged in the management of discontent. As has been illustrated, employees, trade unions, managers, employers and governments will enlist all the resources and methods available in the continual effort to create and maintain order and, where possible, harmony. This is a continuous and permanent problem. Firstly, because the consensual order they seek is fundamentally precarious – the underlying conflict of interests can re-surface at any time. And, secondly, because each of the parties is concerned to create a social order which favours their particular interests or their particular frame of reference. The actual pattern at any point in time, as was suggested in the last chapter, will tend to reflect the parties' access to and control over power resources and the distribution of power between them.

This theoretical problem also highlights why the study of industrial relations is often a central focus for the core social science disciplines, for they too are primarily concerned with understanding how order is maintained in social relations. Most obvious in this respect is the study of law. Laws can be seen as the 'formal rules' which regulate everyday social behaviour. We make laws in order to prohibit and sanction all those kinds of behaviour thought to violate the social fabric; and effective legal controls are seen to be critical to the maintenance of social order. Indeed, respect for the law is often seen as a precondition of social order and a prerequisite of a civilised society. This is reflected in our almost sacred belief in 'the rule of law'; without this, it is often asserted, there would be social chaos.

Political theorists, in their elaboration of political philosophies, often focus upon the kind of social order which characterises different political systems. The degree of individual freedom or the extent to which collective values are promoted will be critically influenced by the prevailing political ordering of social relations. In this respect we are accustomed to the stark contrast which is invariably drawn between liberal democracies and communist regimes. The latter are invariably regarded as requiring an unacceptable degree of subservience to the political order – the absence of 'free' trade unions being thought of as a particular weakness.

Similarly economists, in their concern with the various forms of economic exchange, seek to identify and elaborate the most efficient means of ordering the economic relations in society. Economic markets of goods, labour, money and services can be organised according to different principles, thus presenting us with alternative means of regulating economic affairs. In very general terms there is a continuing argument between free-market economists and those who insist economic activity ought to be planned and carefully controlled. Proponents of the free-market or *laissez-faire* approach claim that maximising individual economic freedom produces not only the most efficient allocation of economic resources but also the most flexible and, moreover, most socially just means of ordering economic relations. Those who favour some degree of planning argue economic resources ought to be distributed according to a set of national priorities identified through the political process. This, they suggest, would not only produce a more efficient allocation of resources according to social need – instead of private profit – but would also permit the creation of a more just economic order.

Among social scientists it is the sociologists who display the most conscious and pre-eminent interest in this question of social order. Indeed, many would define the whole discipline as an inquiry into the sources of social order and instability in society, and the major schools of sociological thought can be differentiated according to how they seek to resolve the problem of accounting for social order. At the extremes this debate is conducted between those who insist social stability derives from a fundamental consensus on certain primary values which receive general, if not unqualified, support from those who make up society and those who operate within a Marxian perspective.[3] The latter, in contrast, maintain that all existing societies are comprised of social classes with historically irreconcilable interests. Social order and stability are the products of a fundamentally coercive, if not always clearly visible, process of control exercised by those in positions of power in society. These not only include private capitalists but might also refer to the Party bosses and bureaucrats of so-called communist societies with centrally planned economies.

It is no accident that all these grand themes and theories find reflection in the various issues and problems discussed in previous chapters. There are two main reasons why industrial relations tends to be of central significance for theories of social order. Firstly, work is a pervasive and fundamental social activity. We all expect to work for some if not the most part of our lives; its rewards determine our life-chances and its character provides our social identities. The way in which we decide to organise work, the means and methods used to administer and control it through the employment relationship are, empirically, critical evidence to the testing and validity of such theories.

Secondly, the sources of social order, stability and harmony cannot be considered in isolation from the sources of social disorder, instability and conflict. They are two sides of the same coin and intimately interrelated both empirically and theoretically. Even in terms of our common-sense understanding of the social world it is not possible to identify the existence of social order unless we have some idea of what social disorder looks like. In the sphere of industrial relations, sad to relate, most people hold very clear ideas as to what might constitute social disorder. As the central mechanism for socio-economic exchange, it is in work and employment relations we find that the prevailing social order experiences its greatest stresses and strains. Industrial conflict, in one form or another, is found in all the industrial societies. This does not mean social order cannot be the product of the fundamental consensus referred to above, for it is rare for such conflict to be consciously directed at the system as such. Indeed, employees who strike for improved wages might be regarded as endorsing the economic values of capitalism, for they are merely pursuing their individual self-interest through a vigorous collaborative endeavour.

What it does mean, however, is that, in the real world, the best test of all our competing accounts or theories of social order will be in the context of the employment relationship. If society *is* held together by a central core of common values and consensual beliefs; if social order emerges out of the rich variety of interdependent social groups and interests which are to be found in society, then the employment relationship is the place to look for such features. Similarly, if society *is* made up of two great warring classes, the capitalists and the proletariat; if capital, with the assistance of the State apparatus, subordinates all before it; and if social order is maintained through a combination of coercive forces and ideological mystifications, then, here also, the employment relationship is the place to look for the evidence.

The purpose of this very brief account of the fundamental question to which social science is directed has been to locate the study of industrial relations in relation to the core disciplines. While it has often been most strongly identified with the seemingly practical questions of how to regulate employment and manage discontent, it should now be clear that, as a field of study, industrial relations occupies the theoretical crossroads of several major social scientific disciplines.

SOCIAL JUSTICE IN EMPLOYMENT

The idea that the primary source of conflict between employer and employee is their respective socio-economic interests is now well established. However, as has been illustrated by the examples, this is an incomplete account for it is impossible to ignore the political and moral dimensions of disagreement. Employees not only have economic interests, but also express political aspirations as to how the employment relationship ought to be regulated, and come to employment with moral expectations about fairness, honour and dignity at work.

For most people, work is the dominant socio-economic focus of their lives and, as such, it is the major social arena – outside of their families – in which they make judgements about the kind of justice they receive from the social order. In the discussion of strikes it was suggested many disputes, despite their apparently economic cause, can only be properly understood if we dig beneath the surface symptoms. Many, if not the majority, might best be regarded as moral disputes. Most wage disputes are not directed to producing an absolute increase in earnings but are often undertaken by employees to maintain their position relative to other groups. As such, they express the belief of the workers involved that, to ensure continued fairness in the social order, they ought to remain where they are in the wages hierarchy.

Nor is it just employees who come armed with notions of fairness and rights attached to their interests. The frame of reference of the employer and managers may contribute equally to the length of disputes. Employees who strike in order to secure the reinstatement of someone deemed to have been victimised often face very considerable resistance from the employer. This is because a managerial concession means accepting that the employer's right to hire and fire labour is conditional on employee agreement. There is no money in it for anyone but, since it is a matter of principle for both parties, the issue must be contested. In this respect it is vital to appreciate that the moral codes and beliefs of employers – often referred to as managerial ideologies – are likely to be equally as fiercely defended as are the presumed rights of employees and trade unions. Just as matters of principle tend to produce the longest and most bitter strikes, so too a managerial commitment to positive employment policies may engender harmonious and productive industrial relations. In the same way as it is often forgotten that employees' economic interests are conditioned by their conceptions of social justice, the moral constraints operating on the employer in pursuit of efficiency and profit also tend to be ignored.

The managerial ideology which informs the employment policies pursued by IBM may well be designed to pre-empt discontent, but their success is likely to depend on continued managerial commitment to such policies even during times when the economic climate might indicate a less generous attitude. Such companies are sometimes described as being 'welfare-capitalist' – a pejorative term implying their very public social conscience is no more than a veneer to cover the venal pursuit of profit. This may be so, but all private companies have to make profit, and this should not detract from the fact that, in making their choice about how to regulate employees, the IBM management chose a path which involved something other than a crude economistic morality.

The precursors of the modern welfare-capitalists were the early paternalistic Quaker family firms whose names – Rowntree and Cadbury – still dominate the confectionary business. Their employment policies were deeply informed by Christian ethics and they too have been accused of hypocrisy in their use of such values to mask the pursuit of profit. An overt commitment to such policies has now gone but their significance lingers on. As recently as 1984, the Chairman of Rowntree Mackintosh remarked, 'The direct Quaker involvement stopped here a long time ago but the attitudes and traditions have not. All companies have their cultures and the Quaker and Methodist values are still regarded inside the company. We think very hard about our people, it is something that hangs in the air from the past. We do not find it easy to make people redundant.'[4] It is possible to scoff at such statements but, nonetheless, that organisational culture and those managerial values stand in stark contrast to the 'macho-management' style adopted by some car manufacturers and the almost exclusive use of economic values to regulate employment in steel and coal in recent years.

None of this is to suggest there are not economic, political or social considerations and constraints which play a marked role in shaping managerial behaviour and employment policy. On occasion, managers may have little choice but to take actions which they themselves regard as unjust and perhaps immoral. The danger is, in emphasising the primacy of the economic interests of employers, it is all too easy to ignore the significance of this moral dimension for the quality, stability and climate of industrial relations. Indeed, as we have seen in recent years, the disproportionately high priority accorded to the pursuit of economic goals can lead to a situation where nothing else seems to matter: the social responsibilities of employers and managers have, in effect, been reduced to that crude economistic morality. A social order in which the employment relationship is treated as nothing *but* an economic exchange is likely to be fragile, unstable and subject to frequent breakdowns. This is confirmed by our experience of the car industry which, despite relatively high earnings, has a fine reputation for poor industrial relations and where there is strong evidence suggesting money is a very poor basis upon which to build a positive employment relationship.[5]

Work and the relationships we construct about it are characterised by economic conflicts, but they are also characterised by conflicting moralities and expectations. One recent study[6] has suggested we can only understand the behaviour of workers if we start by recognising the great variety in the frames of reference held by different occupational work groups. Craftsmen, unskilled workers, peasants, bureaucrats and managers of all kinds are seen as holding different 'world views'. Sabel uses these to draw a series of social and political profiles of each category to demonstrate why they behave differently when looking for jobs, why they hold sometimes radically contrasting expectations of work and why it is they react differently in situations of conflict. One essential element of these world views is what he calls 'our barely articulated ideas about honour and justice', the moral and political dimension of employee action.

The prevailing social order in a factory, an office, a company or even in a society both reflects and incorporates the dominant values and beliefs of those in positions of power and authority. Such values are frequently challenged – though rarely successfully – by those with less power and influence. At its centre, the study of industrial relations is about the ways and means through which governments, managers, employees and all their attendant agencies create and maintain social order in employment. As has been demonstrated, this is not merely a 'technical' problem of administration and control, for a social order is also a moral order. It is for this reason industrial relations are, and will remain, a central focus for public attention and a major issue of political dispute.

References

CHAPTER 1

1 At the time of the laggers' dispute this union was the GMWU. In January 1983 it merged with the boilermakers' union to become the GMBTU. To avoid confusion it will be referred to throughout the discussion by the new name.
2 While not a typical dispute, the 1970 strike at Pilkington's at St Helens in Lancashire is among the best known in the recent history of industrial relations. It provides an excellent example of the complex dynamics of industrial conflict. For a detailed account of the affair, see Lane, T. and Roberts, K. (1971), *Strike at Pilkingtons*, London: Fontana.

CHAPTER 2

1 *Low Pay Review*, No. 12, February 1983.
2 National Consumer Council Report, August 1984.

CHAPTER 3

1 The TUC *General Council's Report* in September 1984 records total membership at 10,076,173. The ten largest unions, in order of size, are the TGWU, AUEW, GMBTU, NALGO, NUPE, USDAW, ASTMS, EETPU, NUT and the NUM. Between them these unions represent 66.4% of all trade unionists affiliated to the TUC. For more detailed discussion of trade unions, their organisation and how they have changed over time see Palmer,

References

G. (1983), *British Industrial Relations*, London: George Allen and Unwin, chapter 3; or Hawkins, K. (1981), *Trade Unions*, London: Hutchinson; or Bain, G. S. (ed.), (1983), *Industrial Relations in Britain*, Oxford: Blackwell, chapters 1–3.

2 Of these, 98 are affiliated to the TUC and represent about 95% of all union members.

3 Somewhat ironically, the advice on which West German trade unionism was reconstructed came from the British TUC.

4 See Hyman, R., 'Trade unions: structure, policies and politics', *in* Bain, *op. cit.* (see note 1). As Hyman points out, neither of these two organisations is 'unambiguously a trade union'. The RCN have forsworn strike action and the Police Federation is legally prevented from advocating strike action or joining the TUC.

5 Donovan, Lord (1968), Royal Commission on Trade Unions and Employers' Associations. *Report*. Cmnd. 3623, London: HMSO.

6 Farnham, D. and Pimlott, J. (1979), *Understanding Industrial Relations*, London: Cassell, p. 164.

7 Palmer, *op. cit.* (see note 1), p. 51.

8 Sissons, K., 'Employers' associations', *in* Bain, *op. cit.* (see note 1)

9 Farnham and Pimlott, *op. cit.* (see note 6), p. 165. Sissons, *op. cit.* (see note 8) suggests that among those enterprises with over 50 employees some 70% to 75% are members of an employers' association.

10 See Sissons, *op. cit.* (note 8), or Palmer, *op. cit.* (note 1), Chapter 4.

11 Sissons, *op. cit.* (note 8), pp. 131–2.

12 *Sunday Times*, 9 November 1980.

13 *Sunday Times*, 5 February 1984, p. 59.

14 The data on Wages Councils are taken from the TUC General Council's Report, 1984, pp. 41 and 319.

CHAPTER 4

1 Wright-Mills, C., *The New Men of Power*, New York: Harcourt-Brace, 1948.

2 Published in 1968, this report presented the findings of a Royal Commission on industrial relations and made a series of recommendations, many of which were ignored by subsequent governments.

3 Nichols, T. and Beynon, H. (1977), *Living with Capitalism*, London: Routledge and Kegan Paul.

4 Bartlett, J. B. (1983), *Success and Failure in Quality Circles*, Occasional Paper 1, Employment Relations Resource Centre, Cambridge.

5 The original findings were reported by Roethlisburger, F. J. and Dickson, W. J. (1939), *Management and the Worker*, Cambridge, Mass.: Harvard University Press. Academics whose work is directed towards, or can be used to increase, managerial control over the workforce are not always warmly regarded by their colleagues. See, for example, Baritz, L. (1960), *The Servants of Power*, New York: Wiley; for a more recent discussion of how employees have been persuaded to work see Anthony, P. (1977), *The Ideology of Work*, London: Tavistock.

6 For a recent detailed account of the legislative framework in industrial relations see Thomason, G. F. (1984), *A Textbook of Industrial Relations Management*, London: IPM.

7 The information on Lonrho is taken from the summary of the 1984 Annual Report to Shareholders, *Observer*, 3 February 1985.

8 *Insurance, Facts and Figures, 1983*, British Insurance Association.

9 *Observer*, 17 March 1985, p. 5.

10 Accurate figures are impossible to gauge because of difficulties in classifying 'public sector' employees. Comparisons with other European nations are equally contentious although all such countries have a similar profile with Britain about average.

CHAPTER 5

1 For a sympathetic account of the employees' side of this affair see Dromey, J. and Taylor, G. (1978), *Grunwick: the Workers' Story*, London: Lawrence and Wishart; for the other interpretation see Clutterbuck, R. (1980), *Britain in Agony*, Harmondsworth: Penguin.

2 The description of IBM which follows is taken from a short article by Peach, L. H. (1983), 'Employee relations in IBM', *Employee Relations*, vol. 5, no. 3, pp. 17–20. Mr Peach, the IBM Director of Personnel and Corporate Affairs, also provided some additional data.

3 Fox, A. (1966), *Industrial Sociology and Industrial Relations*, London: HMSO.

4 This particular example provides a very good illustration of how

even seemingly marginal legal changes can significantly alter the balance of power. Under the original legislation on unfair dismissals the employer had to prove that the dismissal was fair; since the 1980 Employment Act it is now the employee who has to prove that the dismissal was unfair. As an additional disincentive to the employee to take up the case, if the case is lost the employee may also lose his or her right to the 2 weeks severance pay. In effect, having been sacked, the individual can be further penalised for making a fuss over it.

5 There are always exceptions and, on occasion, this convention of mutual protection is deliberately flouted. During the 1984–85 mining dispute the dogmatic public postures adopted by the NUM, the NCB and the government reflected a determination that their opponents had to be *seen* to suffer defeat. This is most unusual, but is indicative of the more forceful approaches which have come to characterise industrial relations in the 1980s.

6 Fox, A. (1973), 'Industrial relations: a social critique of pluralist ideology', in Child, J. (ed.), *Man and Organisation*, London: Allen and Unwin.

7 In 1906, for the first time, a significant number of Labour MPs were returned to Parliament. It was partly this which persuaded the Liberal government to enact the 1906 Trade Disputes Act which made trade unions immune from prosecution for damages in the event of a strike.

8 These recognition rights have since been clearly withdrawn through the 1980 Employment Act. For trade unions the law is not only double-edged but also unreliable.

9 For the best account of how the act worked in practice see Weekes, B., Mellish, M., Dickens, L. and Lloyd, J. (1975), *Industrial Relations and the Limits of the Law*, Oxford: Blackwell.

10 Not all individual rights are cared for so assiduously. No-one is permitted to refuse to pay National Insurance contributions because they are deeply opposed to social security or the National Health Service; and no-one is permitted to refuse to pay part of their taxes because they are fundamentally opposed to contributing to military expenditure. You can be forced to pay for the dole and nuclear weapons but you enjoy an absolute right to refuse to pay union dues.

11 Webb, S. and B. (1898), *Industrial Democracy*, London: Longmans Green.

12 Belloc, H. (1912), *The Servile State*, London and Edinburgh: T. N. Foulis.

273

CHAPTER 6

1 *Sunday Times*, 1 June 1980.
2 *News Line,* 6 December 1980.
3 The survey data are from Taylor, R. (1980), *The Fifth Estate*, London: Pan Books, p. 201.
4 This is less important these days since there is now widespread use of what is called a 'check-off' arrangement through which union dues are automatically deducted from earnings by the employer and remitted to the union.
5 Daniel, N. W. and Millward, N. (1983), *Workplace Industrial Relations in Britain*, London: Heinemann.
6 Taylor, *op. cit.* (see note 3), p. 207.
7 See, for example, Clutterbuck, R. (1980), *Britain in Agony*, Harmondsworth: Penguin.
8 See, for example, Lane, T. (1974), *The Union Makes Us Strong*, London: Arrow Books.
9 The most recent attempt was in early 1984 following a feasibility study which suggested that about £6.7 million would be needed to launch a new newspaper. The trade unions declined to provide the necessary sum, (*The Sunday Times*, 5 February 1984).
10 See, for example, Glasgow Media Group (1982), *Really Bad News*, London: Routledge and Kegan Paul.
11 Taylor, *op. cit.* (see note 3), p 203.
12 Durcan, J. W., McCarthy, W. E. J. and Redman, G. P. (1983), *Strikes in Post-War Britain*, London: Allen and Unwin.

CHAPTER 7

1 A lock-out is when the employer refuses to provide work until the employees return to work on the terms offered. In practice, for reasons we shall come to, it is difficult to distinguish strikes from lock-outs.
2 None of this should be taken to mean it is only strikes which enjoy a highly distorted image. All kinds of social behaviour and social institutions are subject to varying degrees of 'reality-distortion'. For example, in a recent survey, people were asked if they thought the typical household consisted of a husband, wife and two children: 79% of the respondents agreed with this image; in reality only 14% of households are now composed of this idealised combination (*Observer Magazine*, 16 September 1984).

References

3 Hyman, R. (1978), *Strikes*, London: Fontana, p. 34.

4 The base figures for the calculation are taken from those published in the *British Journal of Industrial Relations*.

5 Figures quoted are taken from Thomas, D., 'The secret war against coal', *New Socialist*, no. 19, September 1984, pp. 31–32.

6 One hundred employees on strike for 5 days would produce a 500-day loss. The figures are taken from Durcan *et al.*, (1983), *Strikes in Post-War Britain*, London: Allen and Unwin, pp. 190 and 212.

7 Turner, H. A., Clack, G. and Roberts, G. (1967), *Labour Relations in the Motor Industry*, London: Allen and Unwin.

8 The car industry is notoriously strike-prone but, even there, between 1946 and 1973, when there was the most dramatic increase in strike activity, the average annual loss of working days was only 0.6% of total working time (Durcan *et al.*, *op. cit.* (see note 6), p. 315).

9 The 1980 steel strike also illustrates the definitional problems in distinguishing between strikes – resulting from employee decisions – and lock-outs – resulting from employer decisions. Significantly, the official government data collectors in the Department of Employment did, at one time, try to distinguish between strikes and lock-outs but – because of the difficulty in clearly identifying which party initiates the action, decided to abandon the distinction in 1895! Since strikes are the product of a relationship, such distinctions are, analytically, extremely difficult to make.

10 Durcan *et al.*, *op. cit.* (see note 6), p. 394.

11 For a detailed account of this extremely interesting episode see Lane and Roberts (1971), *Strike at Pilkingtons*, London: Fontana; for a briefer account of the Pilkington strike and others of similar interest, see McCord, N. (1980), *Strikes*, Oxford: Blackwell.

12 Foot, P. (1971), *The Postal Workers and the Tory Offensive*, London: Socialist Worker. See also Hyman, *op. cit.* (see note 3), p. 36.

13 Durcan *et al.*, *op. cit.* (see note 6), p. 182.

14 *Ibid.*, p. 17.

15 *Ibid.*, p. 334.

16 It is not, in practice, as simple as this. Some of the losses will be made up through overtime or increased bonus earnings after the return to work. Strikers can reclaim some tax deductions and their husbands or wives can claim some social security benefits. Nonetheless, the figures do illustrate the dramatic escalation of costs to those on strike.

17 Durcan *et al.*, *op. cit.* (see note 6), p. 188.
18 Despite trade union efforts to reform this procedure no progress was made and, in 1972, the trade unions withdrew unilaterally from the agreement and instructed their local officials to negotiate new procedures at company level.
19 Hyman, *op. cit.* (see note 3); see chapter 3 for his discussion of the various forms in which industrial conflict can be manifest.
20 Cited in Durcan *et al.*, *op. cit.*, (see note 6), p. 327.
21 See Lane and Roberts, *op. cit.* (see note 11).
22 Author's conversation with car workers in 1968.
23 Trist, E. and Bamforth, K. W. (1951), 'Some social and psychological consequences of the longwall method of coal-getting', *Human Relations*, vol. IV.
24 Elsewhere in Europe, notably in France and Italy, the idea that strikes could not be political would be greeted with incredulity; and in Eastern Europe strikes are regarded as fundamentally subversive political acts.
25 For a stimulating and extensive account of the inevitability of trade union involvement in politics, see Crouch, C. (1983), *Trade Unions: The Logic of Collective Action*, London: Fontana.

CHAPTER 8

1 A pre-entry closed shop means prospective entertainers have to be members of the relevant union *before* they are allowed to be employed. In contrast, a post-entry closed shop means new employees have to join the union after they are taken on.
2 Thomas, D., 'The secret war against coal', *New Socialist*, no. 19, September 1984, p. 31. The figures quoted in this example are taken from the same source.
3 'MP's interests', *Labour Research*, vol. 73, no. 6, June 1984, pp. 150–152.
4 'Tory funds', *Labour Research*, vol. 73, no. 8, August 1984, pp. 204–206.
5 Raphael, A., 'A question of interests', *Observer*, 1 July 1984.
6 'Lobbying and MPs' interests', *Labour Research*, vol. 73, no. 7, July 1984, pp. 175–177.
7 In 1980 the social security provisions were changed so that, for workers on strike, it is now assumed that they receive £15 a week in strike pay from their union. No union, unless it is prepared to be bankrupt, can afford to pay such sums for other than very short periods of time.

8 Figures for trade union assets, *Sunday Times*, 5 February 1984; figures for trade union income *General Council's Report 1984*, TUC, pp. 70–71.

9 Lonrho assets, *Observer*, 3 February 1985; Sainsbury's assets, *Management Today*, April 1984, p. 51; private schools income, *Observer*, 18 November 1984; income from privatisation, *Observer*, 18 November 1984; cost of selling British Telecom, *Sunday Times*, 18 November 1984.

10 One of the most recent, from which the data cited in the previous paragraph are taken, is Littler, C. and Salaman, G. (1984), *Class at Work*, London: Batsford.

11 In fact it was not quite as straightforward as this implies. Some policies used percentage increases – which increased differentials and became unacceptable; others used flat-rate increases which decreased differentials to an unacceptable degree; and some used a combination of the two methods, which pleased no-one.

CHAPTER 9

1 Nor is it just free-market economists who fall prey to such delusions. In Eastern Europe, where economists are concerned to create 'planned economies', collective bargaining is vilified because it interferes with and distorts the smooth operation of planned production. Nonetheless it persists, though not in the same form as in the West.

2 There is one rather bizarre qualification to add here. If someone mistakenly assumes that a particular dispute is caused by faulty communication they might, having made a faulty diagnosis, also prescribe a totally inappropriate remedy. This, in turn, might exacerbate the original problem. In this respect the *belief* that ineffective or faulty communications lie at the heart of an issue can be a barrier to finding an appropriate solution.

3 Marxism has a long and respectable intellectual history. As a frame of reference within social science it has provided one of the major explanations of how social order is maintained in societies. It would be a serious mistake to see it simply as the political ideology of the communist world. Indeed, many academic Marxists have advanced substantial Marxian critiques of such societies.

4 Quoted in the *Observer*, 23 September 1984.

5 See Goldthorpe, J., Lockwood, D., Bechoffer, F. and Platt, J.

(1968), *The Affluent Worker*, Cambridge: Cambridge University Press.
6 Sabel, C. F. (1982), *Work and Politics*, Cambridge: Cambridge University Press.

Notes on Further Reading

This *Invitation* is no more than an outline sketch map of the terrain encompassed by industrial relations. As such it is necessarily highly selective and many important issues are omitted completely or only briefly alluded to in the text. If, on finishing the book, the reader concludes that few answers have been provided to the many questions raised, then I will have achieved my purpose. There is nothing more constructive than a healthy state of uncertainty.

One of the few enduring conclusions of social science is that there are always more questions than answers. This may seem disconcerting but it is not, most emphatically, a pessimistic observation. It reflects a well-advised scepticism about the work of social scientists, the permanent need to revise our taken-for-granted ways of seeing and the curious truism that academic knowledge advances more through discrediting existing ideas and conceptions than by making novel discoveries.

So, if you wish to increase your uncertainty and, at the same time, broaden and deepen your understanding of industrial relations, turn to one or more of the following items according to taste. The selection, though based on my own idiosyncratic preferences, includes a mixture of introductory and more advanced references and encompasses a range of academic perspectives.

Journalistic reportage has not fared well in this book but, like Terry Wogan, it is unavoidable and should be understood for what it is. Nearly all contemporary national papers are pro-employer in tone, though occasional exceptions are found in the *Guardian*, the *Daily Mirror* and the *Observer*. The complete exception is the *Morning Star*. By far the most balanced and comprehensive coverage of industrial relations affairs is found in *The Financial Times*, the stockbrokers' daily. Television current affairs programmes try to maintain a balance with Channel 4's weekly 'Union World' programme providing the best-informed analyses.

Periodicals provide more in-depth comment. The *New Statesman* remains the established periodical of the Left and carries much useful discussion; it has lately been challenged by the more racy – and more rhetorical – *New Socialist*. Mention should also be made of *Labour Research*, a monthly publication devoted to digging up the dirt about wicked capitalists. It is sometimes over-conspirational in tone but publishes some invaluable data. On the Right there are fewer publications of equal quality. The best are the *Economist* – which for years has been groaning about excessive trade union power – and the *Spectator*. My own preference is for the latter: it is written with some sparkling wit and never tries to hide its ideological message behind the mystique of demand and supply curves.

Fundamental to understanding contemporary industrial relations is a sound grasp of the historical context. Several 'idiots' guides' are available but these should be avoided – history is never simple nor reducible to the dates of legislative change. A good start might be H. Pelling (1963), *A History of British Trade Unionism*, Penguin. It is not always compelling reading but remains a standard introductory text. Allen and Unwin have published Alan Fox's (1985) *History and Heritage*, an expensive but beautifully written book which is littered with astute if sometimes controversial insights into the historical developments which have shaped modern employment relations. A different kind of history is found in *Class Conflict and the Industrial Relations Crisis*, Heinemann, by C. Crouch (1977). He has provided an intriguing political history of British industrial relations from 1945 to the mid–1970s and his account highlights the dramatic changes that have overtaken employment relations since that time.

A good number of introductory texts are now on sale. One of the best, in my view, is Gill Palmer (1983), *British Industrial Relations*, Allen and Unwin. Unlike some of the others she starts with the employment relationship and avoids the tedium often associated with descriptive material by locating her discussion in a fairly clear and easily comprehended analytical framework. In addition she gives greater attention to the role of managers than is usual, but is weak on the issues of industrial conflict and shop stewards. But no book will give you everything. Alternatively, for a more comprehensive account, see H. Clegg (1979), *The Changing System of Industrial Relations in Great Britain*, Blackwell. This is rarely gripping stuff but, until recently, was undoubtedly the unchallenged introductory text and still contains invaluable detail. A more substantial text – but not one for beginners – is *Industrial Relations in Britain*, Blackwell, edited by George Bain (1983). This contains detailed analyses of most of the key issues, with each chapter being written by a specialist.

Trade unions are unavoidable, and a bewildering variety of books can be found in most bookshops. It might be best to start with a Penguin collection, *Trade Unions*, edited by W. E. J. McCarthy (1985). This is a revised edition including not only extracts from the 'classics' but also some key arguments about the role of trade unions in the economy. A similar but contrasting account of trade unionism can be found in K. Coates and T. Topham (1985), *Trade Unions in Britain*, Spokesman Books. It is more obviously pro-trade union but does highlight the significance of the political dimension of employment relations. After consulting one of these read C. Crouch (1982), *Trade Unions: the Logic of Collective Action*, Fontana, which goes a long way towards explaining many of the apparent contradictions in trade unionism.

On industrial conflict, Richard Hyman's (1984) *Strikes*, Fontana, has become the established introduction; and if you enjoy this you will also find his *Industrial Relations: A Marxist Introduction*, Macmillan (1975) of considerable interest. A more advanced and detailed exposition of the nature of industrial conflict is in P. Edwards and H. Scullion (1982),

The Social Organisation of Industrial Conflict, Blackwell. On shop stewards, some of the most interesting recent research is reported in E. Batstone, I. Boraston and S. Frenkel (1977), *Shop Stewards in Action*, Blackwell.

There are dozens of pro-management texts about industrial relations but they are of highly variable quality. One good and succinct introduction is M. Marchington (1982), *Managing Industrial Relations*, McGraw-Hill. For a more detailed how-to-do-it text, see D. Farnham and J. Pimlott (1982), *Understanding Industrial Relations*, Cassell.

Finally, this book ends where it began, with a last reminder that industrial and employment relations arise out of work and reflect the ever-changing character of work activities. Much can be learned from personal accounts of the experience of work and one good collection of such is S. Terkel (1977), *Working*, Penguin. This could be supplemented by P. Willis (1977), *Learning to Labour*, Saxon House, which demonstrates how young people are socialised for employment. It should be compulsory reading for teachers and politicians. More generally, some knowledge of the sociology of work is essential. T. Watson's (1980), *Sociology, Work and Industry*, Routledge and Kegan Paul, is a useful general text though you might prefer G. Esland and G. Salaman (1975), *People and Work*, Open University Press. This is an edited collection with examples from all the major perspectives which have informed our understanding of work. Lastly, P. Thompson (1983), *The Nature of Work*, Macmillan, provides an excellent summary of the recent more radical accounts of work, though it would be a mistake to start with this book.

Index

absenteeism, 178, 197–8
abstract economists, 220ff
ACAS, 47, 64, 71, 86–7, 98,
    133
arbitration, 87–8
ASLEF, 50
Association of Professional
    Teachers, 230
ASTMS, 57
AUT, 161

BACM, 58
Belloc, H., 145–6
BIM, 58
BMA, 60, 243
British Leyland, 111,
    117–18, 153
British Telecom, 242
BSC, 183, 186

car-delivery industry,
    229–30
car-workers, 55, 115–18,
    182–3, 191–2, 199
CBI, 23, 47, 68–9
Chambers of Commerce,
    69–70

CIR, 86
civil engineering, 113–14
class attitudes, 36, 135
closed shop, 51–2, 132,
    142–3
collective bargaining, 103ff,
    258ff
    bargaining levels, 108
    bargaining process, 121–8
    context of bargaining,
    109–120
    economic significance, 128
    media image, 105–06
    procedural and substantive
    rules, 104, 196
    social significance, 129
conciliation, 87
Conservative
    government, 12, 64, 86,
    91, 235
    Party, 15, 47, 236
    policies, 128, 136, 206, 233
CSEU, 62

Department of
    Employment, 47,
    188–9, 192

283